Thomas Balinger

The BIG Merlin Songbook

100 Songs

for Merlin (M4) in D tuning (D-A-D)

Other titles by Thomas Balinger:

Merlin Songbook for beginners, 65 Campfire Classics
Merlin Songbook for beginners, Christmas Carols
Merlin Songbook for beginners, Hymns & Songs of Worship

The Dulcimer Songbook
The Ukulele Songbook – 50 All Time Classics
The Baritone Ukulele Songbook
American Harmonica Songbook

Thomas Balinger
The Big Merlin Songbook, 100 Songs for Merlin (M4) in D tuning (D-A-D)

All rights reserved.
thomasbalinger@gmail.com

© 2019

Revised Edition 2019-2

ISBN: 9781797478531

Preface

Hello fellow Merlin fans,

welcome to this song collection of classic tunes, arranged for easy Merlin (M4) in D tuning (D-A-D).

These songs cover a wide musical range. From traditional American folk songs to Hymns, Irish songs and children's classics–this is the perfect collection for every Merlin aficionado looking for songs in a wide variety of styles to expand his repertoire.

I've arranged all songs with the beginning player in mind, adding chord symbols, chord diagrams and melody tab to the standard notation to make playing as easy and straightforward as possible.

There's a short section on tuning your Merlin (M4) and reading tablature, along with the basic chords and a selection of easy strumming and picking patterns. You can use these as they are or as a starting point to create your own accompaniments.

So pick up your Merlin and have fun,

Thomas Balinger

Contents

Songs

1. A beautiful life 42
2. All creatures of our God and King 76
3. Amazing Grace 151
4. Animal fair 153
5. Aura Lee 166
6. Beautiful brown eyes 24
7. Billy the kid 34
8. Blood on the saddle 8
9. Boil them cabbage down 6
10. Botany Bay 110
11. Brahms' lullaby 138
12. Brennan on the moor 122
13. Buffalo gals 170
14. Bury me beneath the willow 165
15. Carrickfergus 104
16. Colorado trail 48
17. Come all ye fair and tender ladies 44
18. Come, Thou fount of every blessing ... 86
19. Crawdad song 142
20. Cumberland Gap 16
21. Dink's song 49
22. Don't this road look rough and rocky .. 54
23. Down the road 17
24. Drifting too far from the shore 56
25. East Virginia Blues 28
26. Engine 143 40
27. Finnegan's wake 112
28. Foggy mountain top 59
29. Footprints in the snow 12
30. Frankie and Johnny 46
31. Git along little dogies 68
32. Going down this road 32
33. Hickory dickory dock 154
34. Holy, holy, holy 92
35. Home on the range 174
36. House of the rising sun 172
37. How firm a foundation 80
38. Humpty Dumpty 134
39. I ain't gonna work tomorrow 53
40. I ride an old paint 14
41. I surrender all 88
42. It is well with my soul 84
43. Itsy bitsy spider 145
44. Jack and Jill 150
45. Jack of diamonds 30
46. James Connolly 116
47. Jesse James 66
48. Jesus paid it all 94
49. Jolly good fellow 156
50. Just as I am 78
51. Lavender's blue 136
52. Little Bessie 10
53. London Bridge is falling down 157
54. Long journey home 70
55. Make me down a pallet 74
56. Mary had a little lamb 140
57. Midnight on the stormy deep 20
58. Midnight train 52
59. Molly and Tenbrooks 62
60. My faith looks up to Thee 90
61. My home's across the smoky mountains 164

62.	New river train	26	82.	The farmer in the dell 141
63.	Nine pound hammer	50	83.	The hills of Connemara 127
64.	Nothing but the blood	96	84.	The jolly beggarman 114
65.	Oh! Susanna	168	85.	The last rose of summer 130
66.	Old Black Joe	162	86.	The merry ploughboy 132
67.	Old Dan Tucker	60	87.	The minstrel boy 100
68.	On top of Old Smokey	176	88.	The moonshiner 126
69.	Pease porridge hot	147	89.	There's a hole in the bucket 148
70.	Pop! Goes the weasel	144	90.	The rising of the moon 118
71.	Rain, rain, go away	146	91.	The rose of Mooncoin 128
72.	Rock a-bye, baby	152	92.	The Sally Gardens 102
73.	Roving gambler	18	93.	The star of the County Down 120
74.	Row, row, row	135	94.	This old man 160
75.	Salty dog Blues	36	95.	Three score and ten 108
76.	Saviour, like a shepherd lead us	98	96.	Tom Dooley 177
77.	Shady grove	58	97.	Way down the old plank road 22
78.	Shall we gather at the river	82	98.	Wildwood flower 72
79.	She moved through the fair	106	99.	Wreck of the old 97 38
80.	Shortnin' bread	64	100.	Yankee Doodle 158
81.	The auld orange flute	124		

Appendix

Tuning your Merlin 180
Merlin tablature 181
Basic chords 182
Strumming patterns 186
Picking patterns 188

5

Boil them cabbage down

Boil them cab-bage down, down. Turn them hoe cakes 'round. The

on-ly song that I can sing is boil them cab-bage down.

Went up on a moun-tain, just to give my horn a blow.

Thought I heard my true love say, "Yon-der comes my beau."

2. Possum in a 'simmon tree,
   raccoon on the ground.
   Raccoon says, you son-of-a-gun,
   shake some 'simmons down.
   Boil them cabbage ...

3. Someone stole my old coon dog.
   wish they'd bring him back.
   He chased the big hogs through the fence,
   and the little ones through the crack.
   Boil them cabbage ...

4. Met a possum in the road,
   blind as he could be.
   Jumped the fence and whipped my dog
   and bristled up at me.
   Boil them cabbage ...

5. Once I had an old grey mule,
   his name was Simon Slick.
   He'd roll his eyes, and back his ears,
   and how that mule would kick.
   Boil them cabbage ...

6. How that mule would kick,
   he'd kick with his dying breath.
   He shoved his hind feet down his throat,
   and kicked himself to death,

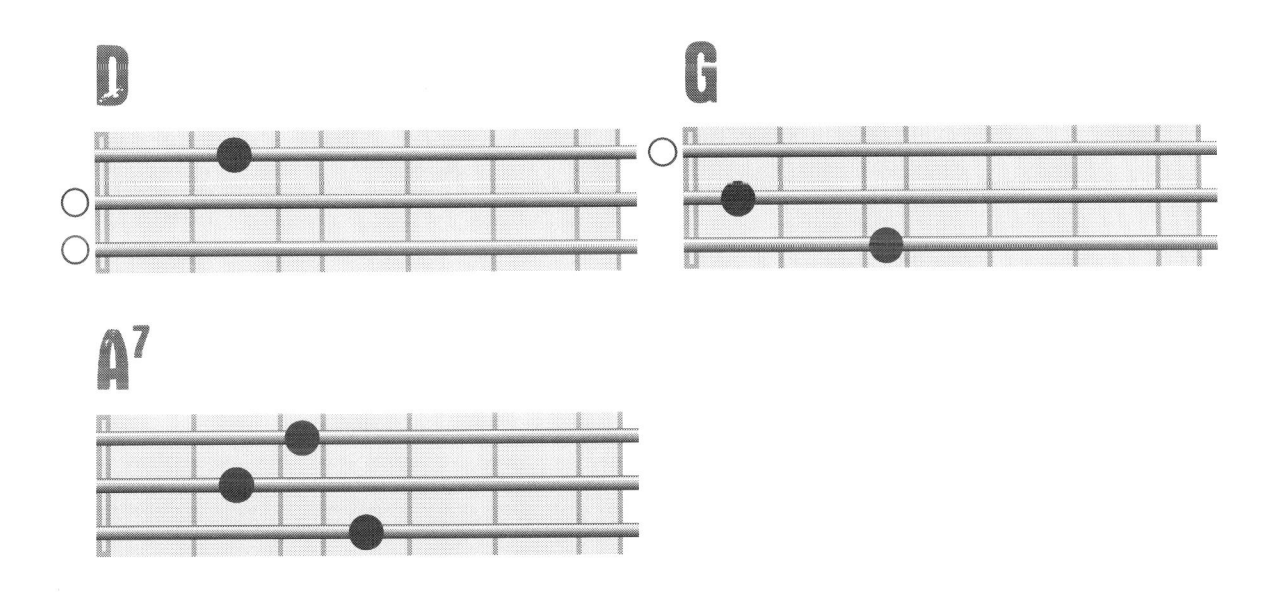

D

G

A⁷

Blood on the saddle

There was blood on the saddle and blood on the ground, and a great big puddle of blood all around. The cowboy lay in it all covered with gore, and he won't go riding no broncos no more. Oh, pity the cowboy, all blood - y and red, _____ for his bron - co fell

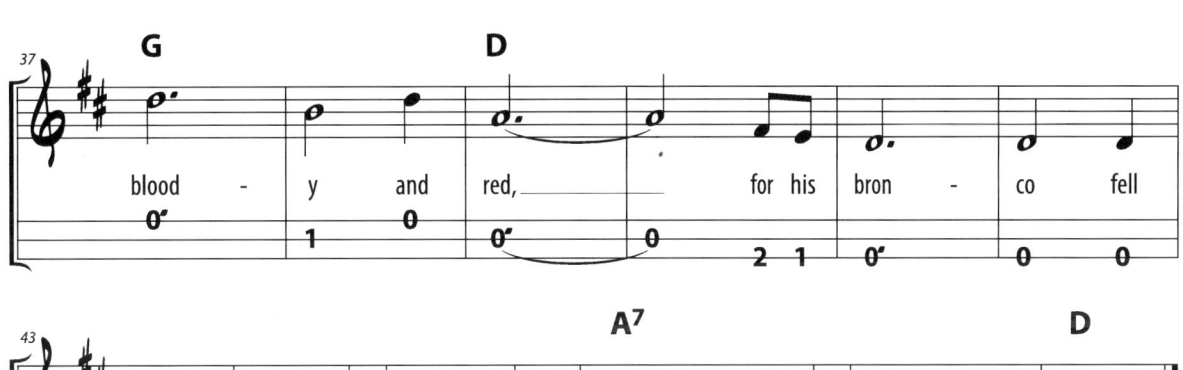

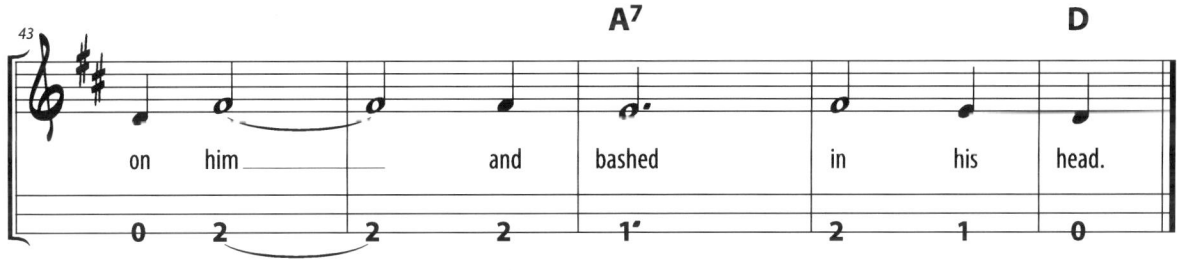

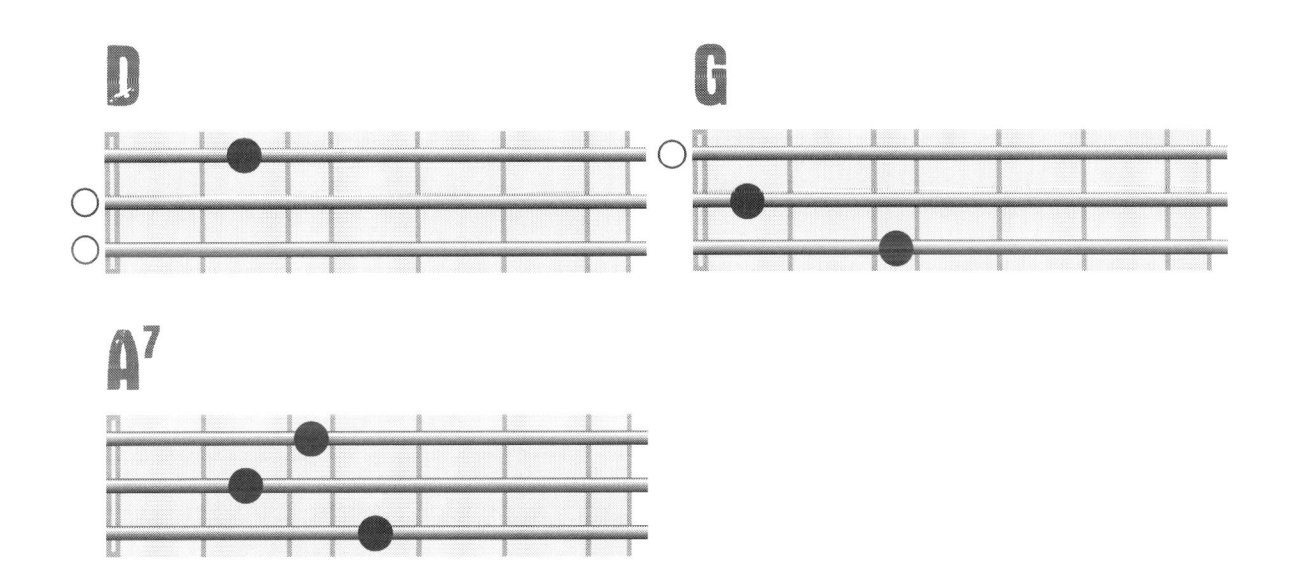

on him _____ and bashed in his head.

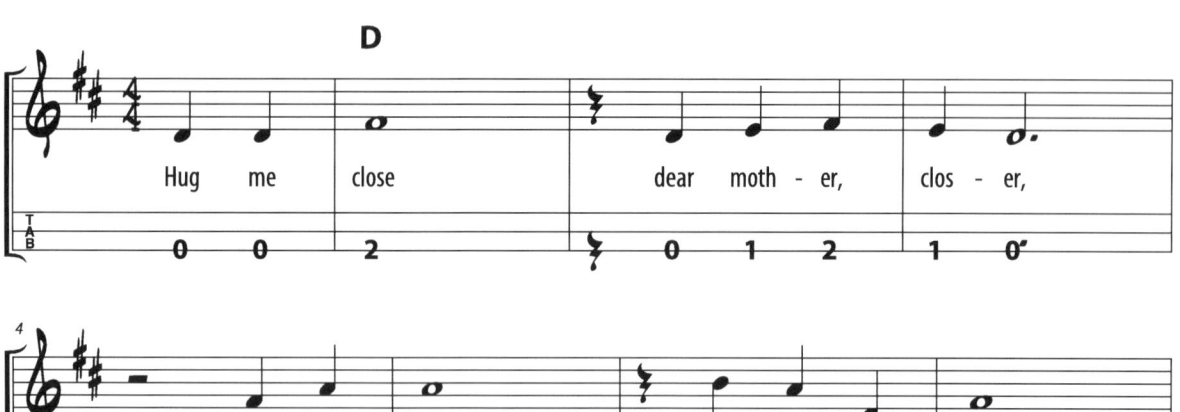

Little Bessie

Lyrics under the music:

Hug me close dear moth-er, clos-er, put your arms a-round me tight. For I'm cold and tired, dear moth-er and I feel so strange to-night.

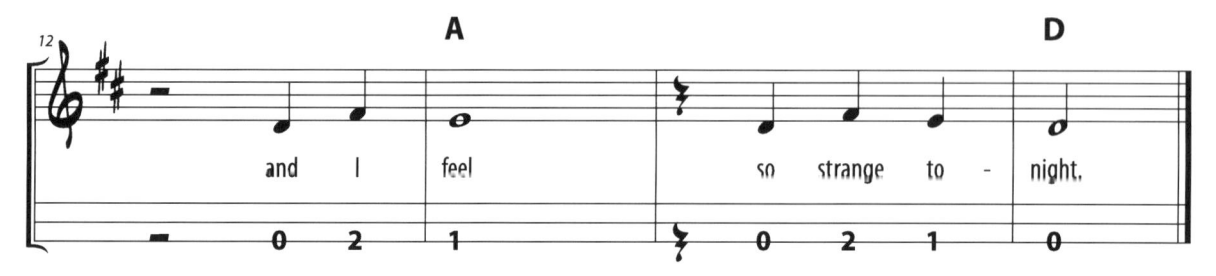

2. Something hurts me here, dear mother,
   like a stone upon my breast.
   Oh I wonder, wonder, mother,
   why it is I cannot rest.

3. All the day as you were working,
   and I lay upon my bed.
   I was trying to be patient,
   and to think of what you said.

4. How the King, Blessed Jesus,
   loves His lambs to watch and keep.
   Oh, I wish He would come and take me
   In His arms that I might sleep.

5. Just before the lamps were lighted,
   just before the children came.
   While the room was very quiet,
   I heard someone call my name.

6. All at once a window opened,
   one so bright upon me smiled
   And I knew it must be Jesus,
   when He said come here, my child.

7. Come up here, little Bessie,
   come up here and live with me.
   Where little children never suffer,
   suffer through eternity.

8. Then I thought of all you told me,
   of that bright and happy land.
   I was going when you called me,
   when you came and kissed my hand.

9. And at first I felt so sorry
   you had called, I would go.
   Oh, to sleep and never suffer,
   mother, don't be crying so.

10. Hug me close dear mother closer,
    put your arms around me tight.
    Oh how much I love you mother,
    and how strong I feel tonight

11. And her mother pressed her closer,
    to her own dear burdened breast.
    On the heart so near its breaking,
    Lay the heart so near Its rest.

12. At the solemn hour of midnight,
    in the darkness calm and deep.
    Laying on her mother's bosom,
    Little Bessie fell asleep.

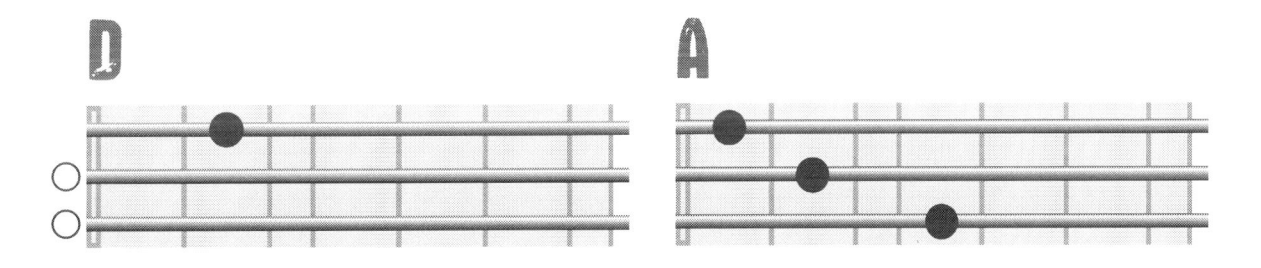

Footprints in the snow

2. I dropped in to see her there was a big round moon,
   her mother said she just stepped out but would be returning soon.
   I found her little footprints and I traced them in the snow,
   I found her when the snow was on the ground.
   I traced her little footprints in the snow ...

3. Now she's up in heaven she's with the angel band,
   I know I'm going to meet her in that promised land.
   But every time the snow falls it brings back memories,
   I found her when the snow was on the ground.
   I traced her little footprints in the snow ...

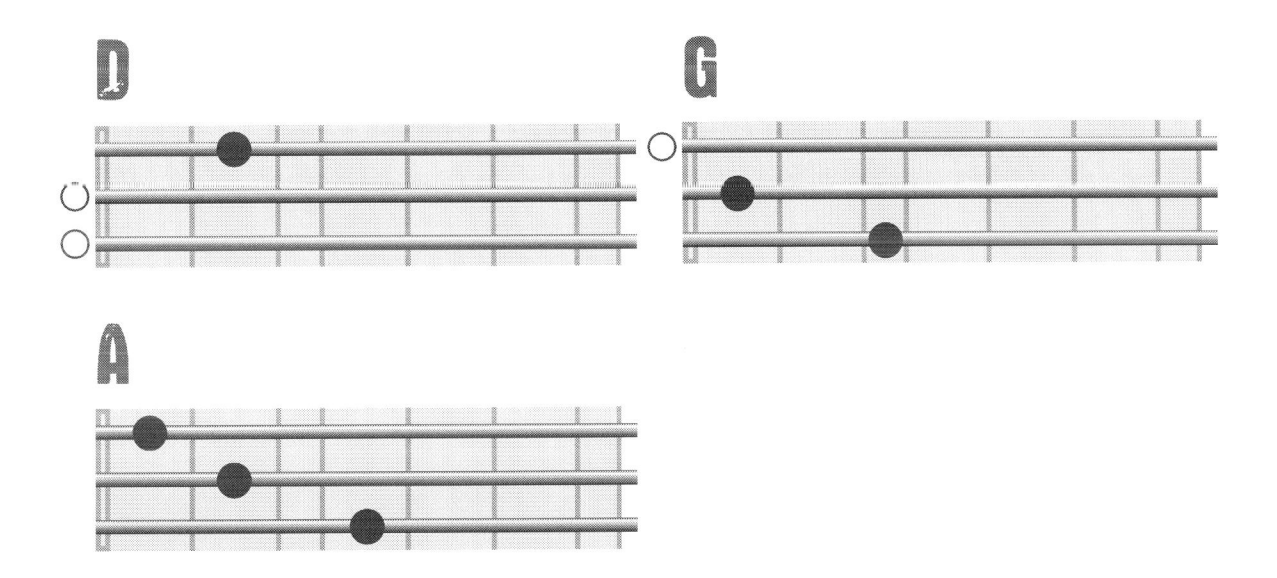

D

G

A

ride an old paint

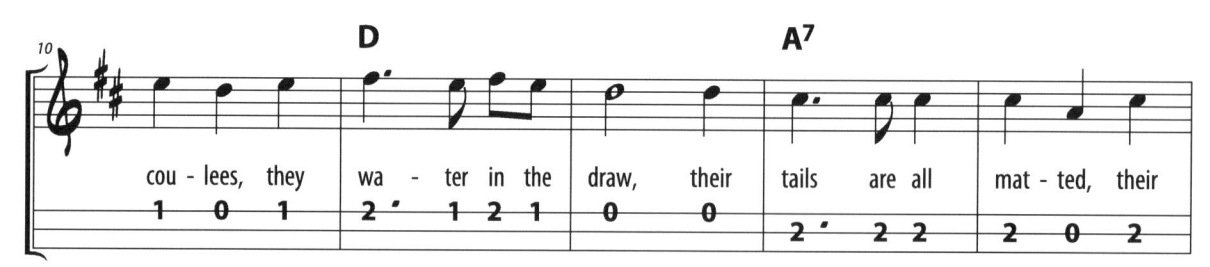

14

2. Old Bill Jones had a daughter and a song,
   one went to Denver, the other went wrong.
   His wife, she died in a poolroom fight,
   but the old man keeps singing from morning till night.
   Ride around, little dogies ...

3. So when I die, take my saddle off the wall,
   put it on my pony, lead my pony from the stall.
   Tie my bones to my saddle, turn our faces to the West,
   and we'll ride the ranges that we love the best.
   Ride around, little dogies ...

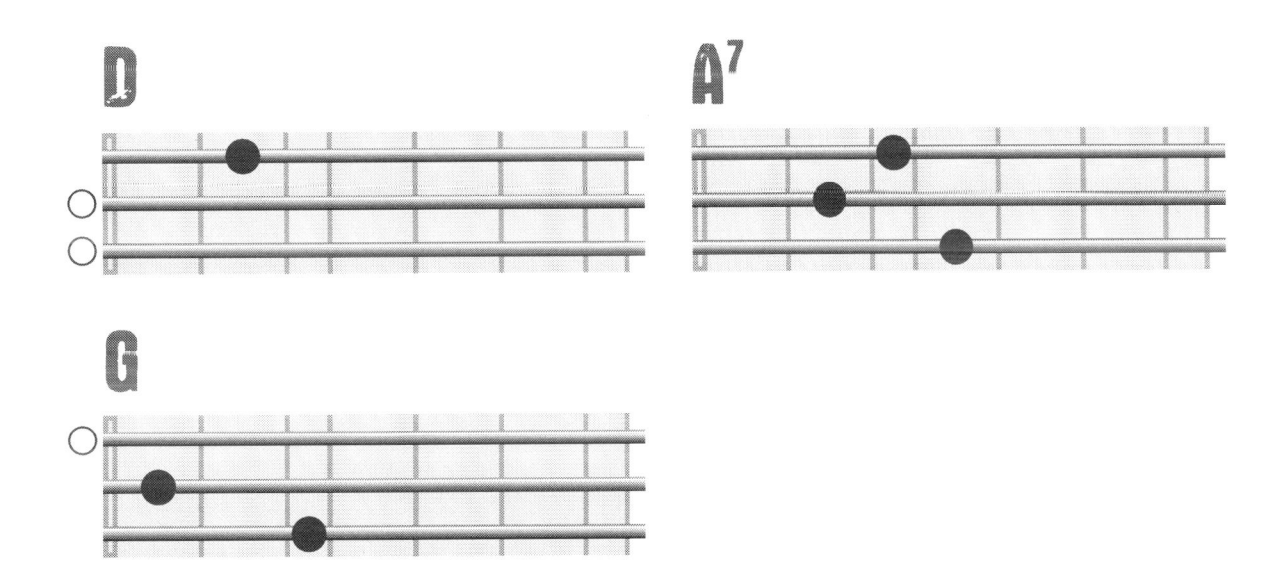

Cumberland Gap

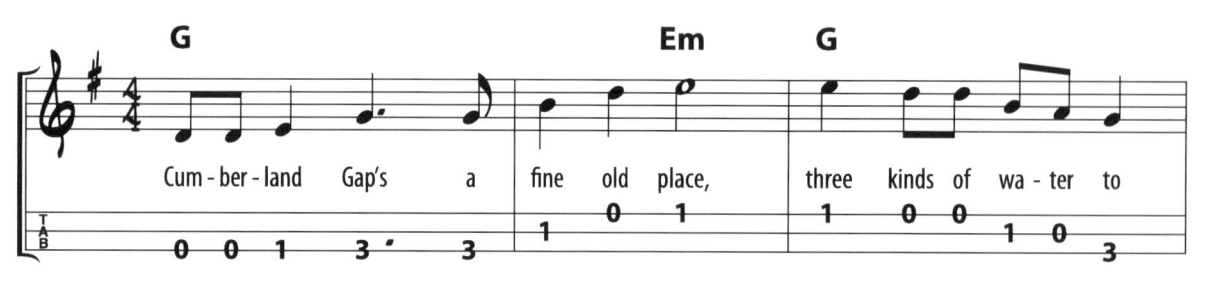

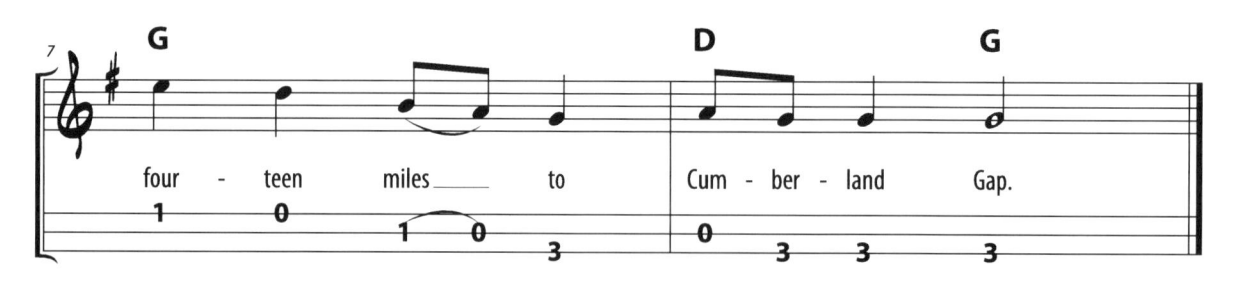

Cum-ber-land Gap's a fine old place, three kinds of wa-ter to wash your face. Lay down boys, take a lit-tle nap, four-teen miles to Cum-ber-land Gap.

2. Me and my wife and my wife's pap,
   we all live down in Cumberland Gap.
   Me and my wife and my wife's pap,
   we all live down in Cumberland Gap.

3. Cumberland Gap with its cliffs and rocks,
   home of the panther, bear and fox.
   Cumberland Gap with its cliffs and rocks,
   home of the panther, bear and fox.

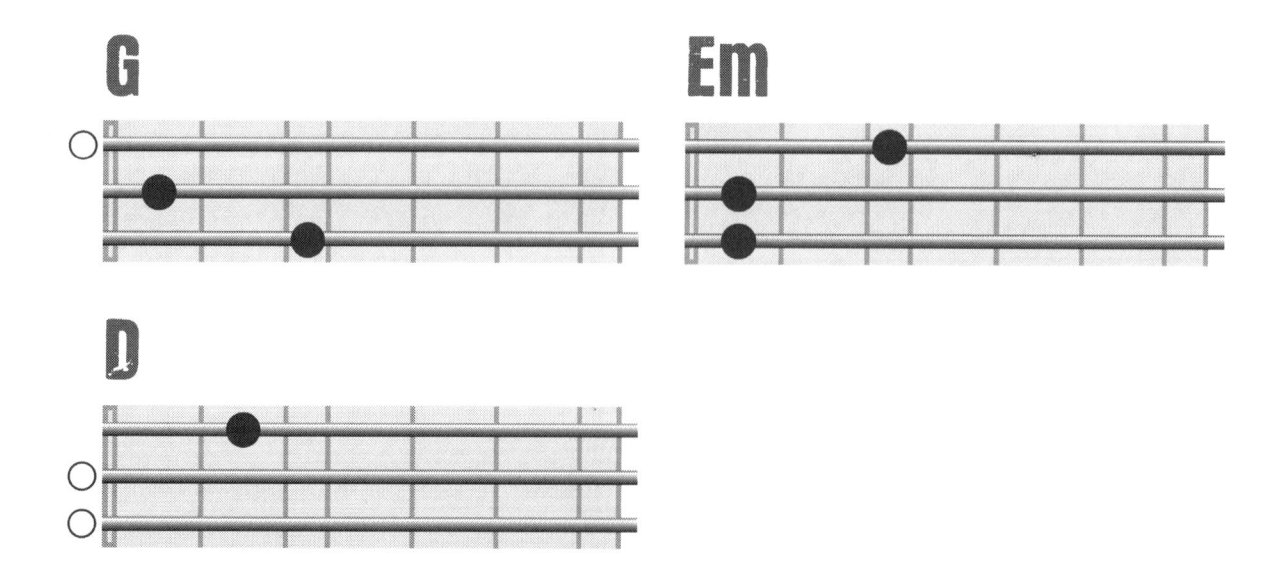

Down the road

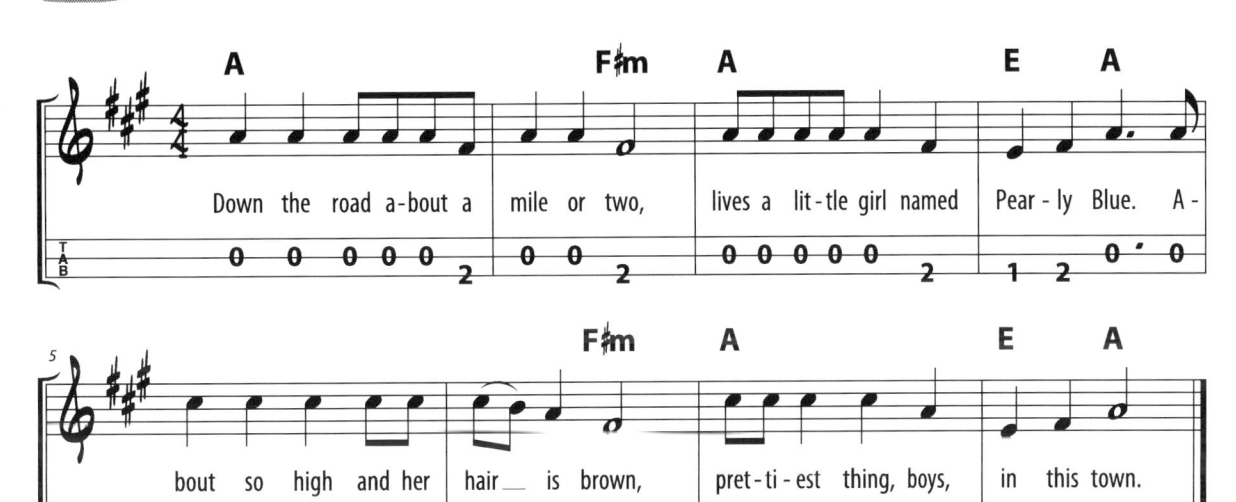

Down the road a-bout a mile or two, lives a lit-tle girl named Pear-ly Blue. A-bout so high and her hair is brown, pret-ti-est thing, boys, in this town.

2. Now anytime you want to know,
   where I'm going, down the road.
   Get my girl on the line,
   you'll find me there most any old time.

3. Now everyday and Sunday too,
   I go to see my Pearly Blue.
   Before you hear that rooster crow,
   you'll see me headed down the road.

4. Now old man Flatt he owned the farm,
   from the hog lot to the barn.
   From the barn to the rail,
   he made his living by carrying the mail.

5. Now every time I get the blues,
   I walk the soles right off my shoes.
   I don't know why I love her so,
   that gal of mine lives down the road.

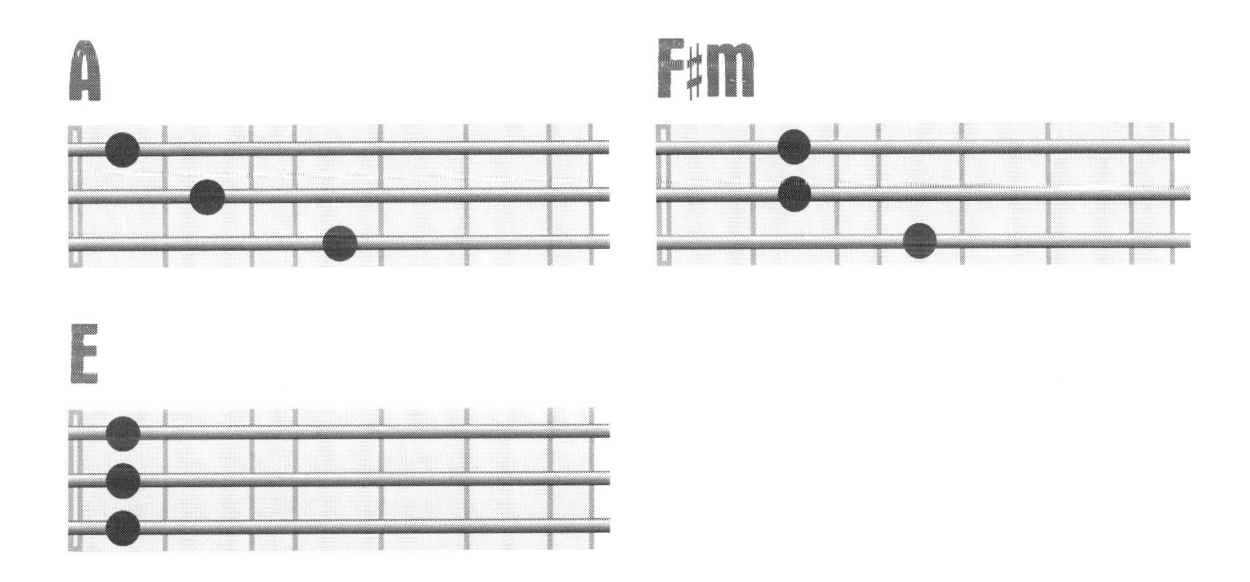

Roving gambler

I am a roving gambler, gambled all around, when-ever I meet with a deck of cards, I lay my money down. Lay my money down, lay my money down.

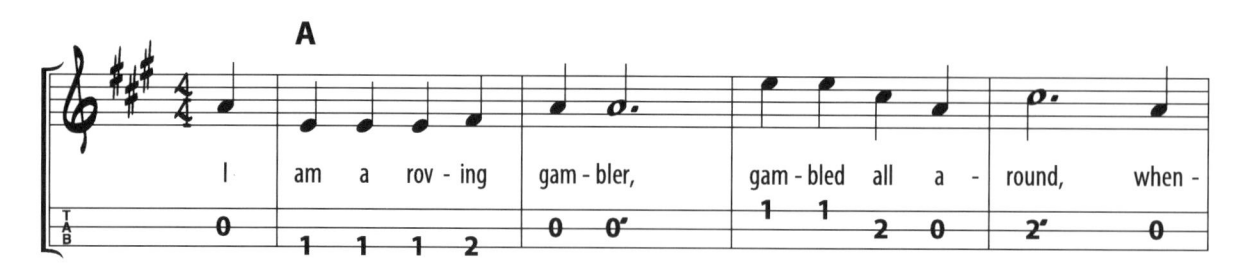

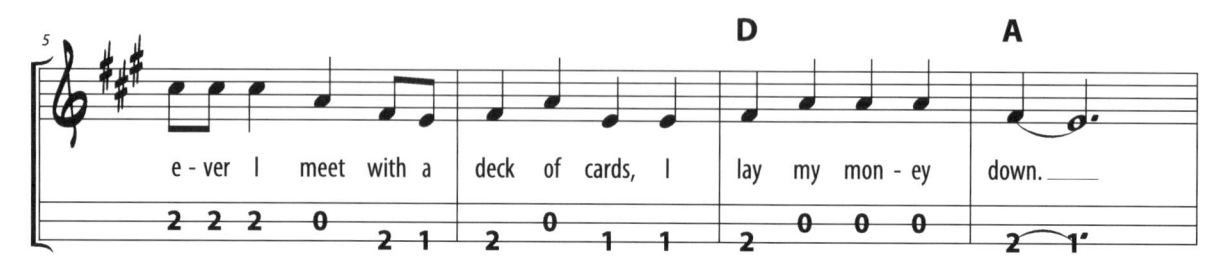

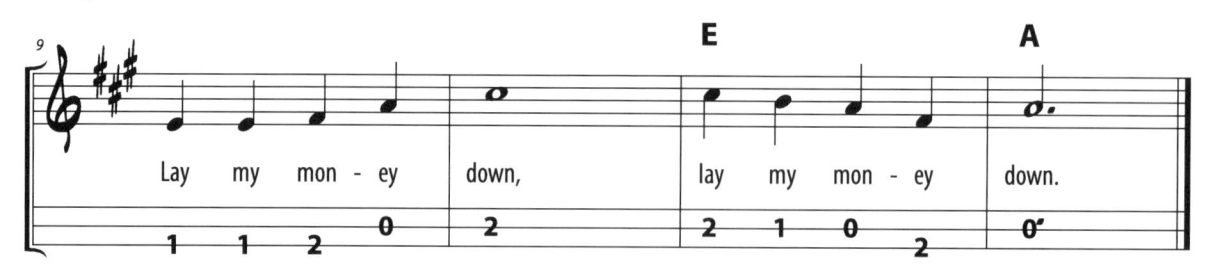

2. I had not been in Frisco many more weeks than three,
   I met up with a pretty little gal,
   she fell in love with me.
   Fell in love with me, fell in love with me.

3. She took me in her parlor, cooled me with her fan,
   whispered low in her mother's ear,
   I love this gambling man.
   Love this gambling man, love this gambling man.

4. Oh daughter oh dear daughter how can you treat me so,
   leave your dear old mother,
   and with a gambler go.
   With a gambler go, with a gambler go.

5. My mother oh my mother you can not understand,
   if you ever see me a-coming back,
   I'll be with a gambling man.
   With a gambling man, with a gambling man.

6. I left her there in Frisco and I wound up in Maine,
   I met up with a gambling man,
   got in a poker game.
   Got in a poker game, got in a poker game.

7. We put our money in the pot and dealt the cards around,
   I saw him deal from the bottom of the deck,
   and I shot that gambler down.
   Shot the gambler down, shot the gambler down.

8. Well, now I'm in the jailhouse got a number for my name,
   the warden said as he locked the door,
   you've gambled your last game.
   Gambled your last game, gambled your last game.

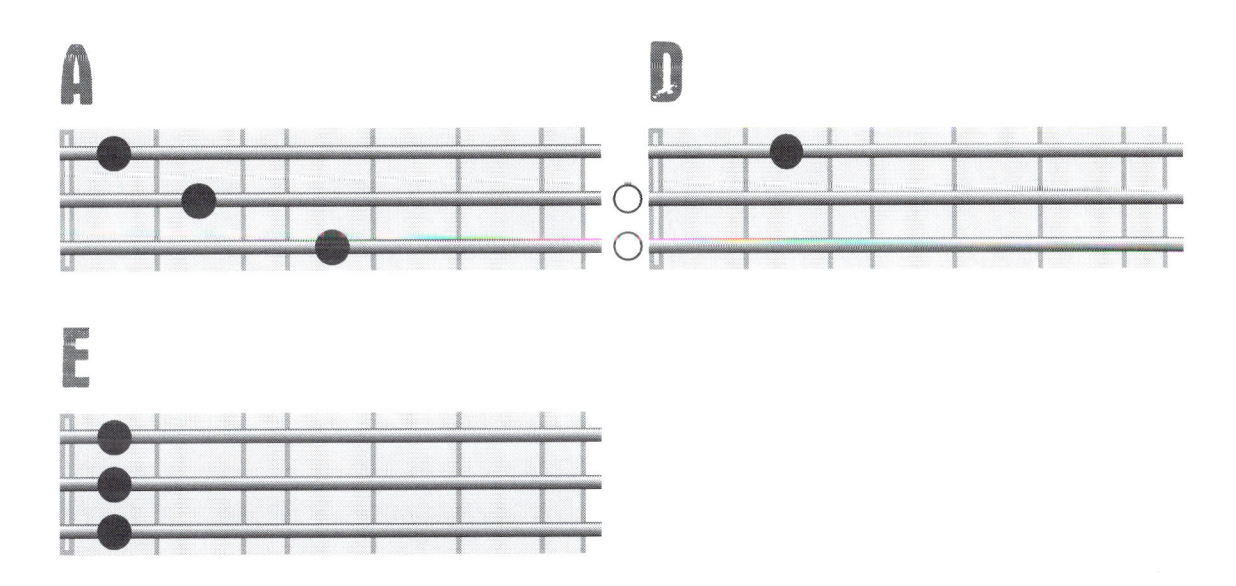

A

D

E

Midnight on the stormy deep

T'was mid-night on the storm-y deep, my soli-ta-ry watch I'd keep. And I think of her I'd left behind, and asked if she'd be true and kind.

2. I never shall forget the day,
   that I was forced to go away.
   In silence there my head she'd rest,
   and press me to her loving breast.

3. Oh Willy don't go back to sea,
   there's other girls as good as me.
   But none can love you true as I,
   pray don't go where the bullets fly.

4. The deep, deep sea may us divide,
   and I may be some other's bride.
   But still my thoughts will sometimes stray,
   to thee when thou art far away.

5. I never have proved false to thee,
   the heart I gave was true as thine.
   But you have proved untrue to me,
   I can no longer call thee mine.

6. Then fare-thee-well I'd rather make,
   my home upon some icy lake.
   Where the southern sun refused to shine,
   then to trust a love so false as thine.

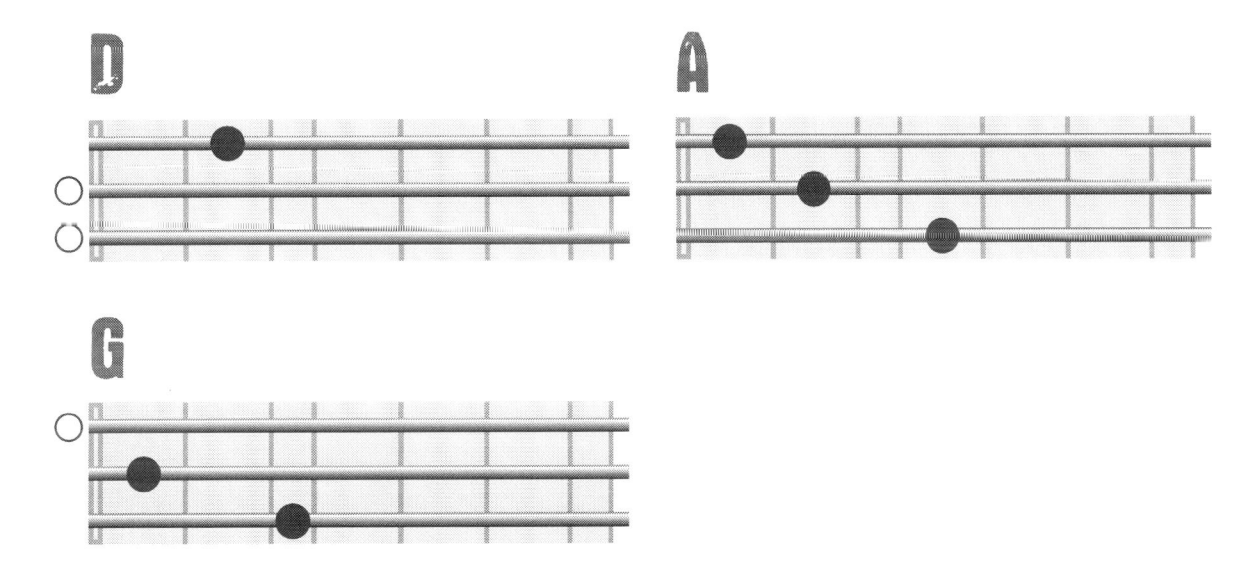

Way down the old plank road

I'd rath-er be in Rich-mond with all the hail and rain, than to be in Geor-gia, boys, tied to a ball and chain. Won't get drunk no more, boys, won't get drunk no more. Won't get drunk no more, boys, way down the old plank road.

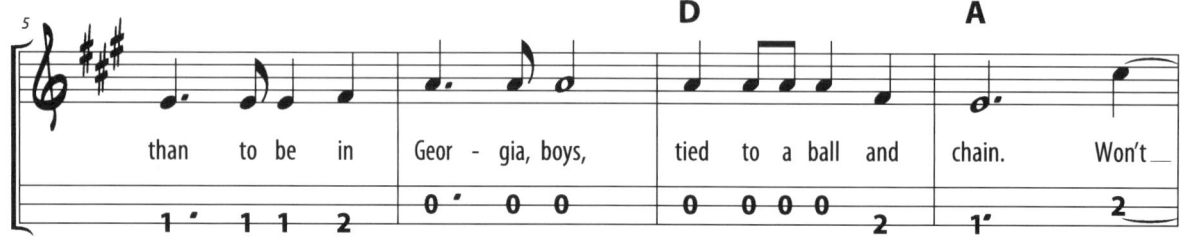

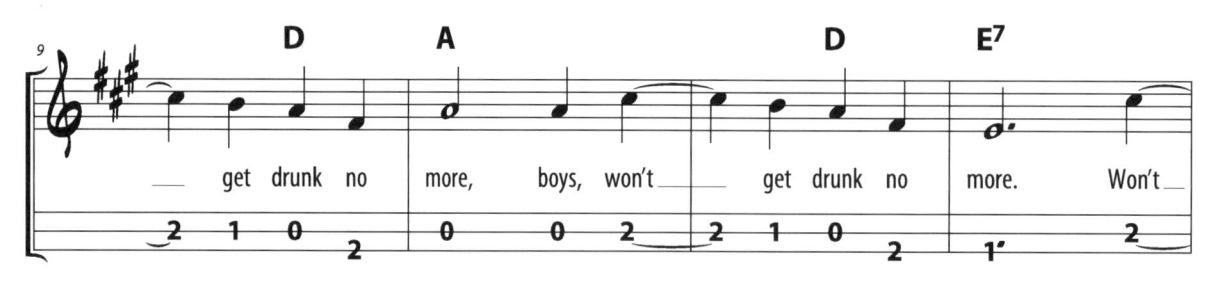

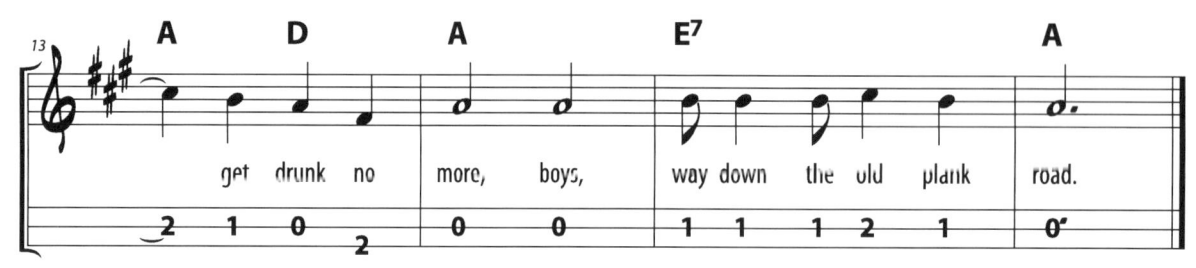

2. I went down to Mobile, but I got on the gravel train,
   very next thing they heard of me, had on that ball and chain.
   Won't get drunk no more, boys ...

3. Doney, oh dear Doney, what makes you treat me so,
   caused me to wear that ball and chain, now my ankle's sore.
   Won't get drunk no more, boys ...

4. Knoxville is a pretty place, Memphis is a beauty,
   wanta see them pretty girls, hop to Chattanoogie.
   Won't get drunk no more, boys ...

5. I'm going to build me a scaffold on some mountain high,
   so I can see my Doney girl as she goes riding by.
   Won't get drunk no more, boys ...

6. My wife died on Friday night, Saturday she was buried,
   Sunday was my courtin' day, Monday I got married.
   Won't get drunk no more, boys ...

7. Eighteen pounds of meat a week, whiskey here to sell,
   how can a young man stay at home, pretty girls look so well.
   Won't get drunk no more, boys ...

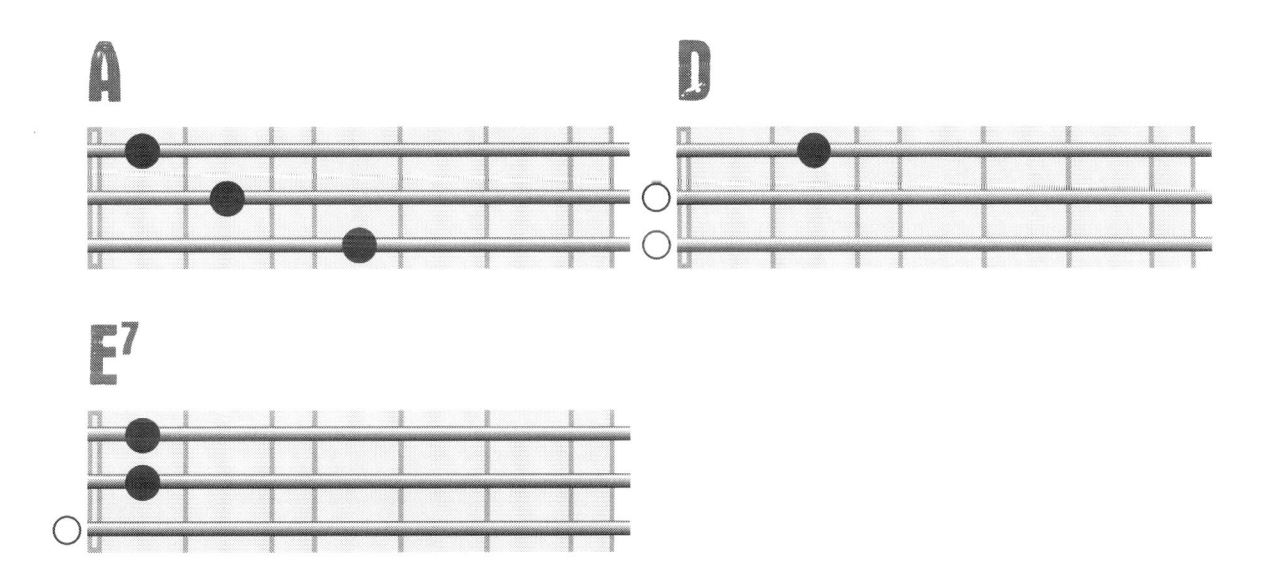

A

D

E⁷

Beautiful brown eyes

Willie, my darling, I love you, I love you with all my heart. Tomorrow we were to be married, but liquor has kept us apart.

Beautiful, beautiful brown eyes, beautiful, beautiful brown eyes, beautiful, beautiful brown eyes, I'll never love blue eyes again.

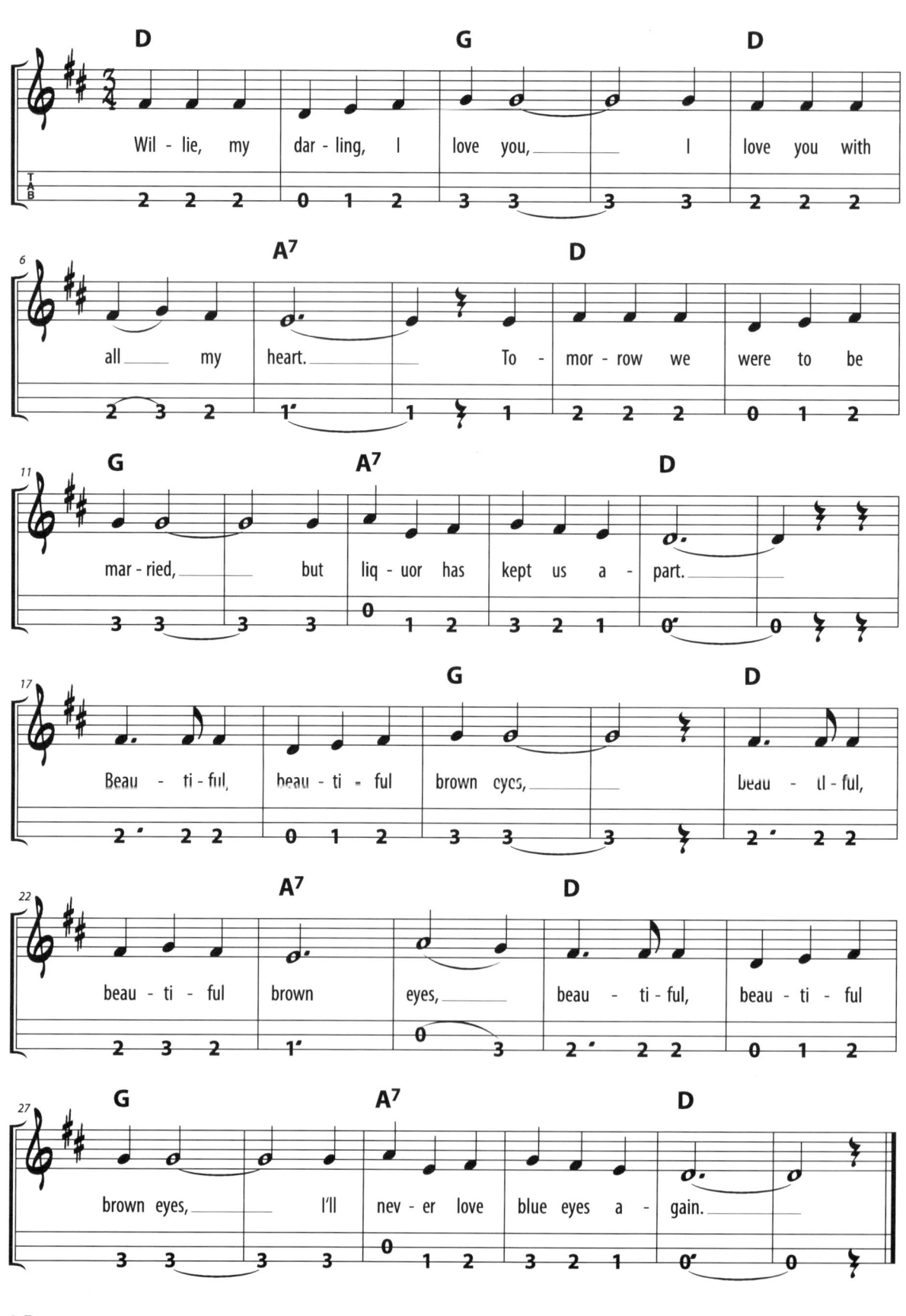

24

2. I staggered into the barroom,
   I fell down on the floor.
   And the very last words that I uttered,
   "I'll never get drunk any more."
   Beautiful, beautiful brown eyes ...

3. Seven long years I've been married,
   I wish I was single again.
   A woman don't know half her troubles,
   until she has married a man.
   Beautiful, beautiful brown eyes ...

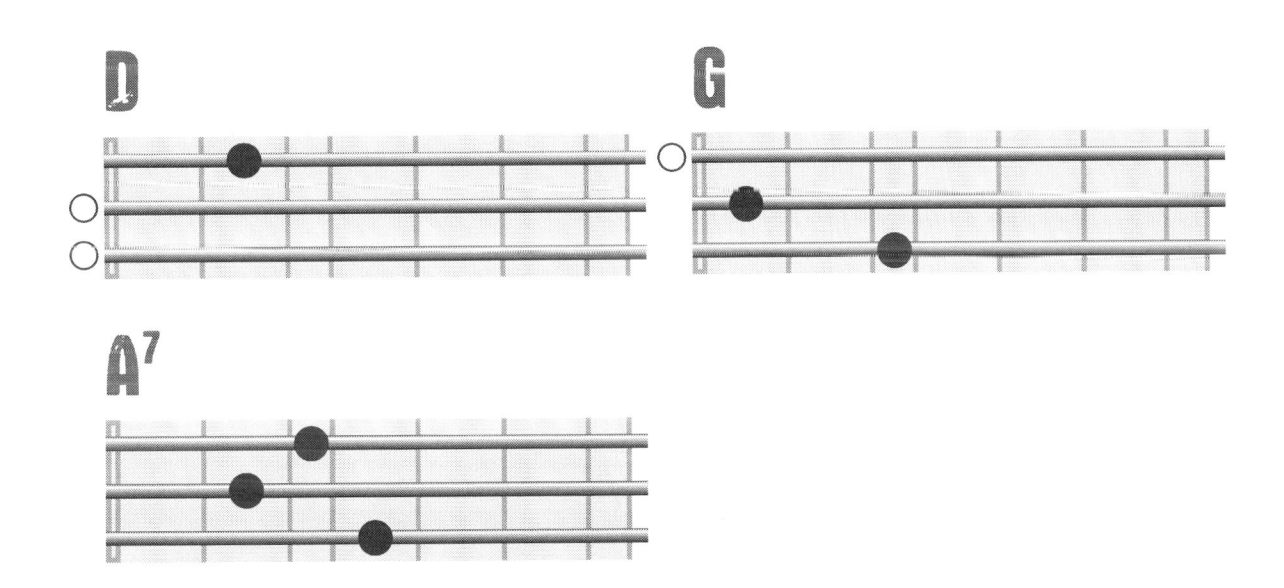

New river train

I'm riding on that new river train, I'm riding on that new river train. That same old train that brought me here, gonna take me away again.

2. Darling you can't love one,
   darling you can't love one.
   You can't love one and have any fun,
   oh darling you can't love one.

3. Darling you can't love two,
   darling you can't love two.
   You can't love two and your little heart be true,
   Oh darling you can't love two.

4. Darling you can't love three,
   darling you can't love three.
   You can't love three and still love me,
   oh darling you can't love three.

5. Darling you can't love four,
   darling you can't love four.
   You can't love four and love me anymore,
   oh darling you can't love four.

6. Darling you can't love five,
   darling you can't love five.
   You can't love five and get money from my hive,
   oh darling you can't love five.

7. Darling you can't love six,
   darling you can't love six.
   You can't love six, for that kind of love don't mix,
   oh darling you can't love six.

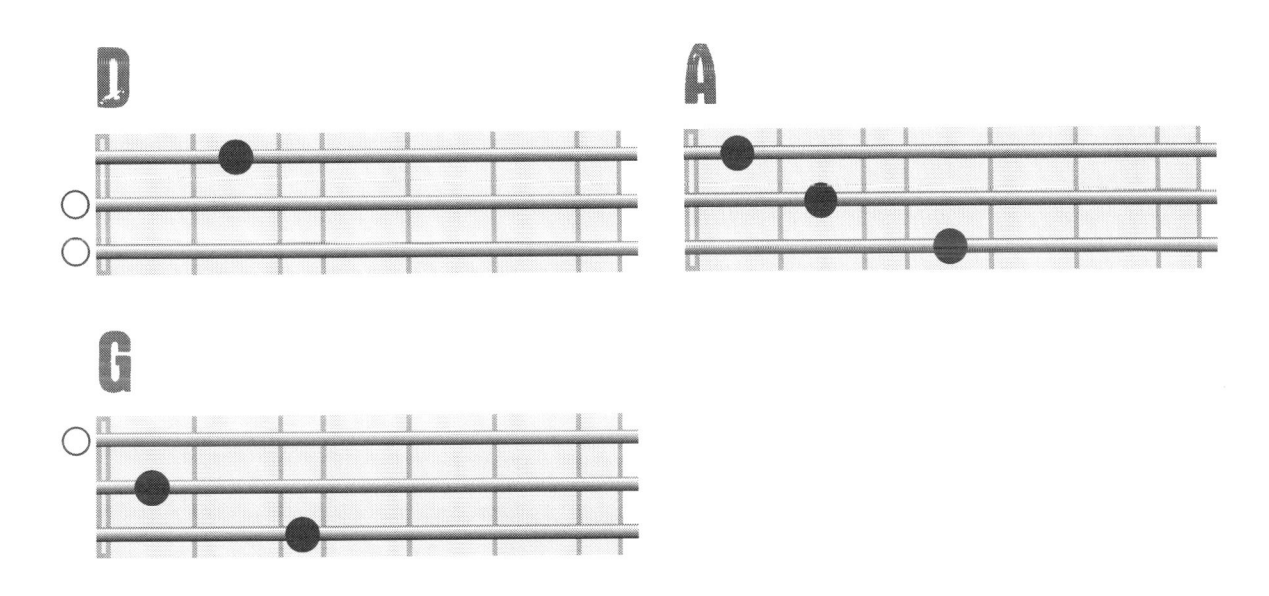

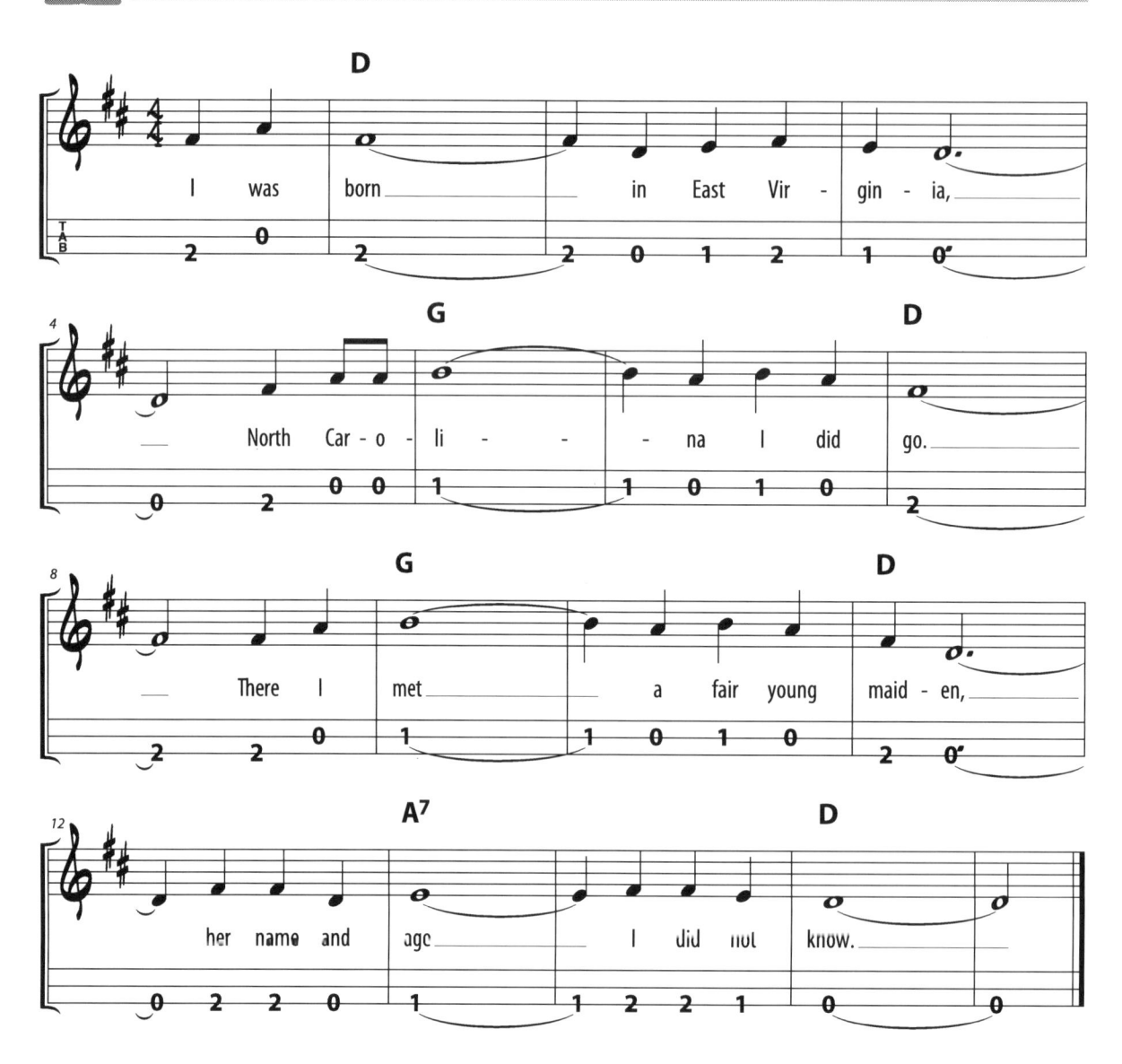

East Virginia Blues

2. And her hair was dark and curly,
   and her cheeks were rosy red.
   On her breast she wore white lilies
   and there I longed to lay my head.

3. I don't want your greenback dollar,
   I don't want your watch and chain.
   All I want is your heart, darling,
   and to see my home again.

4. I'll go back to East Virginia,
   North Carolina ain't my home.
   I'll go back to East Virginia,
   leave them north Carolina alone.

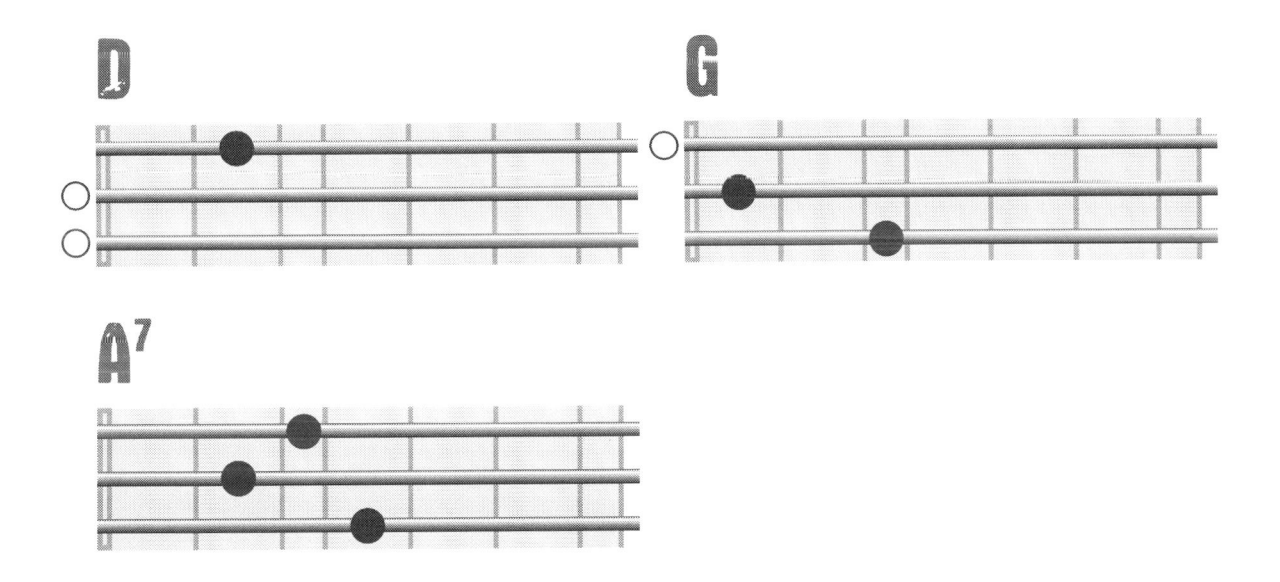

D

G

A⁷

Jack of diamonds

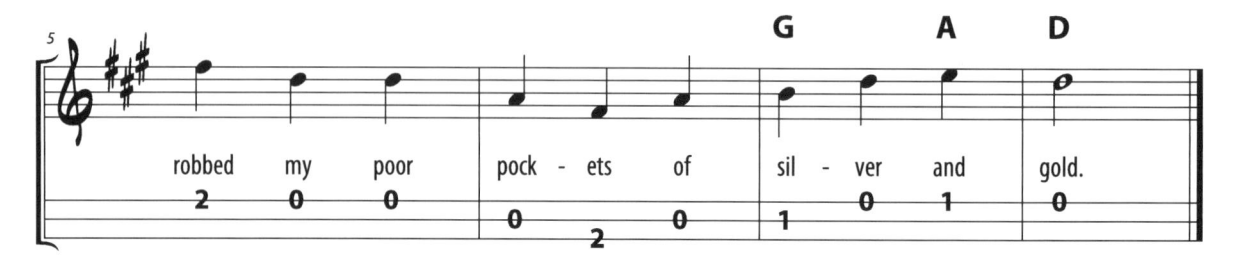

[Sheet music with lyrics: "Jack of dia-monds, Jack of dia-monds, I've known you of old. You've robbed my poor pock-ets of sil-ver and gold."]

2. Whiskey you villain,
   you've been my downfall.
   You've kicked me, you've cuffed me,
   but I love you for all.

3. Her parents don't like me,
   they say I'm too poor.
   They say I'm unworthy,
   to enter her door.

4. They say I drink whiskey,
   but my money's my own.
   And them that don't like me,
   can leave me alone.

5. I'll eat when I'm hungry,
   I'll drink when I'm dry.
   And when I get thirsty,
   I'll lay down and cry.

6. Rye whiskey, rye whiskey,
   rye whiskey I cry.
   If I don't get rye whiskey,
   I surely will die.

7. O baby, O baby,
   I've told you before
   Do make me a pallet,
   I'll lay on the floor.

8. I'm a rabble soldier
   and Dixie's my home
   I'll get up in my saddle,
   my quirt in my hand.

9. If the ocean was whiskey
   and I was a duck
   I'd dive to the bottom
   to get sweet sup

10. But the ocean ain't whiskey,
    and I ain't no duck
    So I'll play Jack O'Diamonds
    and try to change my luck.

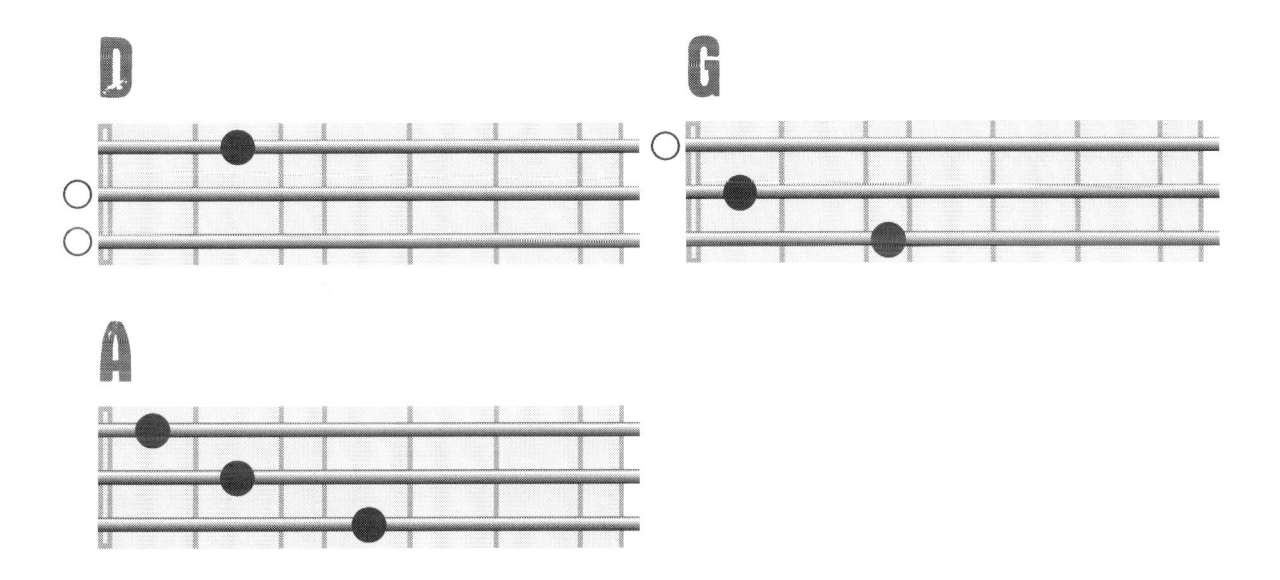

D

G

A

Going down this road

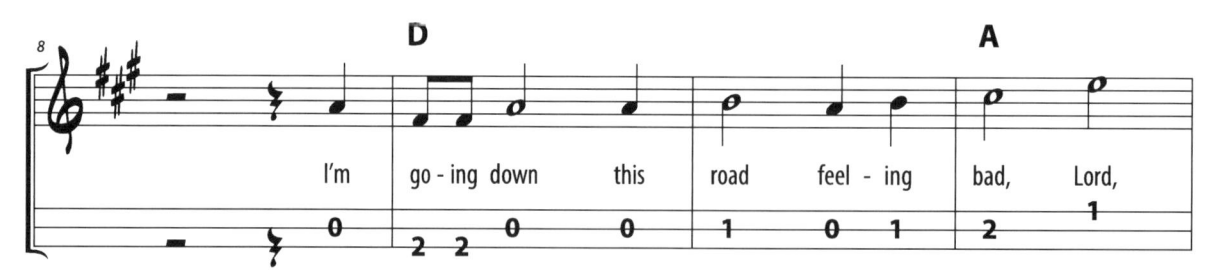

I'm going down this road feeling bad,

I'm going down this road feeling bad,

I'm going down this road feeling bad, Lord,

Lord, and I ain't a-gonna be treated this a way.

2. I'm down in the jailhouse on my knees,
   down in the jailhouse on my knees,
   down in the jailhouse on my knees, Lord, Lord,
   and I ain't a-gonna be treated this a-way.

3. They feed me on corn bread and beans,
   they feed me on corn bread and beans,
   they feed me on corn bread and beans, Lord, Lord,
   and I ain't a-gonna be treated this a-way.

4. Got two dollar shoes on my feet,
   got two dollar shoes on my feet,
   two dollar shoes they hurt my feet, Lord, Lord,
   and I ain't a-gonna be treated this a-way.

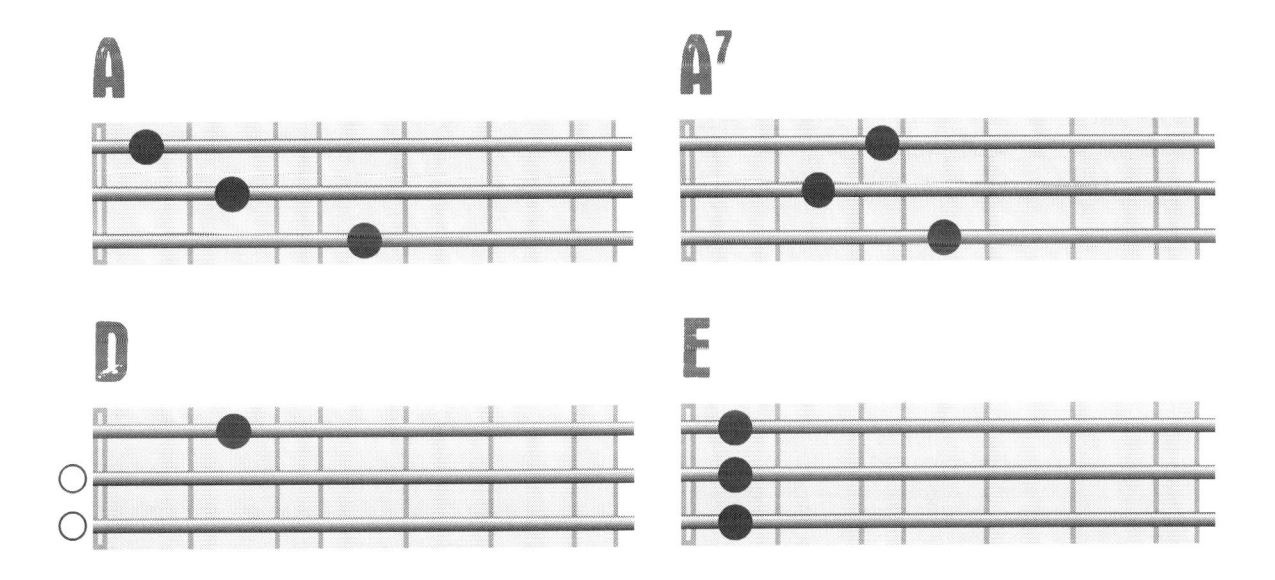

5. I'm going where the weather fits my clothes,
   I'm going where the weather fits my clothes,
   I'm going where the weather fits my clothes, Lord, Lord,
   and I ain't a-gonna be treated this a-way.

Billy the Kid

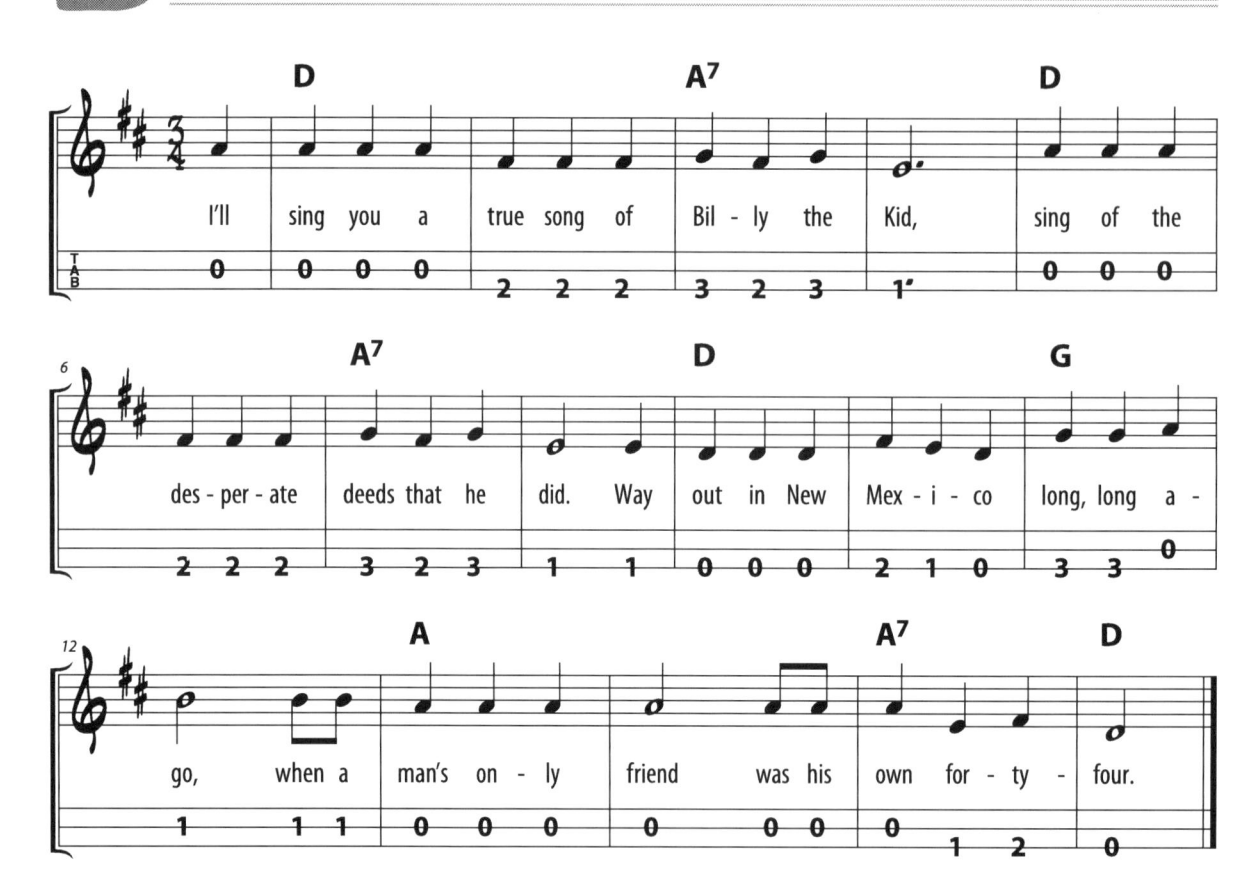

I'll sing you a true song of Bil-ly the Kid, sing of the des-per-ate deeds that he did. Way out in New Mex-i-co long, long a-go, when a man's on-ly friend was his own for-ty - four.

2. When Billy the Kid was a very young lad,
   in old Silver City he went to the bed.
   Way out in the west with a knife in his hand,
   at the age of twelve years he killed his first man.

3. Fair Mexico maidens play guitars and sing,
   songs about Billy their boy bandit king.
   Now here is young manhood that reached its sad end,
   de'd notches on his pistol for twenty-one men.

4. Now 'twas on the same night that poor Billy died,
   he said to his friends: "I'm not satisfied.
   It's twenty-one men that I've put bullets through,
   and sherriff Pat Garrett's gonna make twenty-two".

5. Now this is how Billy the Kid met his fate,
   the bright moon was shining and the hour was late.
   Shot down by Pat Garrett who once was his friend,
   the poor outlaw's life had reached its sad end.

6. There's many a fine boy with a face fine and fair,
   who starts out in life with a chance to be square.
   But just like poor Billy he wanders astray,
   then he loses his life in the very same way.

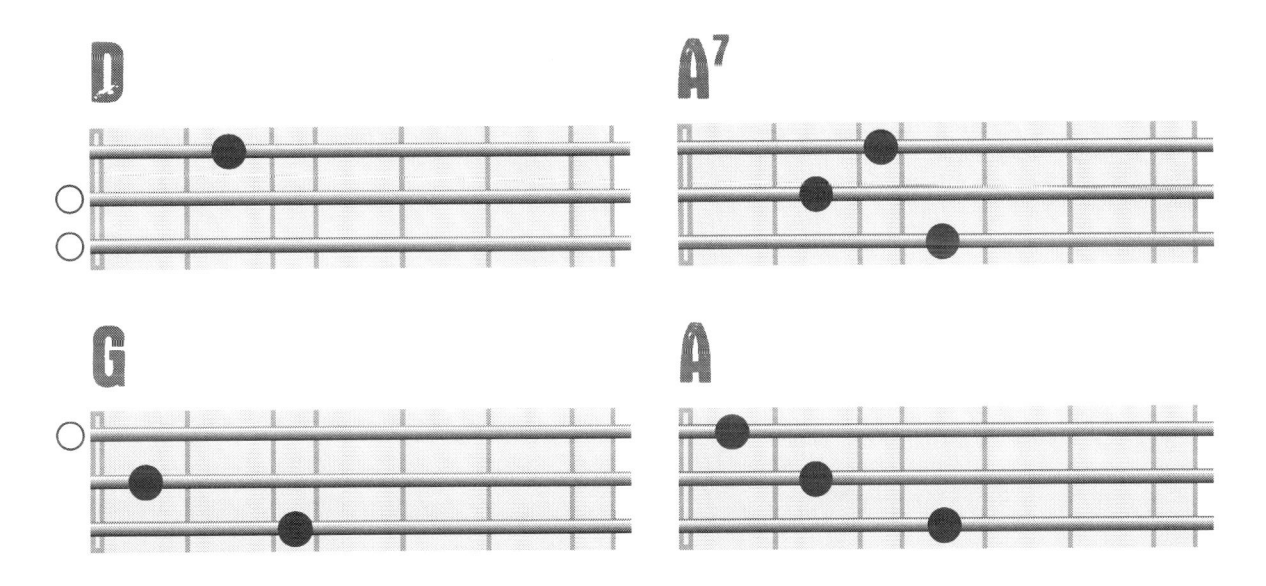

Salty dog Blues

2. Now look-a hear, Sal, I know you,
   run-down stockin' and a worn-out shoes.
   Honey, let me be your salty dog.
   Let me be your salty dog ...

3. I was down in the wildwood settin' on a log,
   finger on the trigger and an eye on the hog
   Honey let me be your salty dog.
   Let me be your salty dog ...

4. I pulled the trigger and the gun said go,
   shot fell over in Mexico.
   Honey let me be your salty dog.
   Let me be your salty dog ...

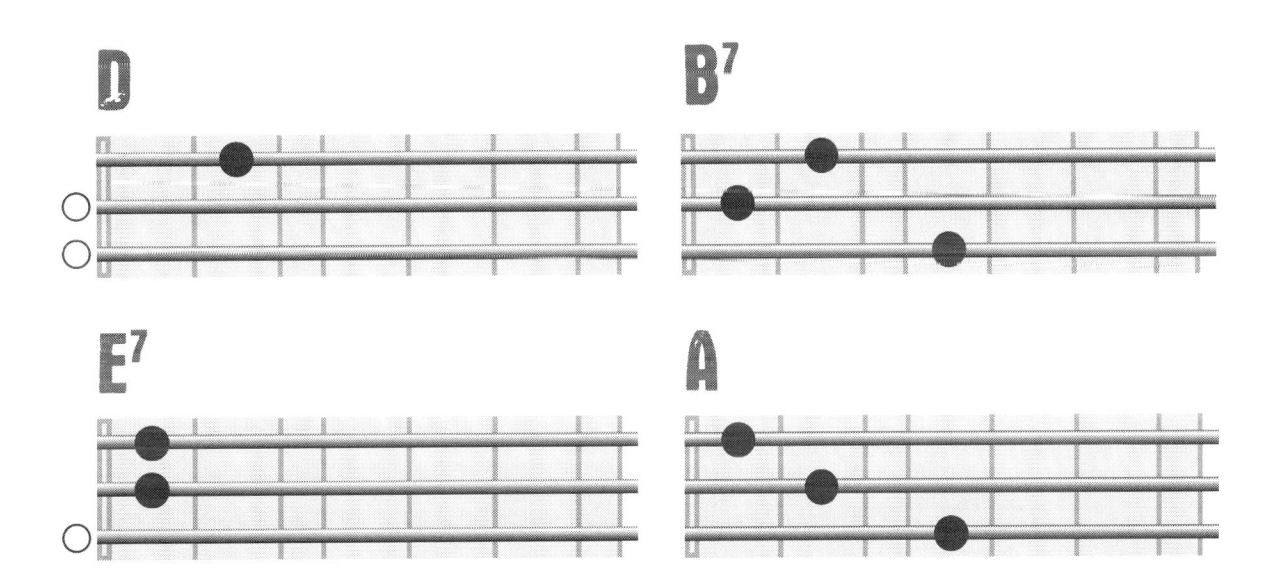

D

B⁷

E⁷

A

Wreck of the old 97

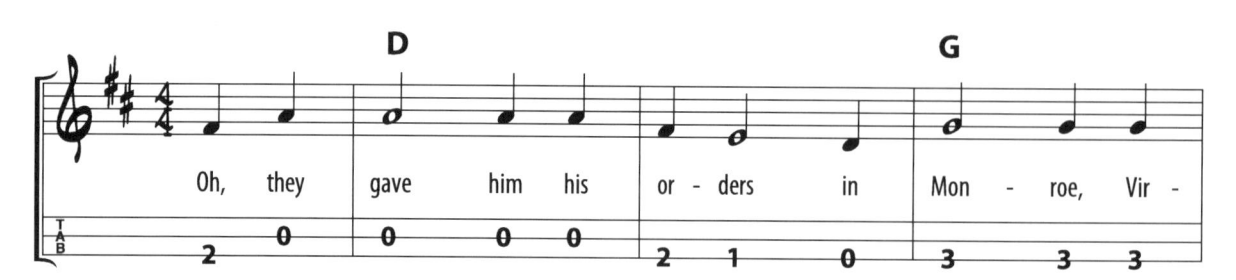

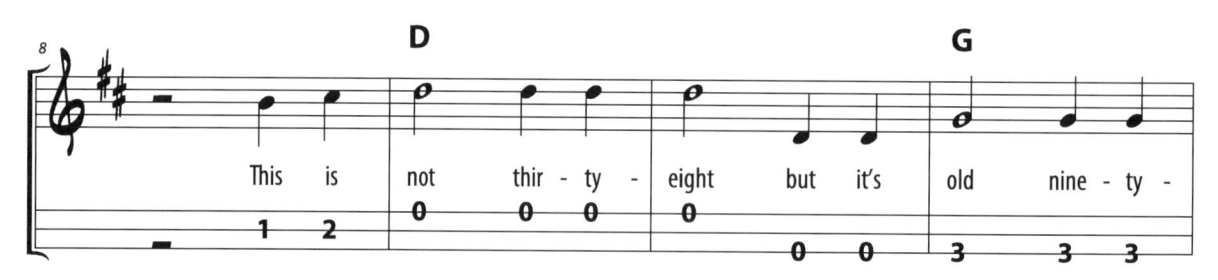

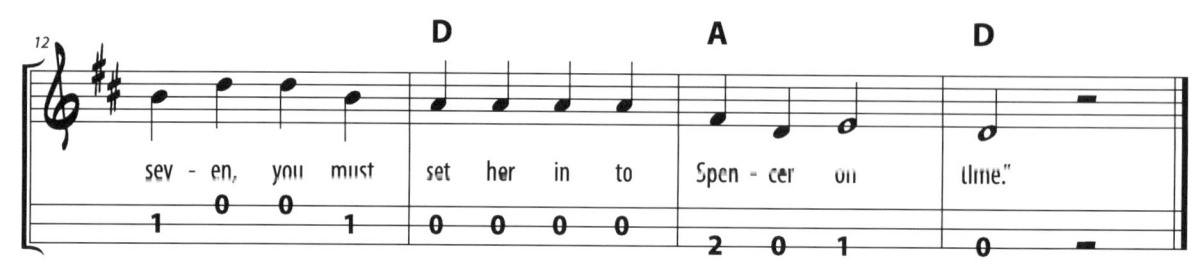

Oh, they gave him his or-ders in Mon-roe, Vir-gin-ia say-ing, "Steve, you're way be-hind time; This is not thir-ty-eight but it's old nine-ty-sev-en, you must set her in to Spen-cer on time."

2. But he turned around to his black greasy fireman,
said: "Heave in a little more coal,
when we reach that White Oak Mountain,
you just watch old 97 roll."

3. It's a mighty rough road from Lynchburg to Danville,
and Lima's on a three-mile grade;
It was on that grade that he lost his air brakes,
you can see what a jump he made.

4. He was going down the grade, doing ninety miles an hour,
when his whistle began to scream;
and they found him in the wreck, with his hand on the throttle,
he was scalded to death by the steam.

5. Oh, ladies, you must take warning,
from this time on and learn:
Never speak harsh words to your true loving husband,
He may leave you and never return.

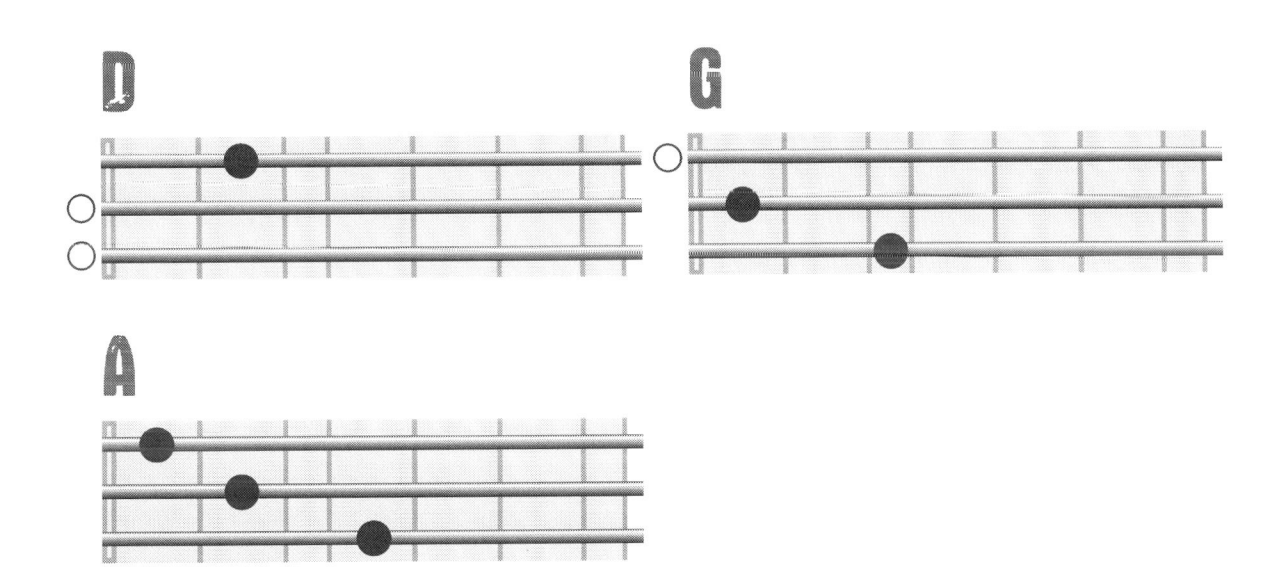

Engine 143

Along came the F. F. V., the swiftest on the line, running o'er the C. 'n' O. Road, just twenty minutes behind. Running into Souville, headquarters on the line, receiving their strict orders from the station right behind.

2. Georgie's mother came to him, a bucket on her arm,
   saying to her darling son, be careful how you run.
   Many a man that's lost his life trying to make lost time,
   And if you run your engine right, you'll get there right on time.

3. Up the tracks she darted against a rock she crashed,
   upside down the engine turned and Georgie's head was smashed.
   His head against the firebox door and the flames were rolling high,
   I'm glad I was born for an engineer on the C. 'n' O. Road to die.

4. The doctor said to Georgie, my darling boy be still,
   your life may yet be saved, if it is God's precious will.
   Oh no, said George, that will not do, I want to die so free,
   I want to die for the engine I love: One Hundred and Forty-Three.

5. The doctor said to Georgie, your life cannot be saved,
   murdered on a railway and laid in a lonesome grave.
   His face was covered up with blood, his eyes they could not see,
   and the very last words poor Georgie said were, Nearer, my God, to Thee.

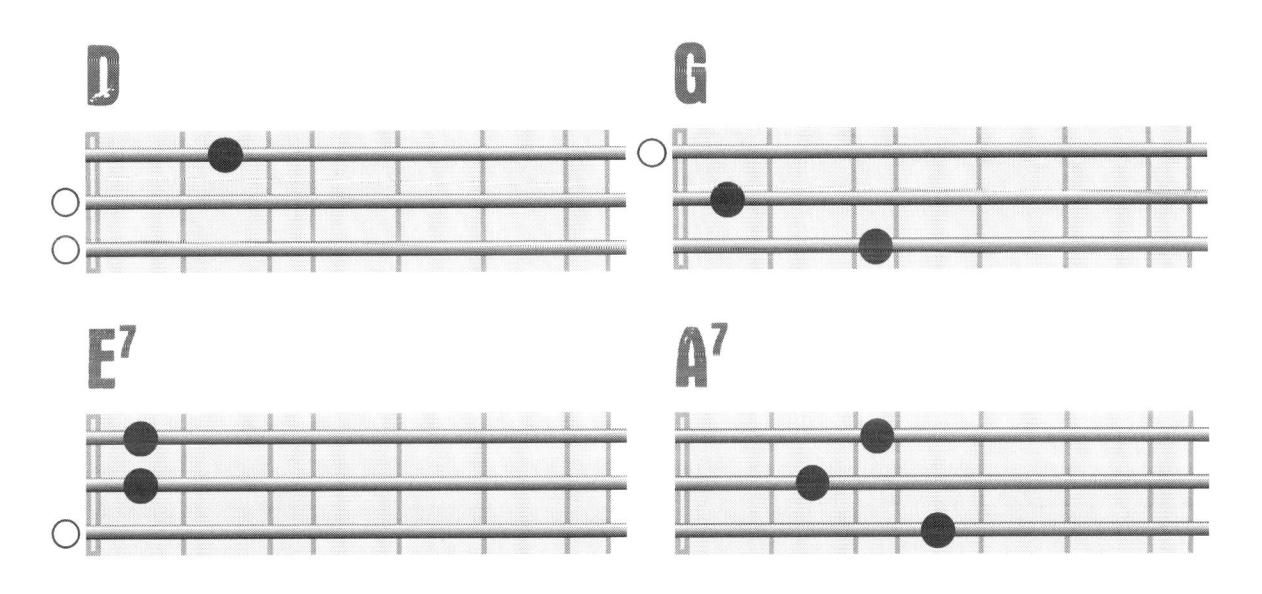

A beautiful life

Each day I'll do a gol-den deed, by help-ing those who are in need; My life on earth is but a span, and so I'll do the best I can. life's even-ing sun is sink-ing low, a few more days, and I must go. To meet the deeds that I have done, where there will be no set-ting sun.

2. To be a child of God each day,
   my light must shine along the way;
   I'll sing His praise while ages roll,
   and strive to help some troubled soul.
   Life's evening sun is sinking low ...

3. The only life that will endure,
   is one that's kind and good and pure;
   And so for God I'll take my stand,
   each day I'll lend a helping hand.
   Life's evening sun is sinking low ...

4. I'll help someone in time of need,
   and journey on with rapid speed;
   I'll help the sick and poor and weak,
   And words of kindness to them speak.
   Life's evening sun is sinking low ...

5. While going down life's weary road,
   I'll try to lift some trav'ler's load;
   I'll try to turn the night to day,
   make flowers bloom along the way.
   Life's evening sun is sinking low ...

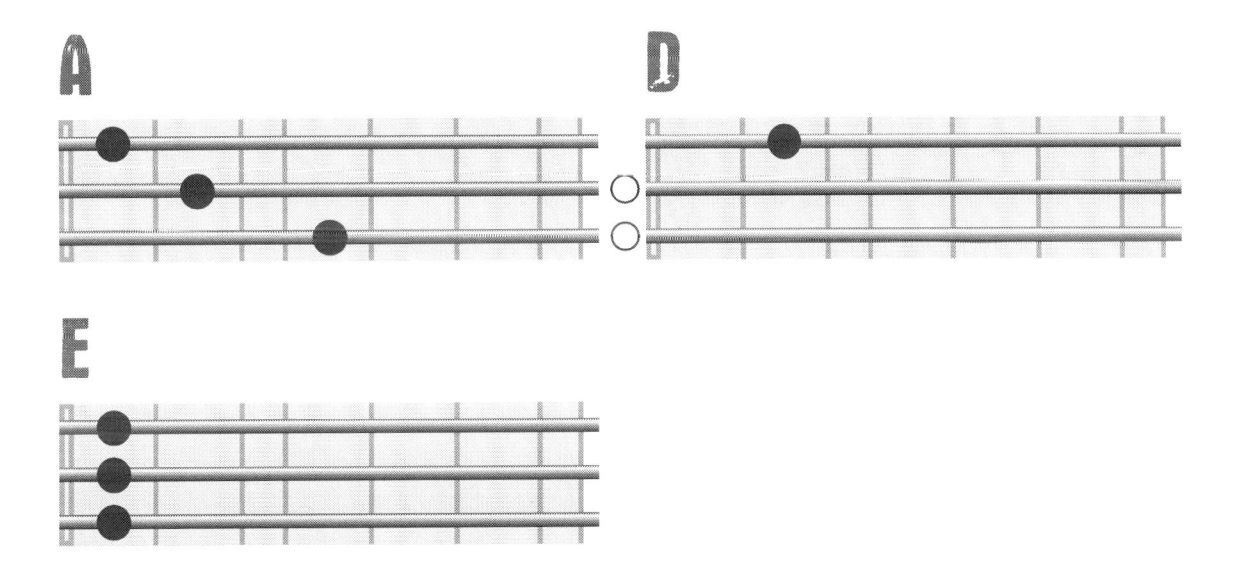

Come all ye fair and tender ladies

D

Come all ye fair and ten-der la-dies,

A7

take warn-ing how you court your men.

Em **D**

They're like a star on a sum-mer morn-ing,

Em **D**

they first ap-pear and then they're gone.

2. They'll tell to you some loving story,
   and they'll make you think that they love you well.
   And away they'll go and court some other,
   and leave you there in grief to dwell.

3. I wish I was on some tall mountain,
   where the ivy rocks are black as ilk.
   I'd write a letter to my false true lover,
   whose cheeks are like the morning pink.

4. I wish I was a little sparrow,
   and I had wings to fly so high.
   I'd fly to the arms of my false true lover,
   and when he'd ask, I would deny.

5. Oh love is handsome, love is charming,
   and love is pretty while it's new.
   But love grows cold as love grows old,
   and fades away like morning dew.

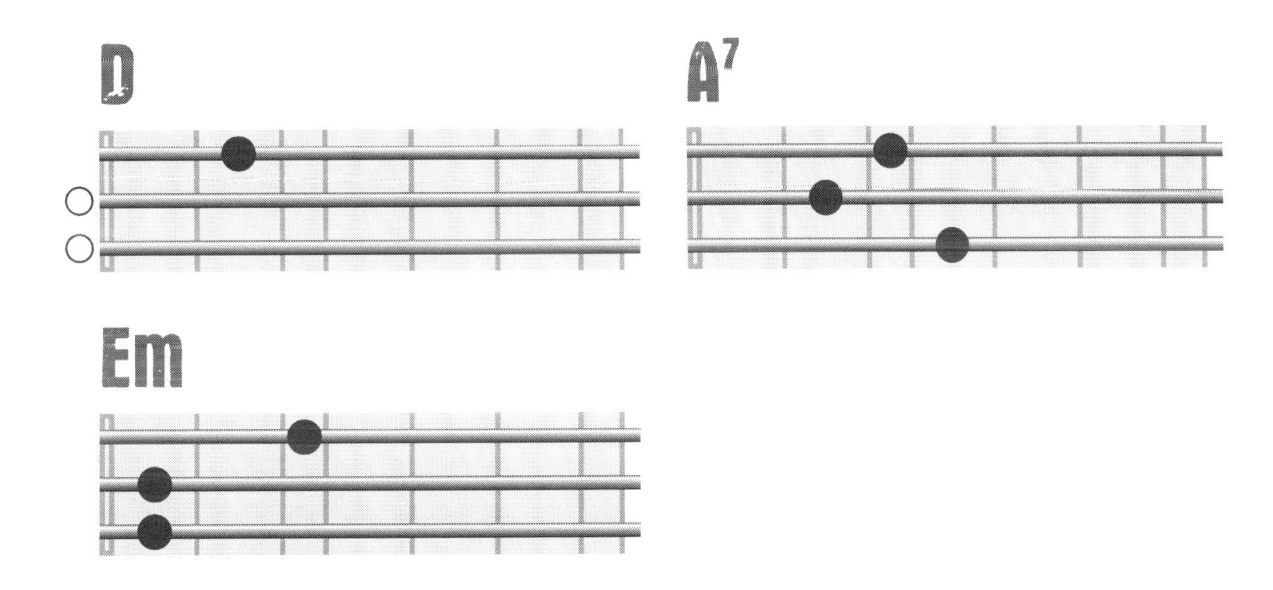

D

A⁷

Em

Frankie and Johnny

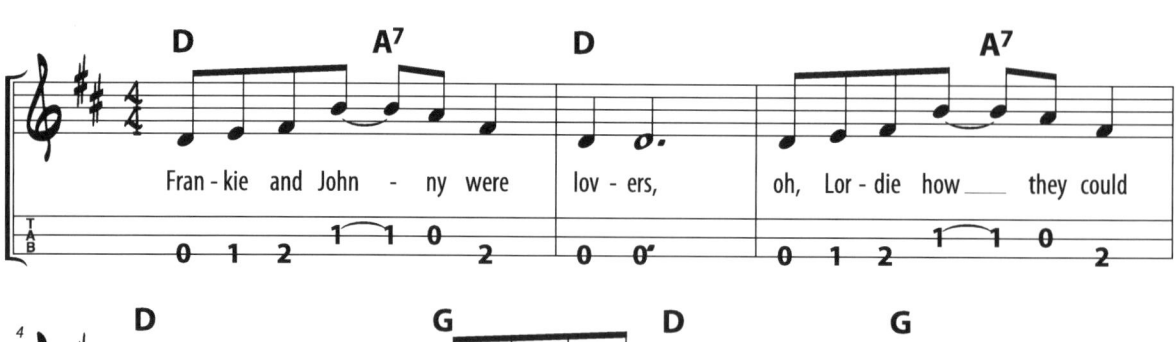

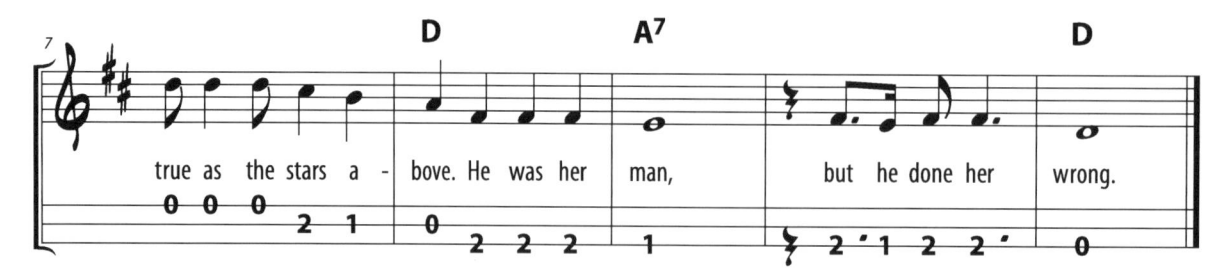

Fran-kie and John-ny were lov-ers, oh, Lor-die how they could love! They swore to be true to each o-ther, just as true as the stars a-bove. He was her man, but he done her wrong.

2. Frankie and Johnny went walking
   John in his brandnew suit.
   Then, "oh good Lawd," says Frankie,
   "Don't my Johnny look real cute!"
   He was her man, but he done her wrong.

3. Frankie she was a good woman,
   and Johnnie was a good man.
   And every dollar that she made,
   went right into Johnny's hand.
   He was her man, but he done her wrong.

4. Frankie went down to the corner,
   just for a bucket of beer.
   She said to the fat bartender,
   "Has my loveliest man been here?"
   He was her man, but he done her wrong.

5. "I don't want to cause you no trouble,
   I don't want to tell you no lie.
   But I saw your man an hour ago
   with a gal named Alice Bly.
   And if he's your man, he's a-doing you wrong."

6. Frankie looked over the transom,
   and found, to her great surprise,
   that there on the bed sat Johnny,
   a-lovin' up Alice Bly.
   He was her man, but he done her wrong.

7. Frankie drew back her kimono;
   She took out her little forty-four.
   Root-a-toot-toot, three times she shot,
   right through that hardwood floor,
   She shot her man, 'cause he done her wrong.

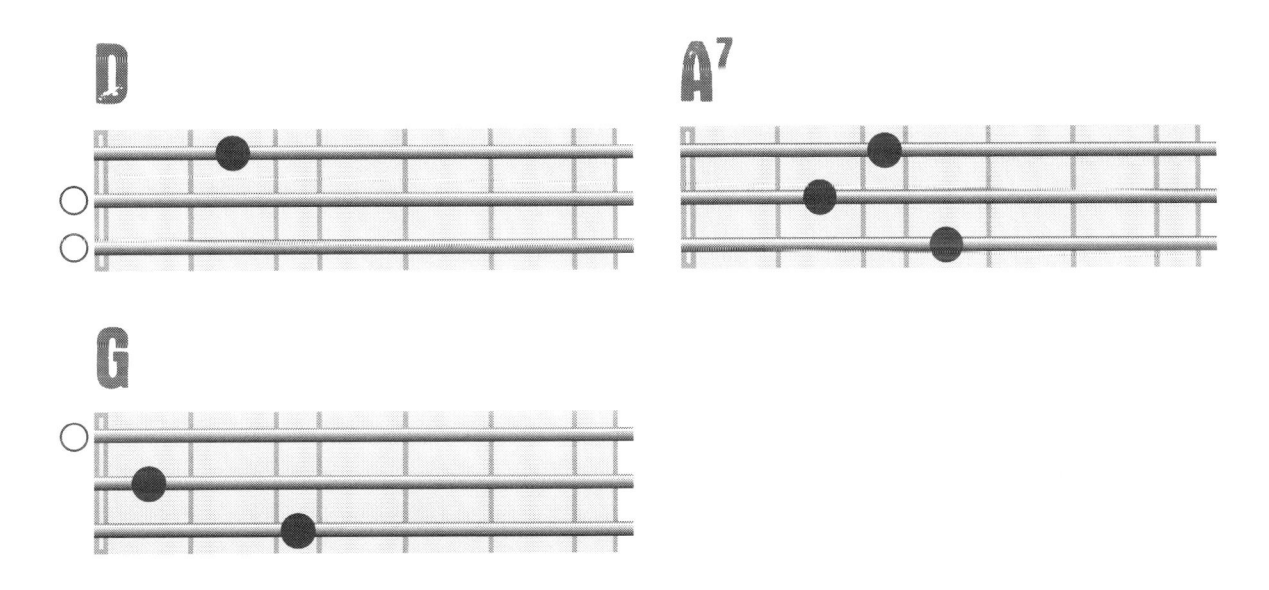

D

A⁷

G

Colorado trail

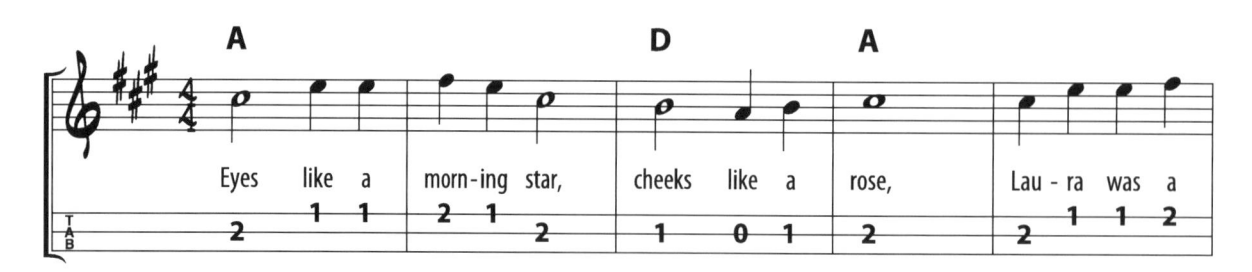

Eyes like a morning star, cheeks like a rose, Laura was a pretty girl God Al-might-y knows! Weep all you lit-tle rains, wail, winds, wail, all a-long, a-long, a-long the Col-o-rad-o trail.

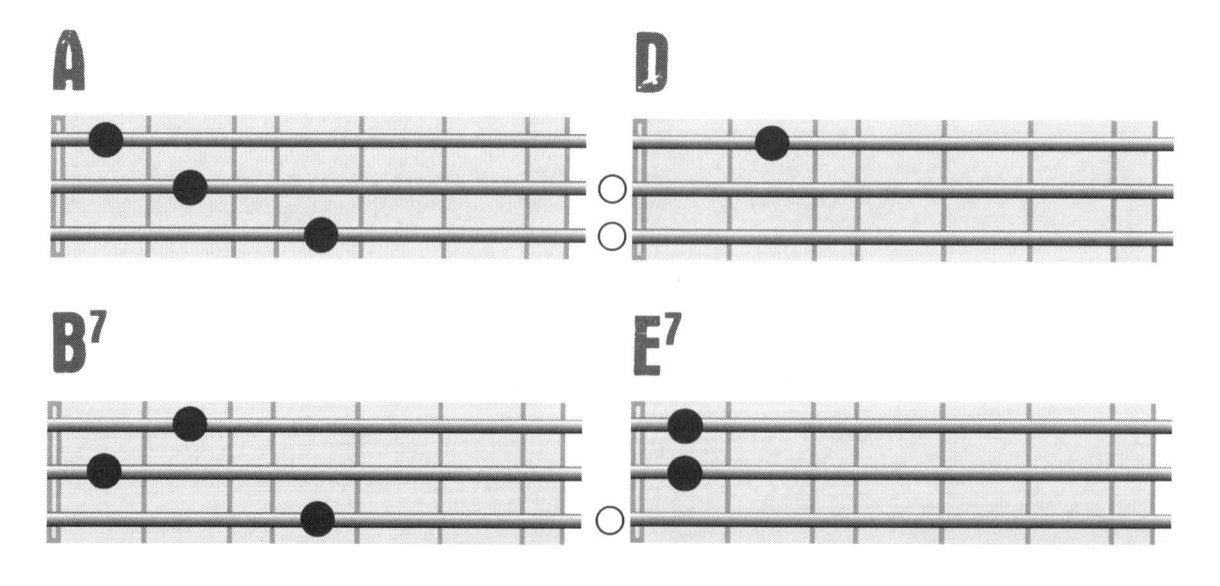

Dink's Song

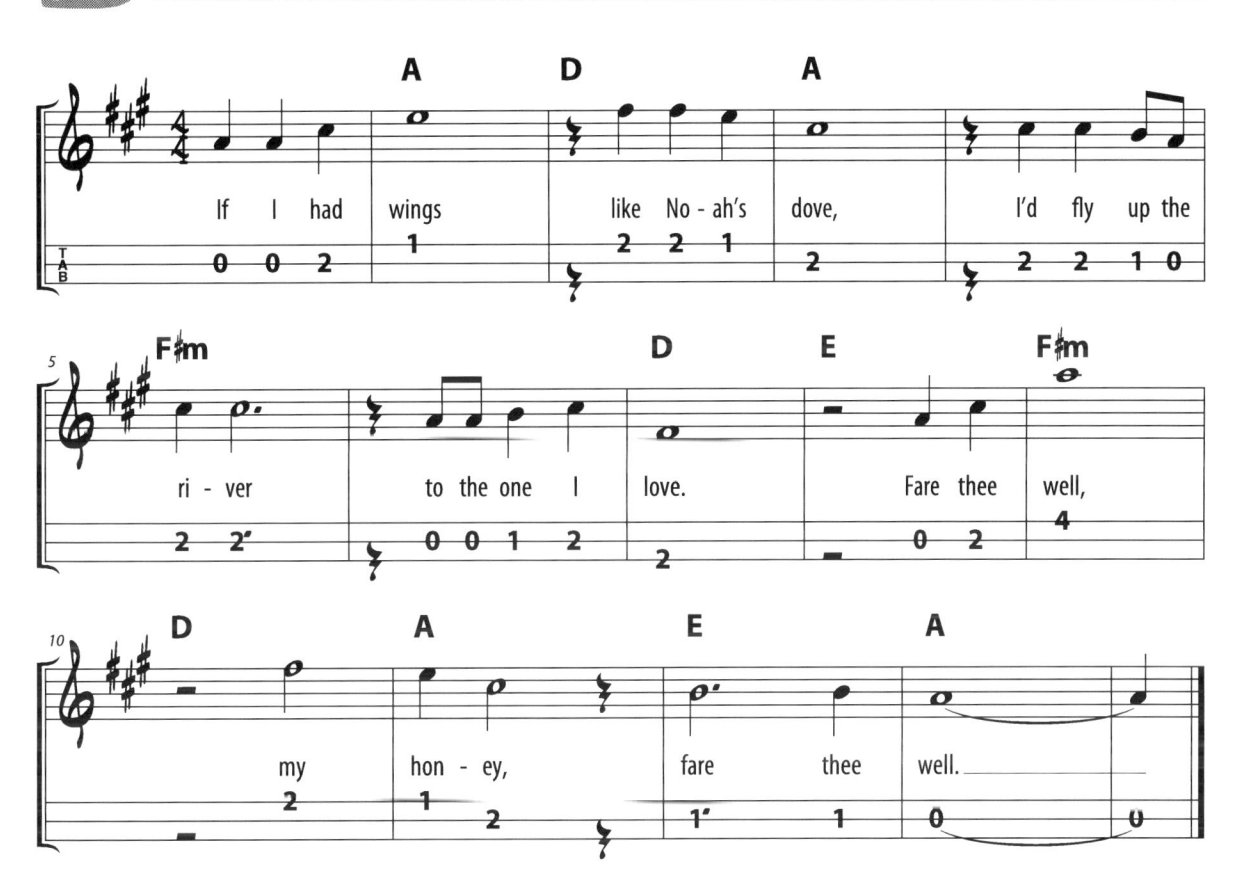

2. I've got a man and he's long and tall,
   he moves his body like a cannon ball.
   Fare thee well, my honey, fare thee well.

3. I remember one night, it was drizzling rain,
   and in my heart, I felt an aching pain.
   Fare thee well, my honey, fare thee well.

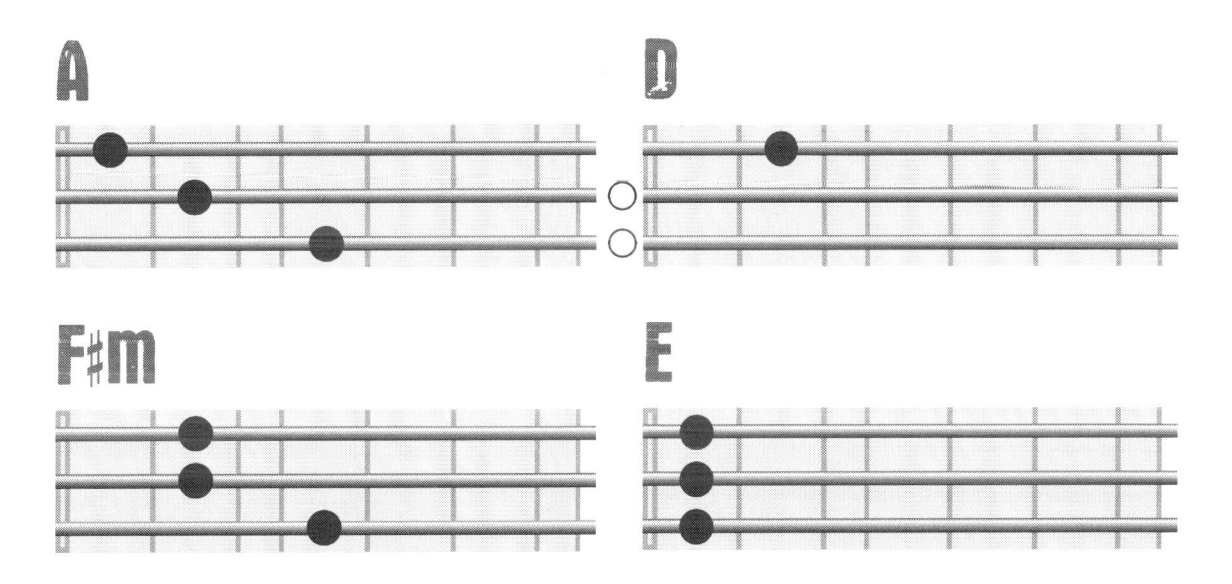

Nine pound hammer

This nine pound hammer is a little too heavy, buddy, for my size, buddy, for my size.

(Chorus): Roll on, buddy, don't you roll so slow. How can I roll when the wheels won't go?

2. I'm going on the mountain just to see my baby,
   and I ain't coming back, no, I ain't coming back.
   Roll on buddy ...

3. There ain't one hammer down in this tunnel,
   that can ring like mine, that can ring like mine.
   Roll on buddy ...

4. Rings like silver, shines like gold,
   rings like silver, shines like gold.
   Roll on buddy ...

5. This old hammer it killed John Henry,
   ain't gonna kill me, ain't gonna kill me.
   Roll on buddy ...

6. It's a long way to Harlan, it's a long way to Hazard,
   just to get a little brew, just to get a little brew.
   Roll on buddy ...

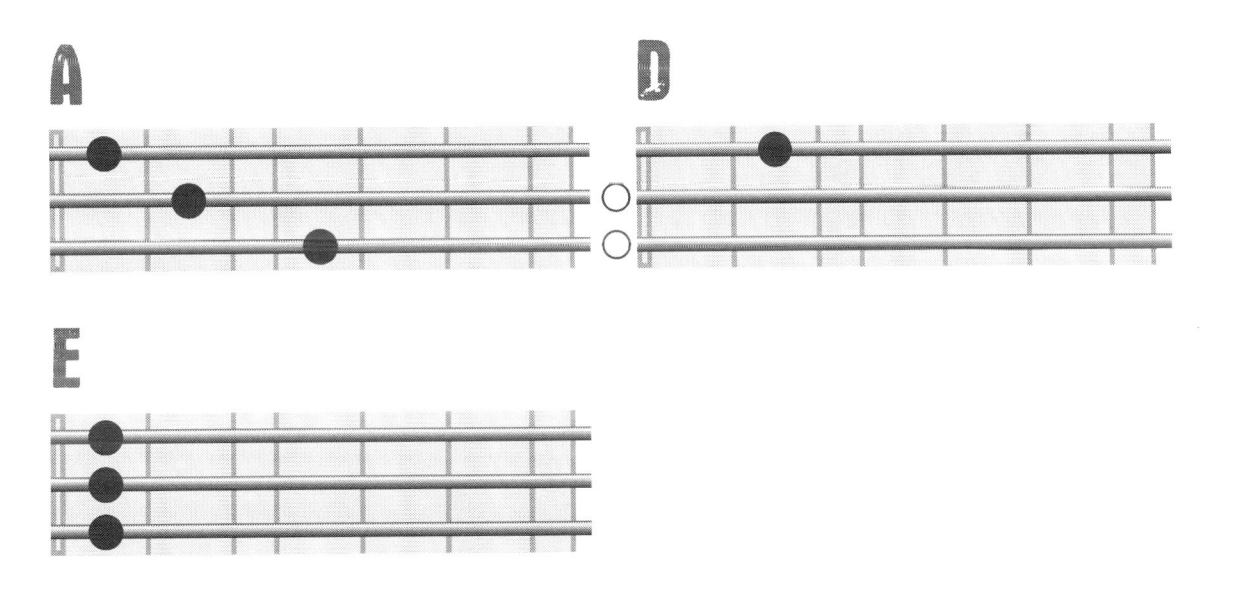

A

D

E

Midnight train

A
I'm rid - ing on that mid - night train, my
D
A
head is sink - ing low. These lone - some
E
A
blues will fol - low me, where - e - ver I may go.

2. No matter what I say or do,
   you're never satisfied.
   I tried and tried so many times,
   I'm leaving you now goodbye.

3. Oh, why on Earth was I ever born,
   I'll never understand.
   To fall in love with a woman like you,
   in love with another man.

A

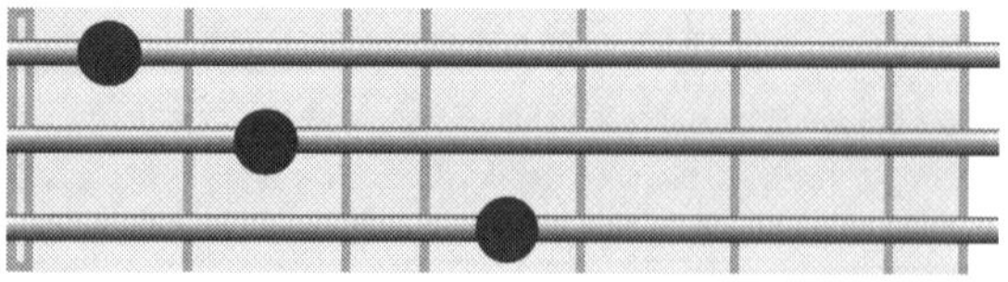

D

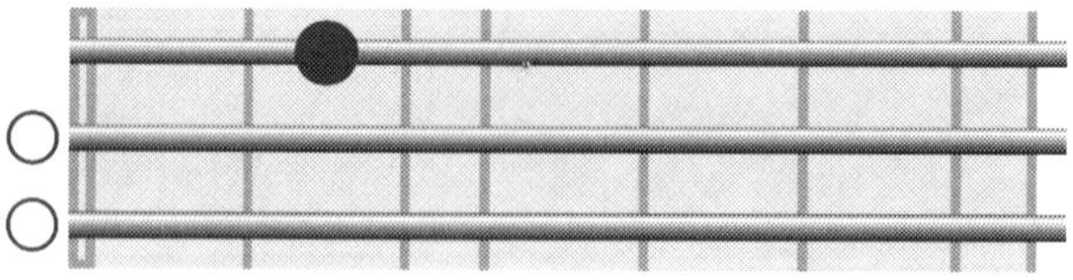

E

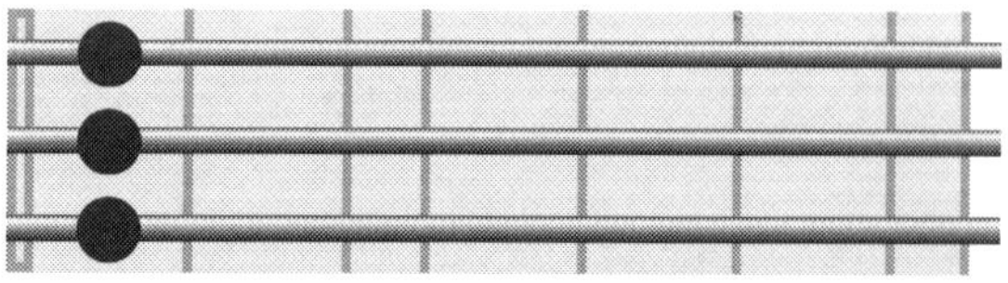

ain't gonna work tomorrow

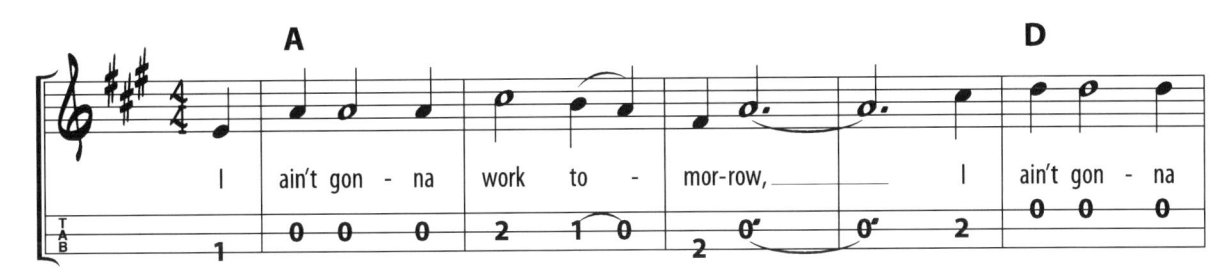

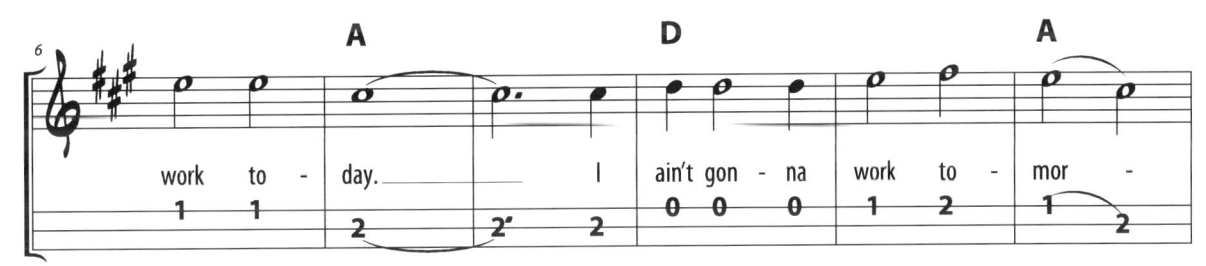

2. I love my mama and papa, too,
   I love my mama and papa, too.
   I love my mama and papa too,
   but I'd leave them both to go with you.

3. I've been all around this country,
   I've been all around this world.
   I've been all around this country,
   For the sake of one little girl.

4. I'm leaving you this lonesome song,
   I'm leaving you this lonesome song.
   I'm leaving you this lonesome song,
   'cause I'm gonna be gone before long.

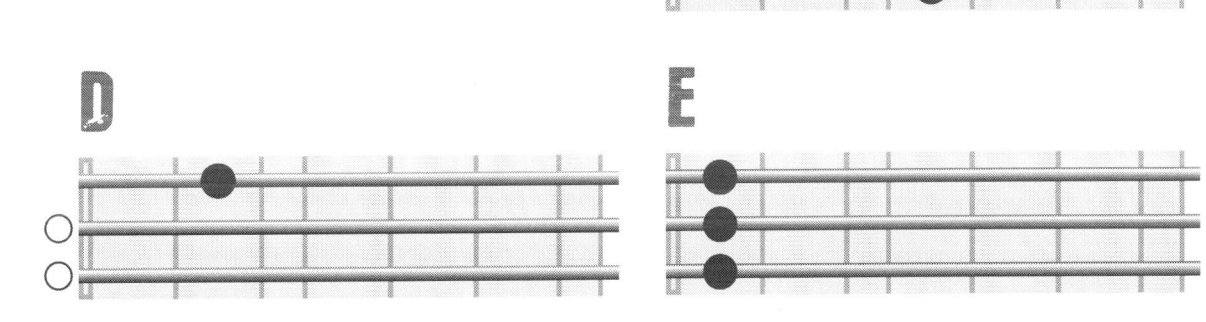

Don't this road look rough and rocky

Darling, I have come to tell you, though it almost breaks my heart,

but before the morning, darling, we'll be many miles apart.

Don't this road look rough and rocky, don't that sea look wide and deep?

Don't my baby look the sweetest, when she's in my arms asleep!

54

2. Can't you hear the night birds crying,
   far across the deep blue sea?
   While of others you are thinking,
   won't you sometimes think of me?
   Don't this road look rough and rocky ...

3. One more kiss before I leave you,
   one more kiss before we part.
   You have caused me lots of trouble,
   darling you have broke my heart.
   Don't this road look rough and rocky ...

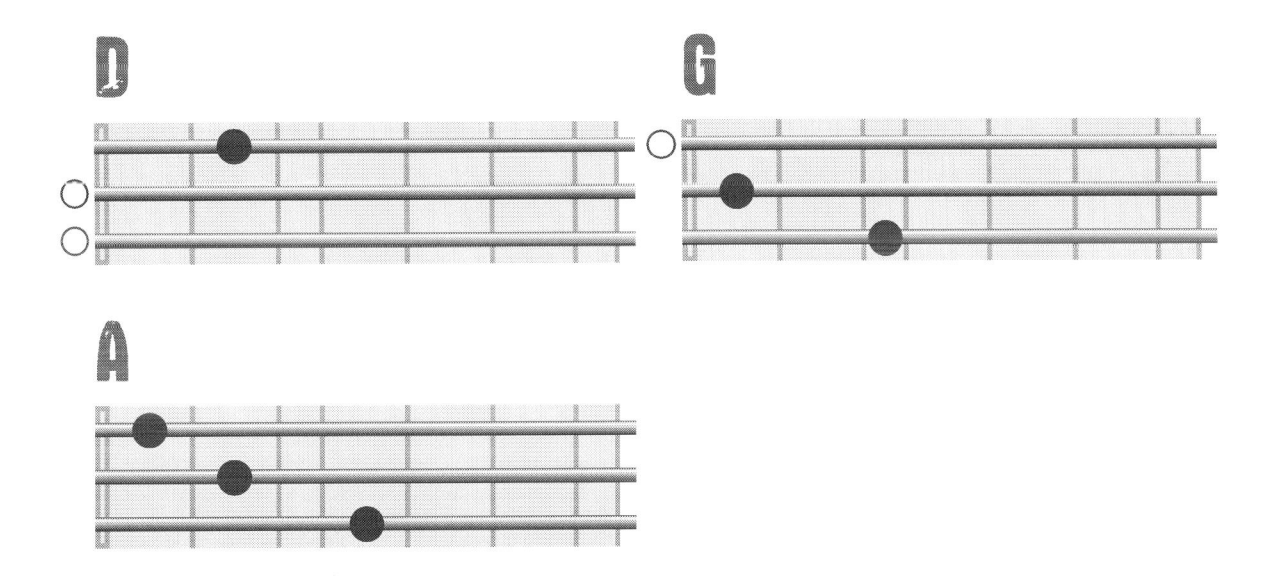

D

G

A

Drifting too far from the shore

Out on the perilous deep, where danger silently creeps, and storms so violently sweeping, you're drifting too far from the shore. Drifting too far from the shore, you're drifting too far from the shore. Come to Jesus today, let him show you the

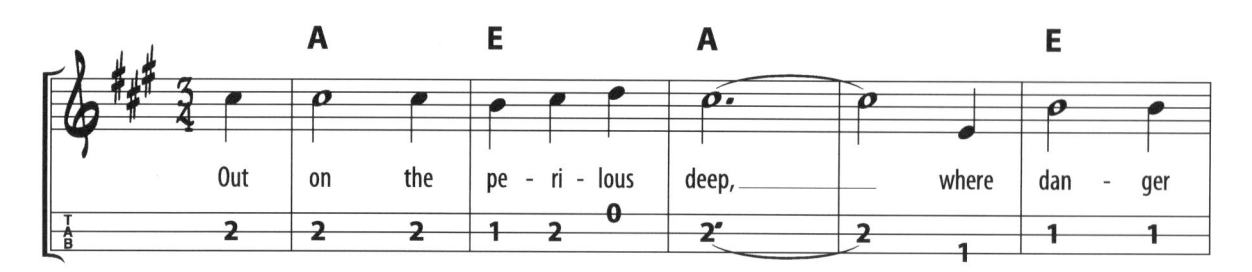

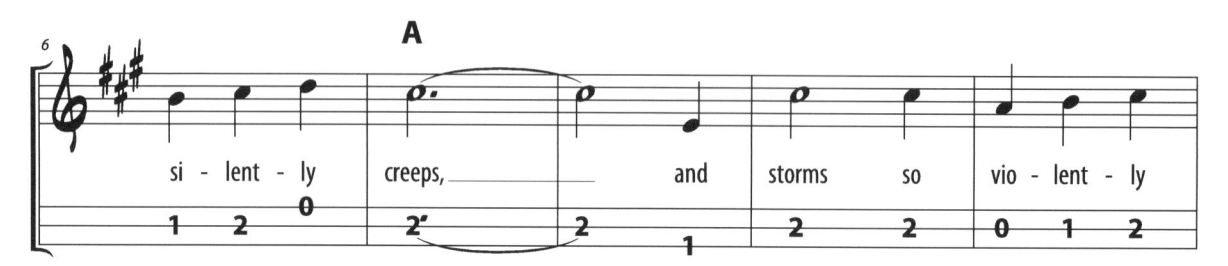

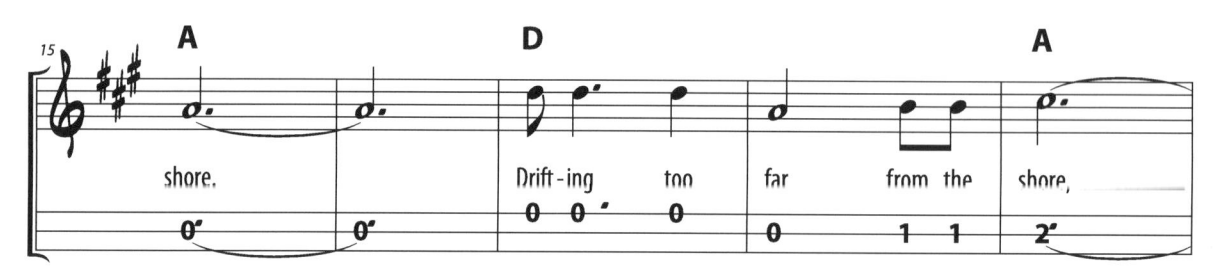

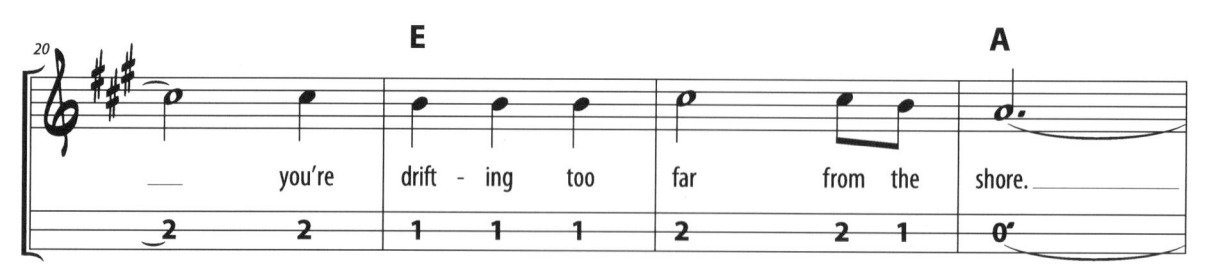

2. Today the tempest rolls high,
   and clouds overshadow the sky.
   Sure death is hovering nigh,
   drifting too far from the shore.
   Drifting too far from the shore ...

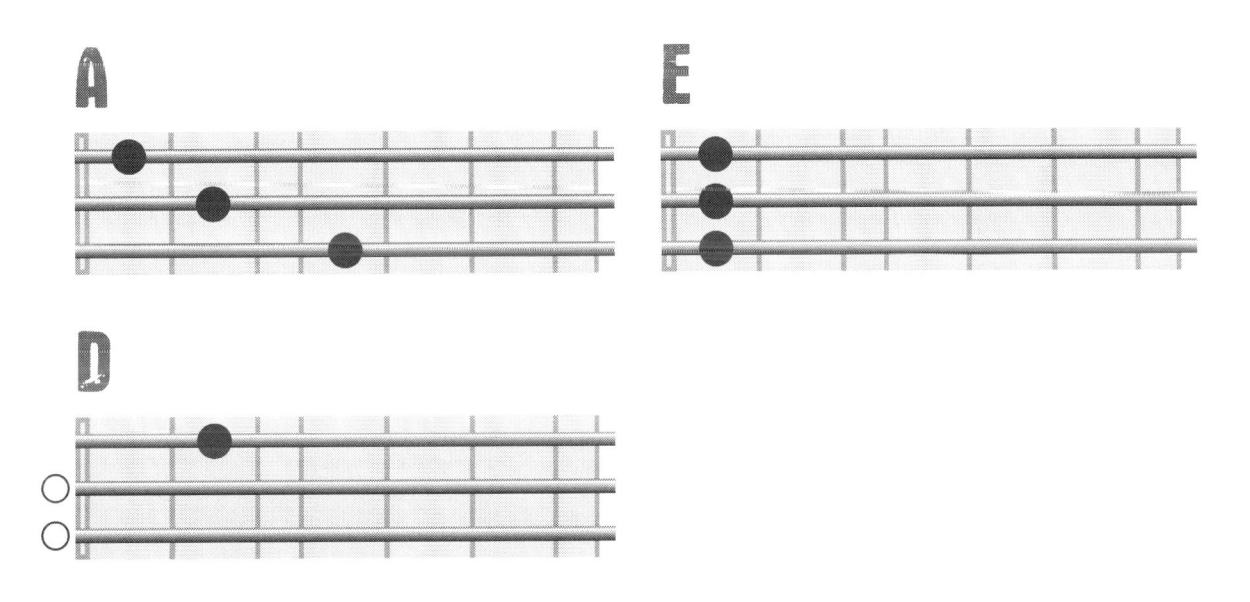

Shady grove

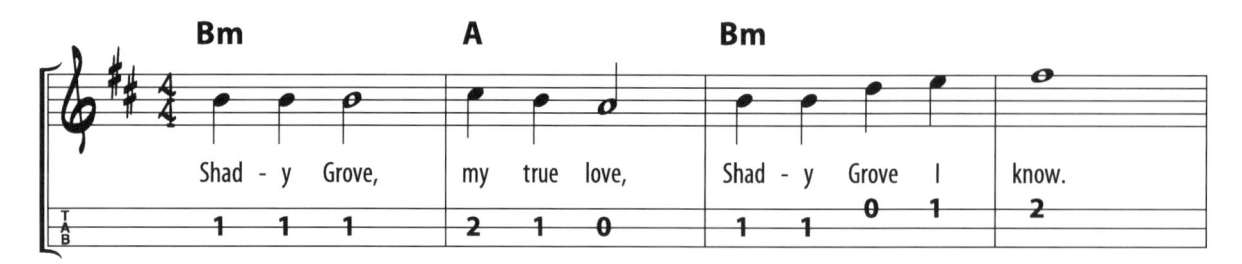

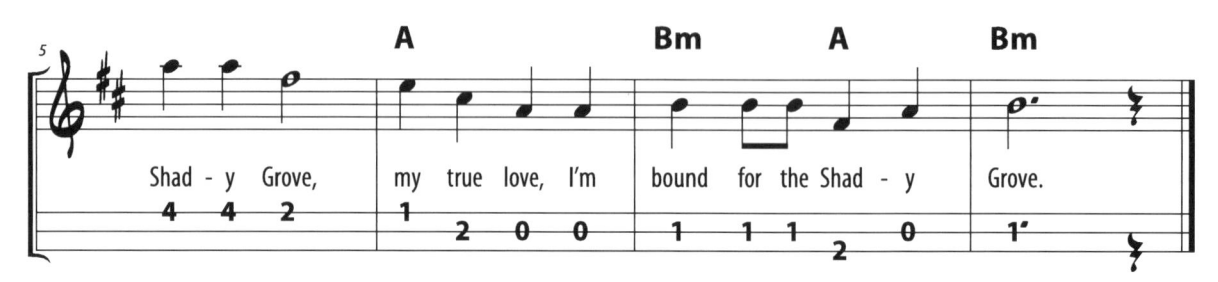

2. Peaches in the summertime,
   apples in the fall.
   If I can't have my Shady Grove,
   I'll have no one at all.

3. Cheeks as red as a blooming rose,
   eyes of the deepest brown.
   She is the darling of my heart,
   prettiest girl in town.

4. The first time I saw Shady Grove,
   she was standing at the door.
   Shoes and stockings in her hand,
   little bare feet on the floor.

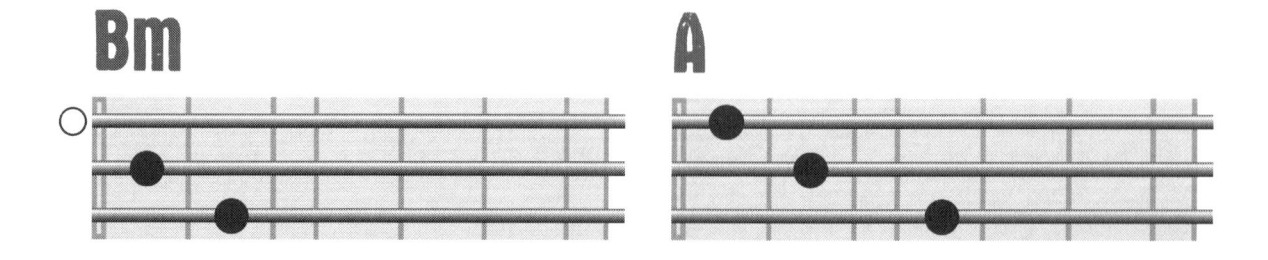

Foggy mountain top

If I was on some foggy mountain top, I'd sail a-way to the West. I'd sail all a-round this whole wide world, to the girl I love the best.

2. If I'd only listened to what my mama said,
   I would not be here today.
   Lying around this old jailhouse,
   wasting my poor life away.
   If I was on some foggy mountain top …

3. Oh she caused me to weep, she caused me to mourn,
   she caused me to leave my home.
   Oh the lonesome pines and the good old times,
   I'm on my way back home.
   If I was on some foggy mountain top …

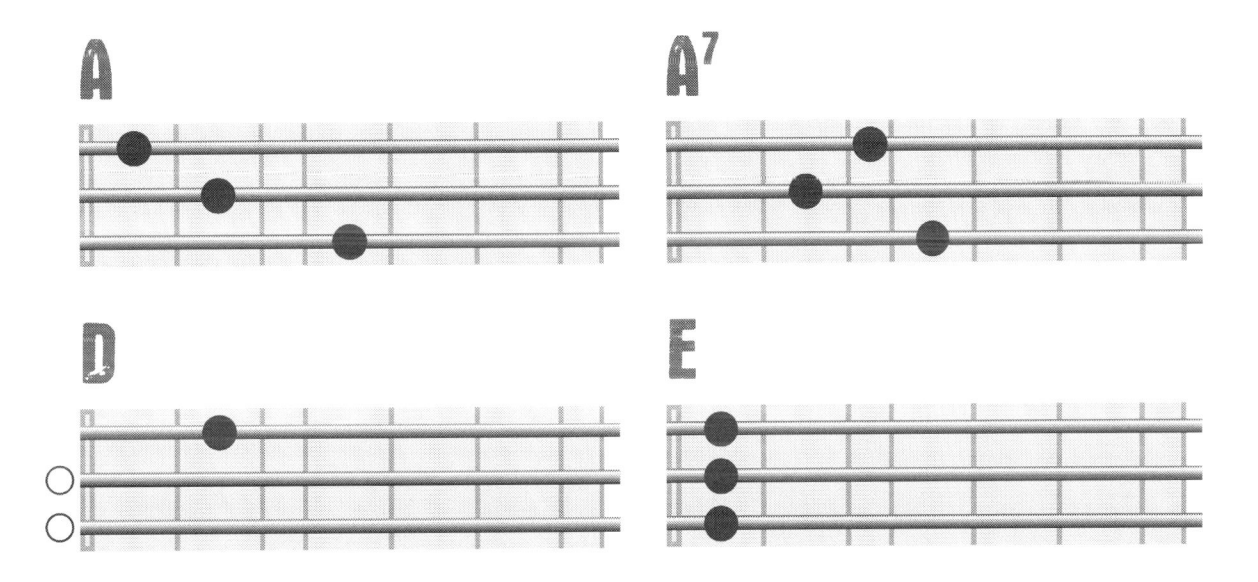

59

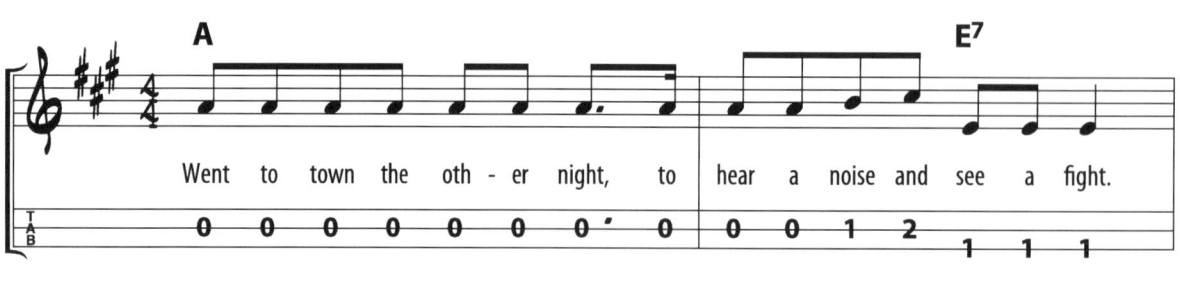

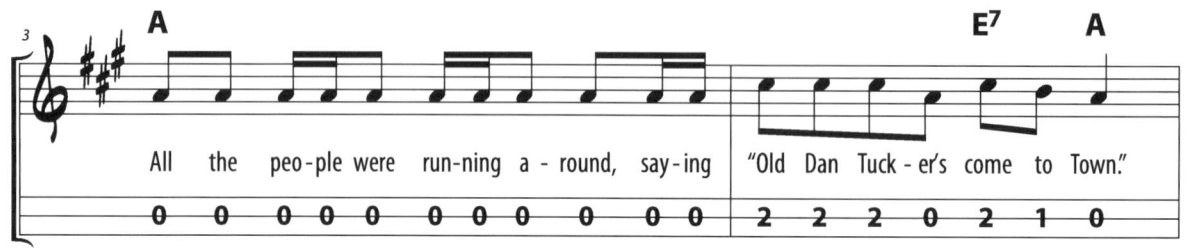

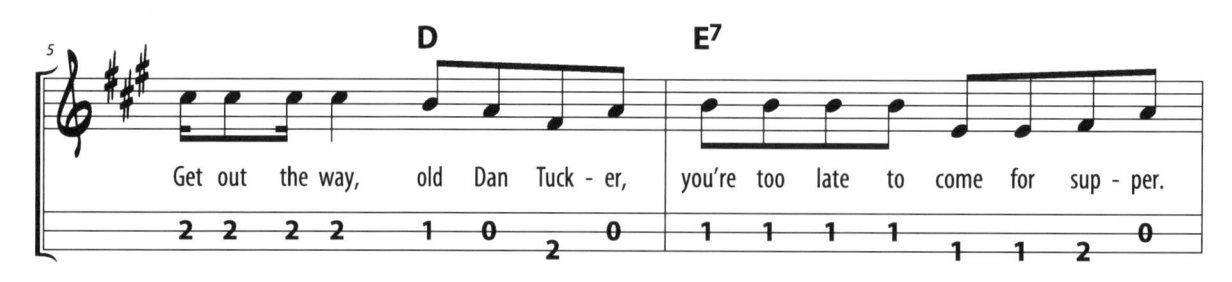

Old Dan Tucker

2. Old Dan Tucker's a fine old man,
   washed his face in a frying pan.
   Combed his hair with a wagon wheel,
   died of toothache in his heel.
   Get out the way, old Dan Tucker ...

3. Old Dan Tucker he come to town,
   riding on a billygoat, leading a hound.
   Hound dog bark and the billygoat jump,
   throwed Dan Tucker on top of a stump.
   Get out the way, old Dan Tucker ...

4. Old Dan Tucker, he got drunk,
   fell in the fire and he kicked up a chunk.
   Red hot coal got in his shoe,
   oh my Lawdy how the ashes flew.
   Get out the way, old Dan Tucker ...

5. Old Dan Tucker, he come to town,
   swinging the ladies round and round,
   first to the right and then to the left,
   and then to the gal that he loved best.
   Get out the way, old Dan Tucker ...

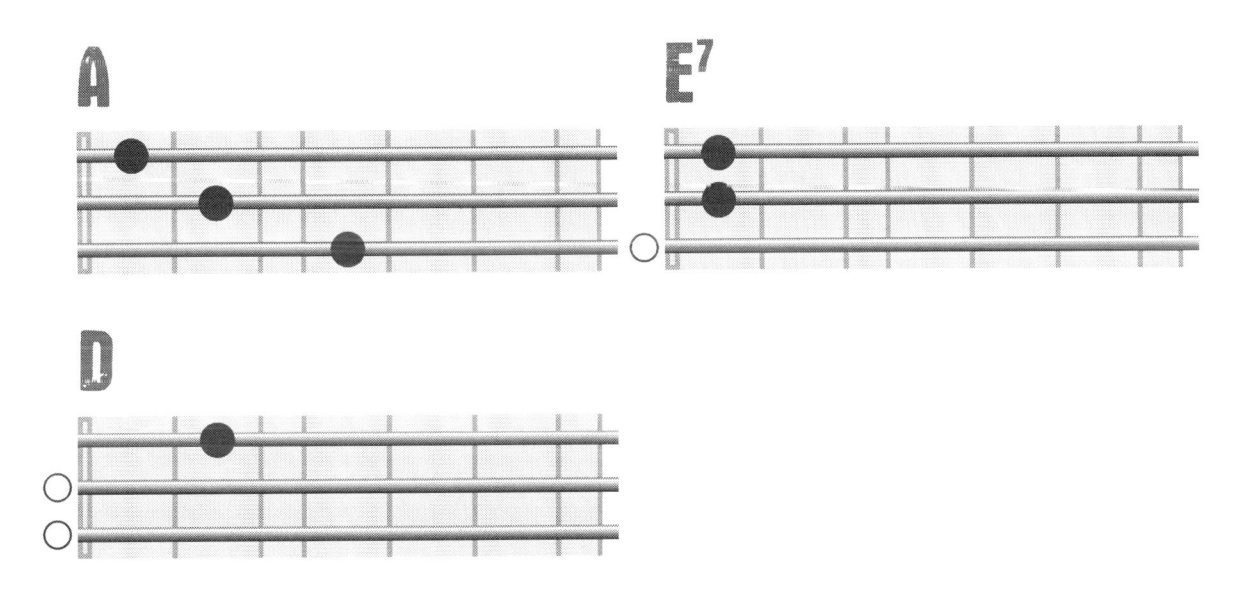

A

E⁷

D

61

Molly and Tenbrooks

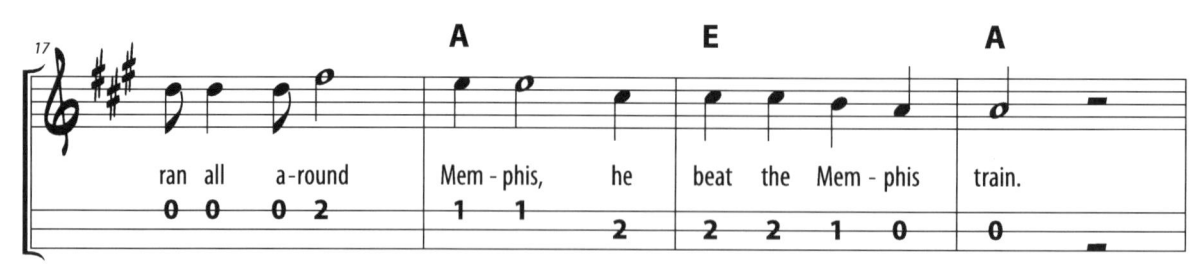

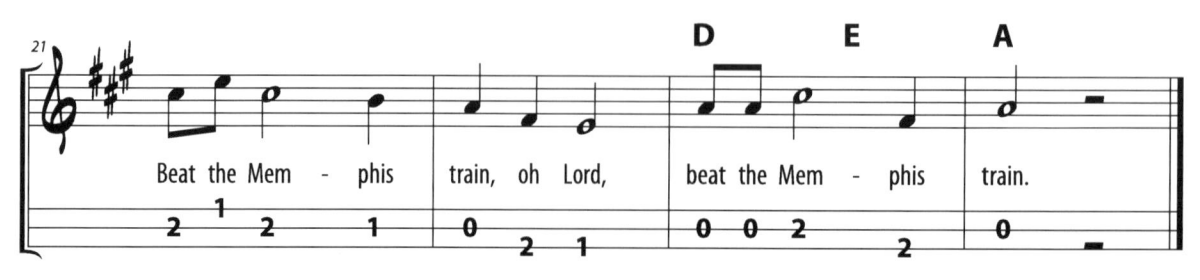

Run old Mol-ly run, run old Mol-ly run, Ten-brooks go-nna beat you to the bright shin-ing sun, to the bright shin-ing sun, oh Lord, to the bright shin-ing sun.

Ten-brooks was a big bay horse, he wore a shag-gy mane. He ran all a-round Mem-phis, he beat the Mem-phis train. Beat the Mem-phis train, oh Lord, beat the Mem-phis train.

62

2. Tenbrooks said to Molly, what makes your head so red?
   Running in the hot sun with a fever in my head.
   Fever in my head, oh Lord, fever in my head.

3. Molly said to Tenbrooks you're looking mighty squirrel,
   Tenbrooks said to Molly I'm leaving this old world.
   Leaving this old world, oh Lord, leaving this old world.

4. Out in California where Molly done as she pleased,
   she come back to old Kentucky, got beat with all ease.
   Beat with all ease, oh Lord, beat with all ease.

5. The women's all a-laughing, the children all a-crying,
   men's all a-hollering old Tenbrooks a-flying.
   Old Tenbrooks a-flying, oh Lord, Old Tenbrooks a-flying.

6. Kaiper, Kaiper, you're not riding right,
   Molly's a beating old Tenbrooks clear out of sight.
   Clear out of sight, oh Lord, clear out of sight.

7. Kaiper, Kaiper, Kaiper my son,
   give old Tenbrooks the bridle and let old Tenbrooks run.
   Let old Tenbrooks run, oh Lord, let old Tenbrooks run.

8. Go and catch old Tenbrooks and hitch him in the shade,
   we're gonna bury old Molly in a coffin ready made.
   In a coffin ready made, oh Lord, in a coffin ready made.

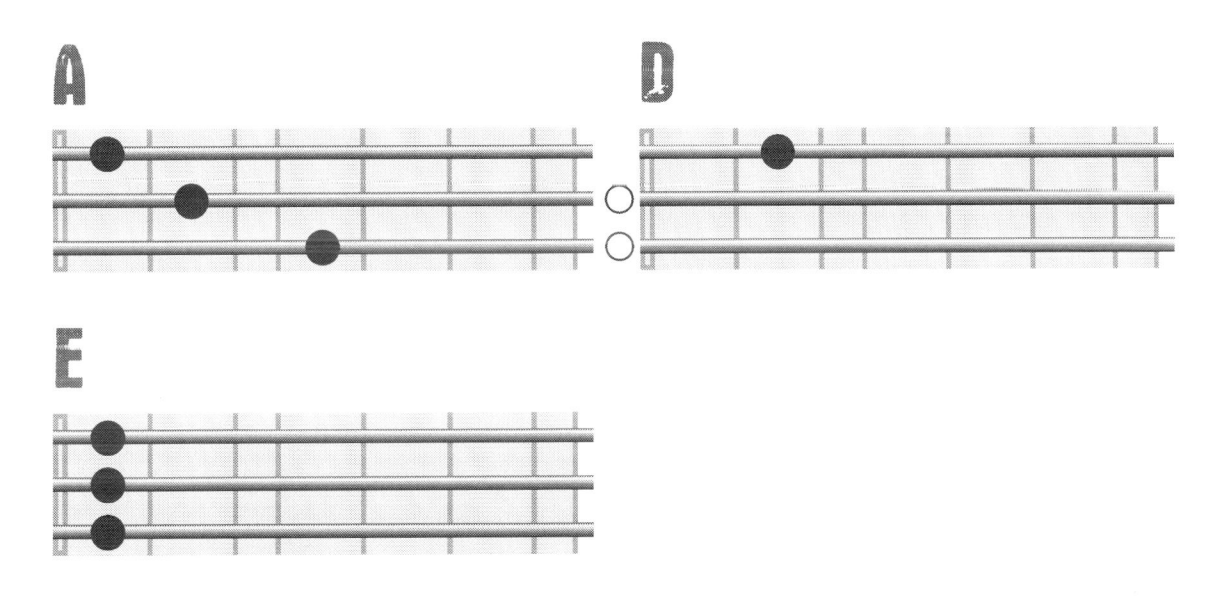

A

D

E

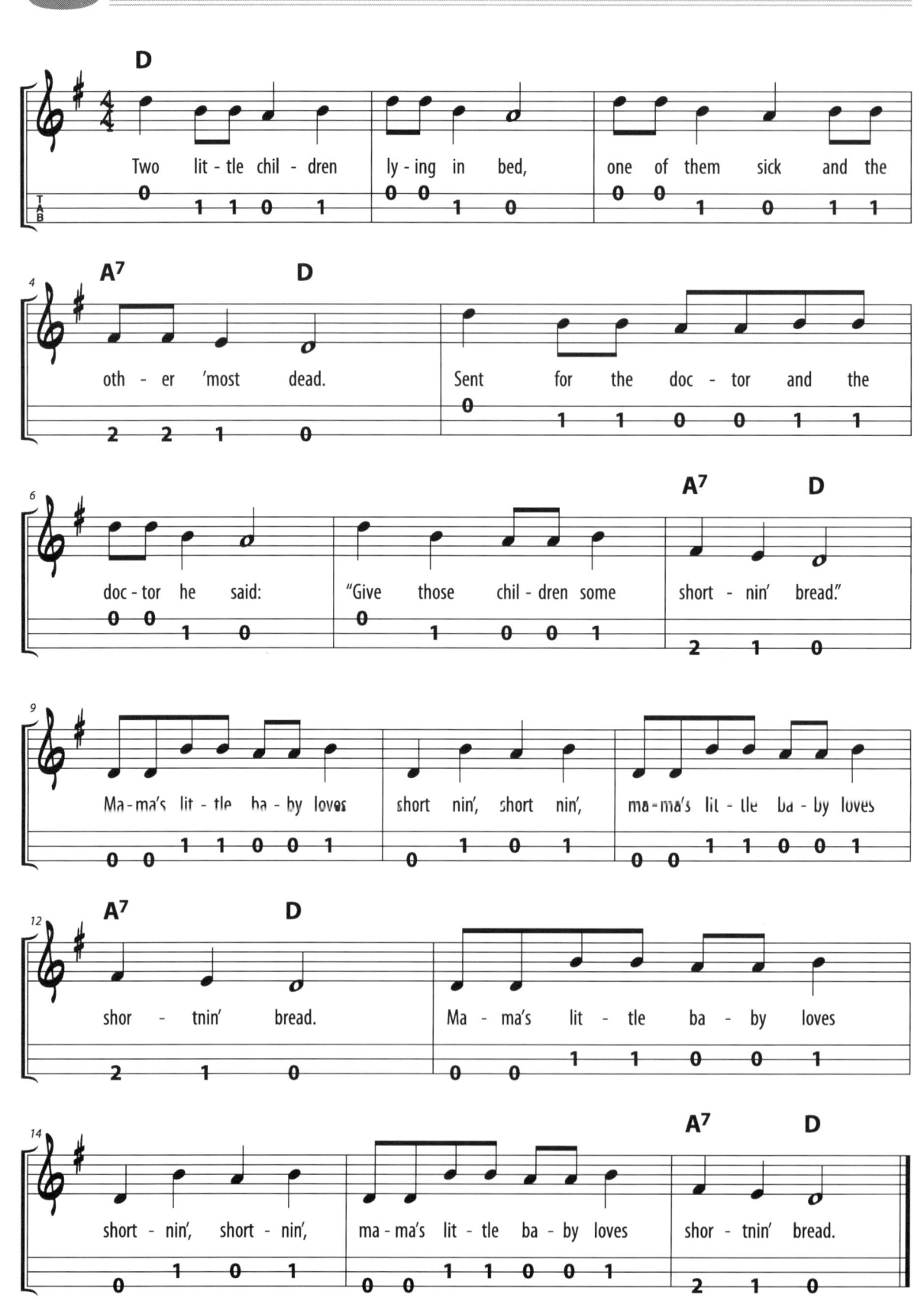

Shortnin' bread

Two little children lying in bed, one of them sick and the other 'most dead. Sent for the doctor and the doctor he said: "Give those children some shortnin' bread."

Mama's little baby loves shortnin', shortnin', mama's little baby loves shortnin' bread. Mama's little baby loves shortnin', shortnin', mama's little baby loves shortnin' bread.

2. Put on the skillet, slip on the lid,
   mama's gonna bake a little shortnin' bread.
   This ain't all she's gonna do.
   Mama's gonna make a little coffee, too.
   Mama's little baby loves ...

3. When those children, sick in bed,
   heard that talk about shortnin' bread.
   Popped up well, to dance and sing,
   skipped around and cut the pigeon wing.

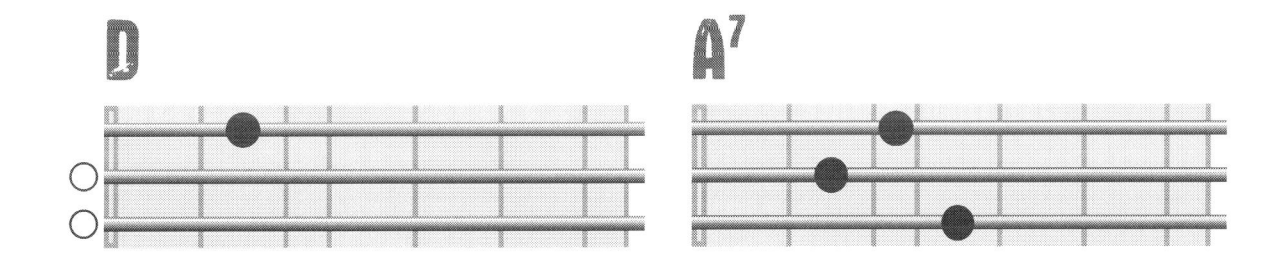

D

A⁷

Jesse James

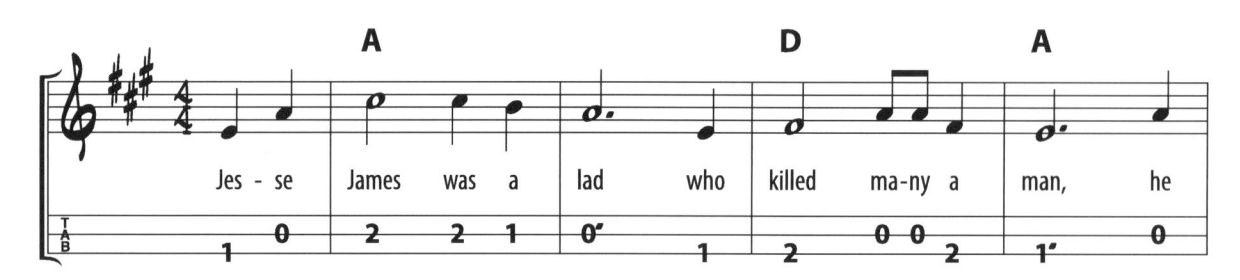

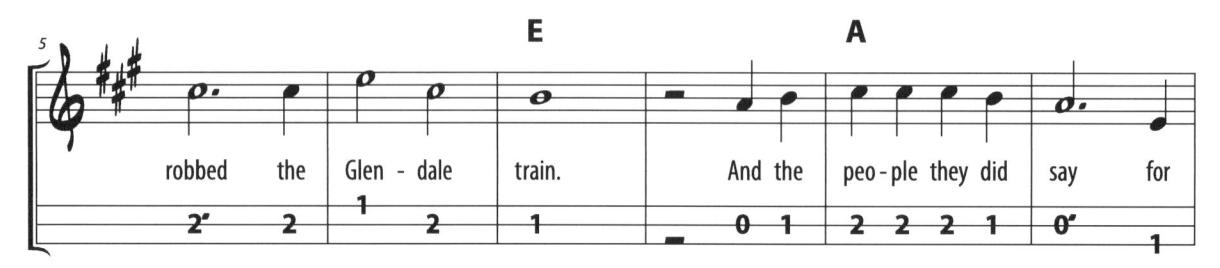

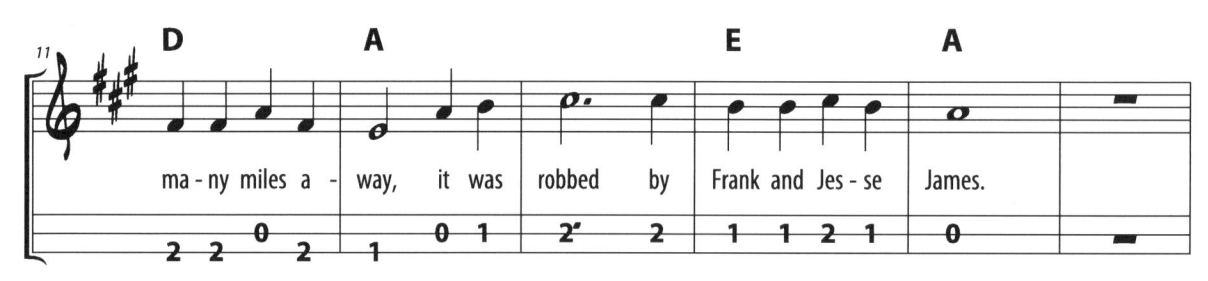

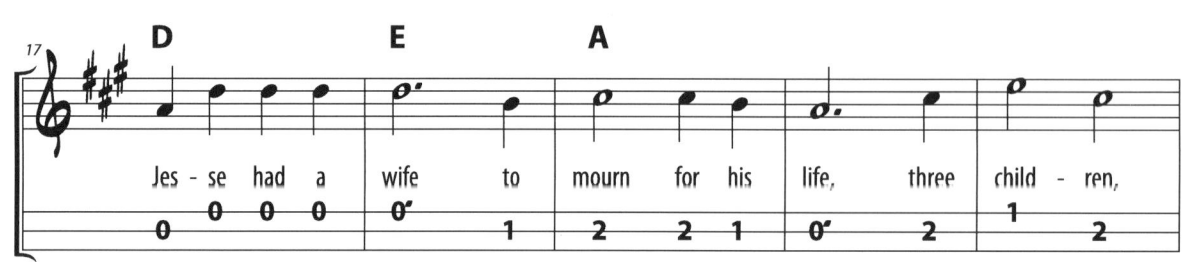

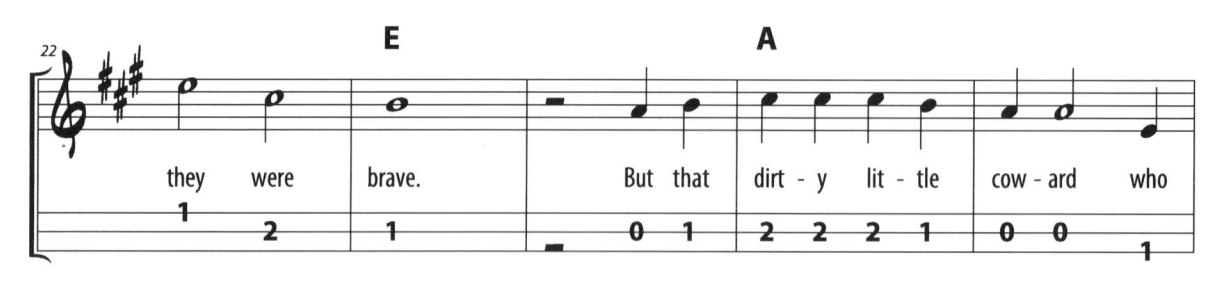

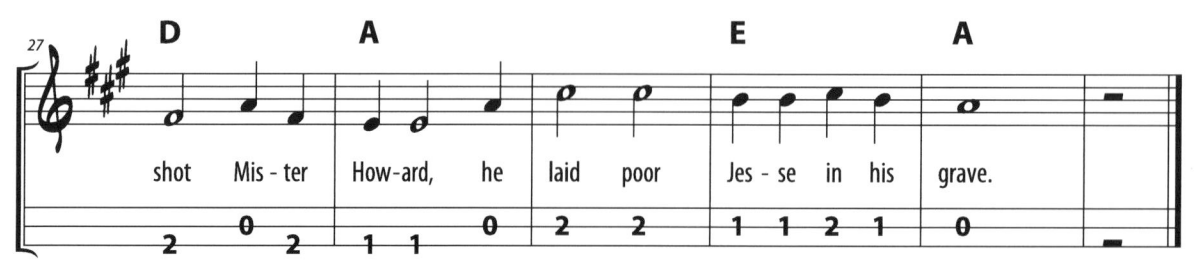

Jes-se James was a lad who killed ma-ny a man, he robbed the Glen-dale train. And the peo-ple they did say for ma-ny miles a-way, it was robbed by Frank and Jes-se James. Jes-se had a wife to mourn for his life, three chil-dren, they were brave. But that dirt-y lit-tle cow-ard who shot Mis-ter How-ard, he laid poor Jes-se in his grave.

2. Well it was Robert Ford, that dirty little coward,
   I wonder how he feels.
   For he ate of Jesse's bread and he slept in Jesse's bed,
   and he laid poor Jesse in his grave.
   Jesse had a wife ...

3. Jesse was a man, a friend to the poor,
   he'd never rob a mother or a child.
   There never was a man with the law in his hand,
   that could take Jesse James alive.
   Jesse had a wife ...

4. People held their breath when they heard of Jesse's death,
   and wondered how he ever came to fall,
   Robert Ford, it was a fact, he shot Jesse in the back,
   while Jesse hung a picture on the wall.
   Jesse had a wife ...

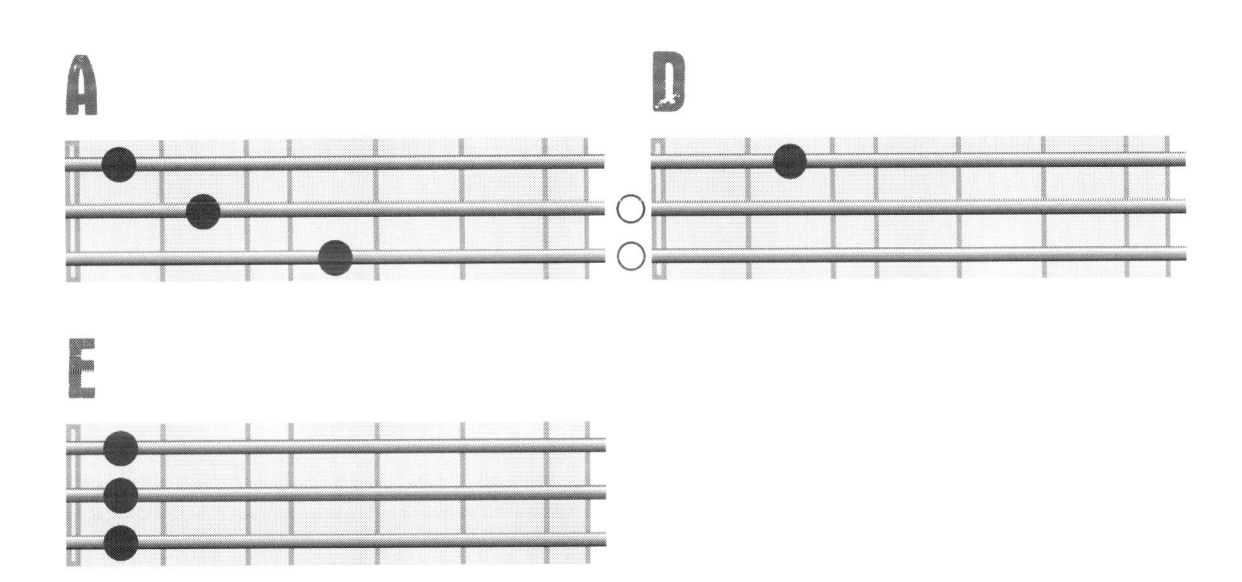

Git along little dogies

As I went a-walkin' one mornin' for pleasure, I spied a cow-puncher come ridin' along. His hat was throwed back and his spurs were a-jinglin' and as he approached he was singin' this song Whoop-ee ti-yi-yo, git along, little dogies, it's your misfortune and none of my own. Whoop-ee ti-yi-yo, git along, little dogies, you know that Wyoming will be your new home.

2. It's early in spring that we round up the dogies,
   and mark 'em and brand 'em and bob off their tails;
   We round up our horses and load the chuckwagon,
   and then throw them dogies out onto the trail.
   Whoopee-ti-yi-yo, git along ...

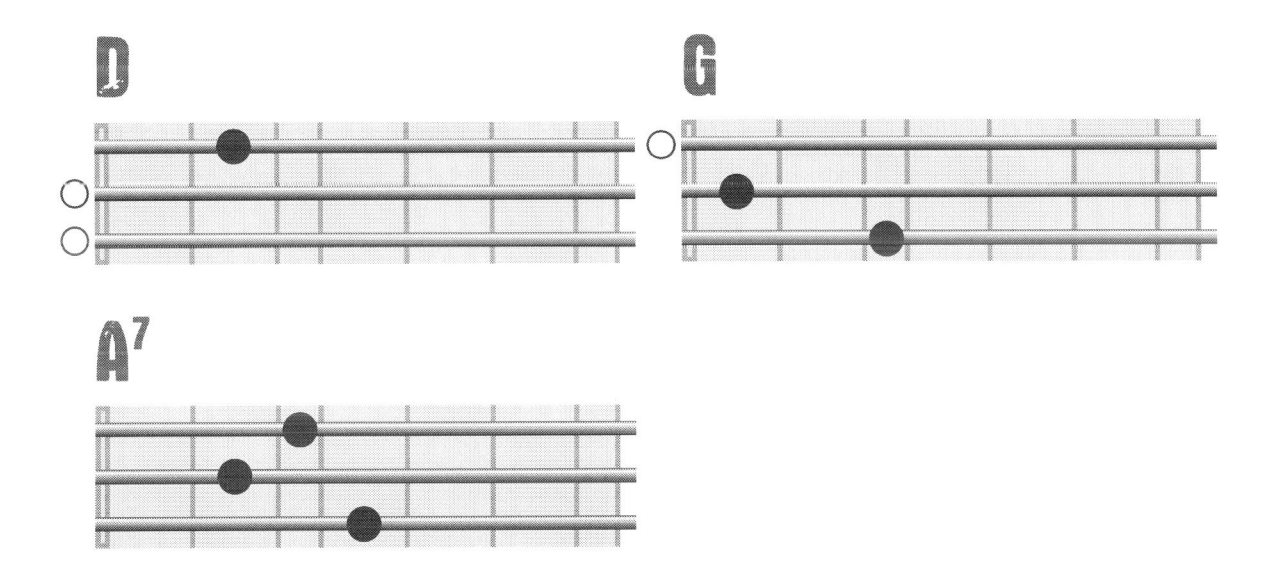

D

G

A⁷

Long journey home

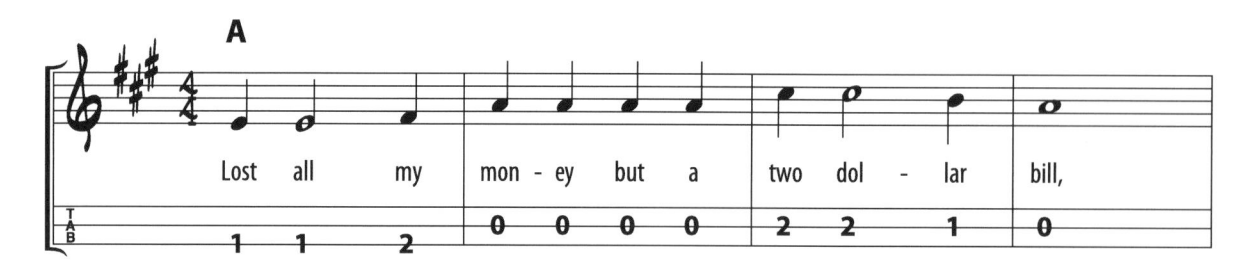

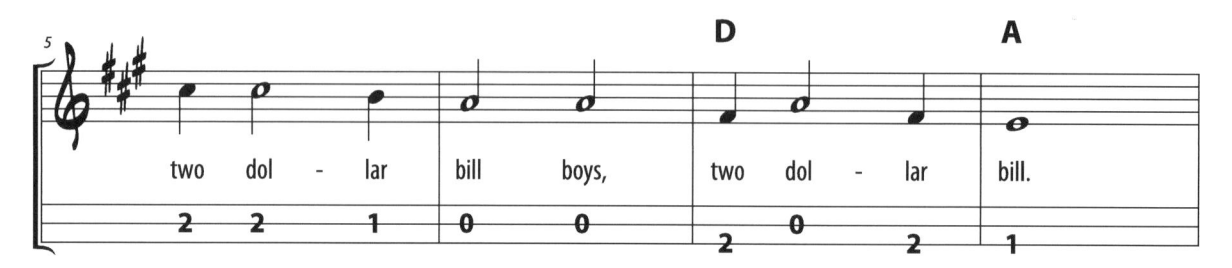

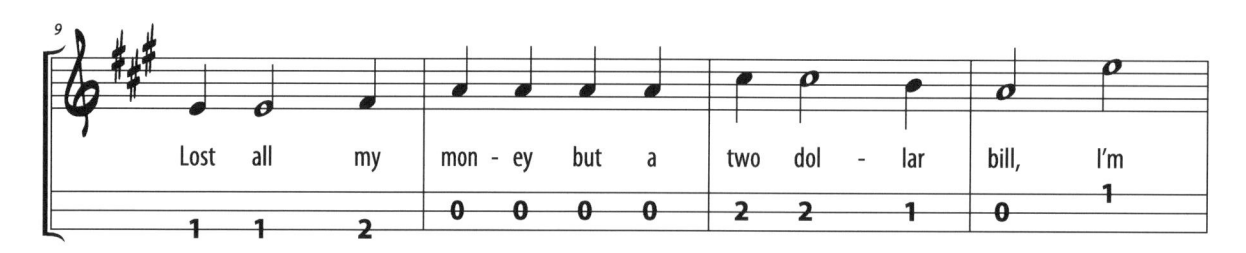

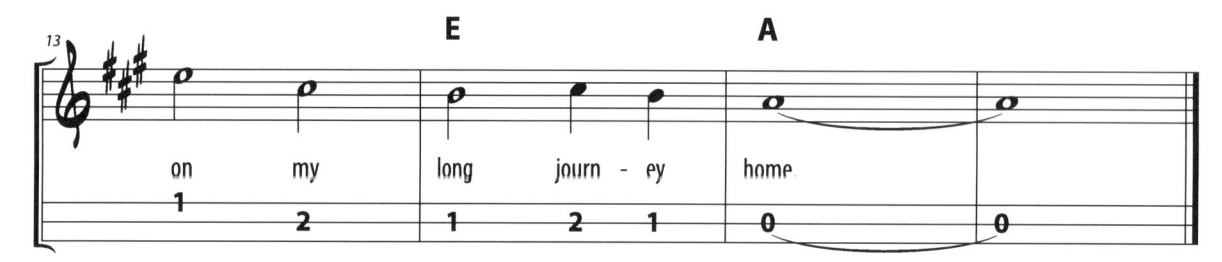

Lost all my mon-ey but a two dol-lar bill, two dol-lar bill boys, two dol-lar bill. Lost all my mon-ey but a two dol-lar bill, I'm on my long jour-ney home

2. Cloudy in the west and it looks like rain,
   looks like rain boy, looks like rain.
   Cloudy in the west and it looks like rain,
   I'm on my long journey home.

3. Black smoke a-rising and it surely is a train,
   surely is a train boys, surely is a train.
   Black smoke a-rising and it surely is a train,
   I'm on my long journey home.

4. Homesick and lonesome and I'm feeling kind of blue,
   feeling kind of blue boys, feeling kind of blue.
   Homesick and lonesome and I'm feeling kind of blue,
   I'm on my long journey home.

5. It's starting raining and I've got to go home,
   I've got to go home boys, I've got to go home.
   It's starting raining and I've got to go home,
   I'm on my long journey home.

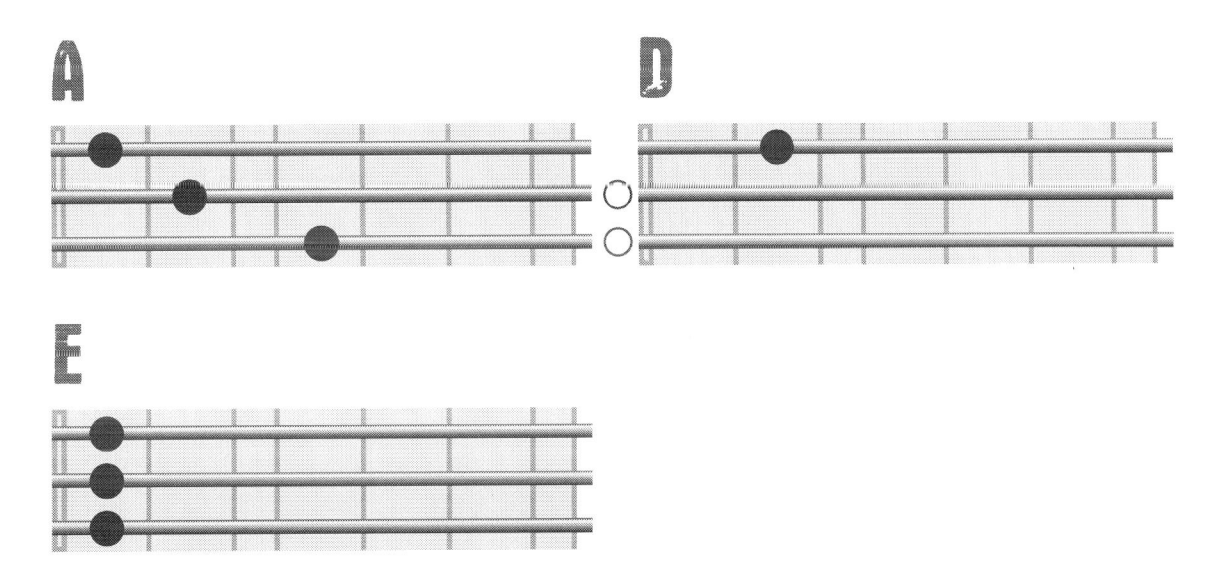

Wildwood flower

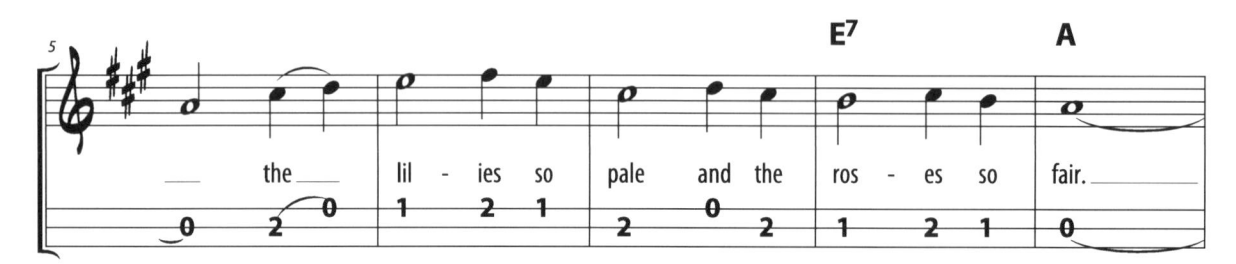

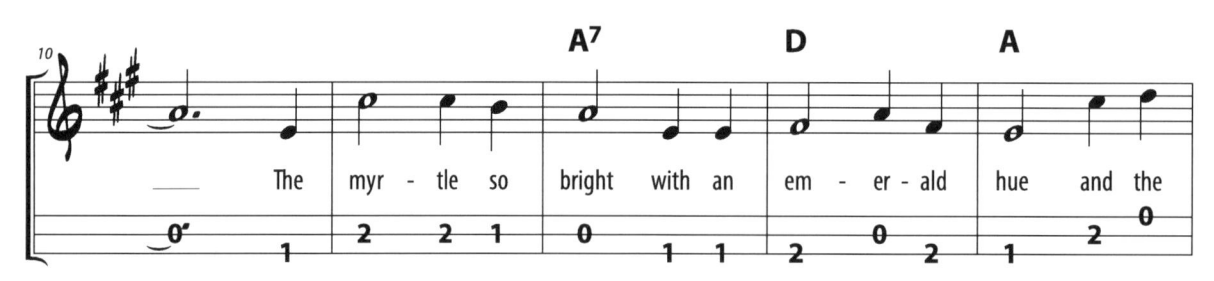

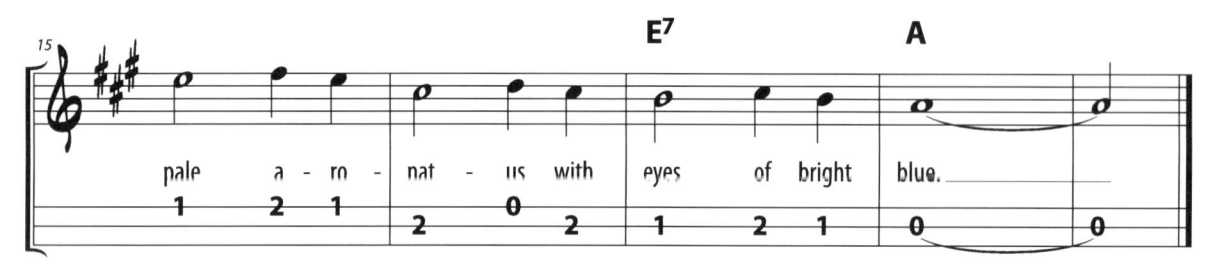

I'll twine 'mid the ring-lets of my ra-ven black hair, the lil-ies so pale and the ros-es so fair. The myr-tle so bright with an em-er-ald hue and the pale a-ro-na-tus with eyes of bright blue.

2. I'll sing, and I'll dance, my laugh shall be gay,
   I'll cease this wild weeping drive sorrow away.
   Tho' my heart is now breaking he never shall know,
   that his name made me tremble and my pale cheek to glow.

3. I'll think of him never I'll be wildly gay,
   I'll charm ev'ry heart and the crowd I will sway.
   I'll live yet to see him regret the dark hour,
   when he won, then neglected the frail wildwood flower.

4. He told me he loved me and promis'd to love,
   through ill and misfortune all others above.
   Another has won him, Ah! misery to tell;
   He left me in silence no word of farewell!

5. He taught me to love him he call'd me his flower,
   that blossom'd for him all the brighter each hour;
   But I woke from my dreaming my idol was clay;
   My visions of love have all faded away.

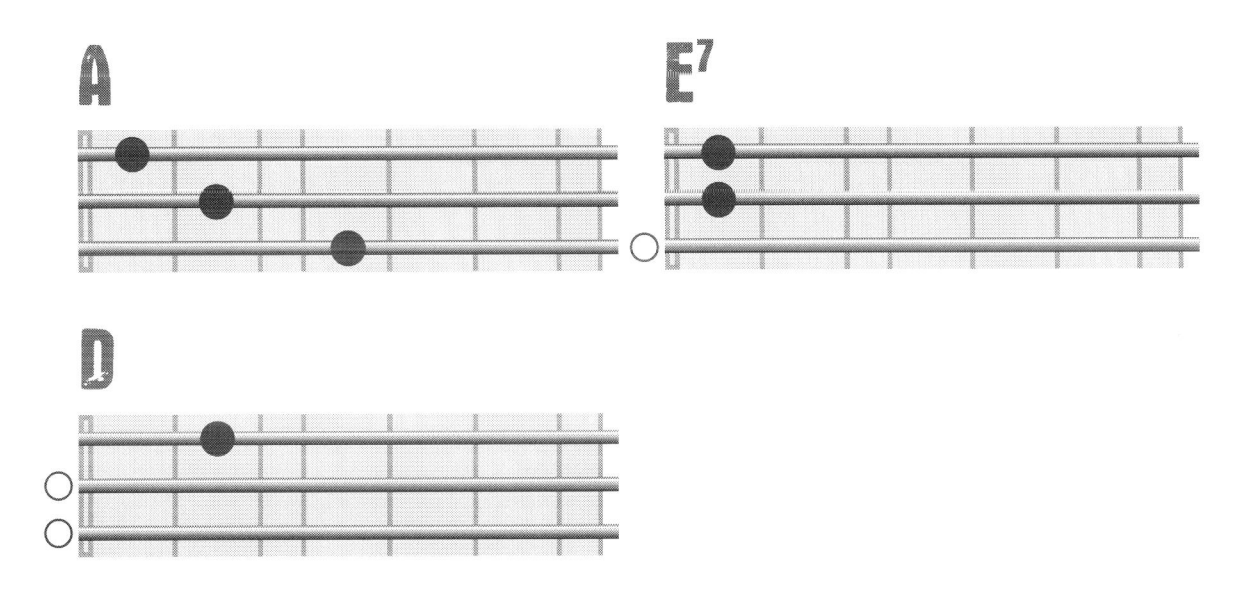

Make me down a pallet

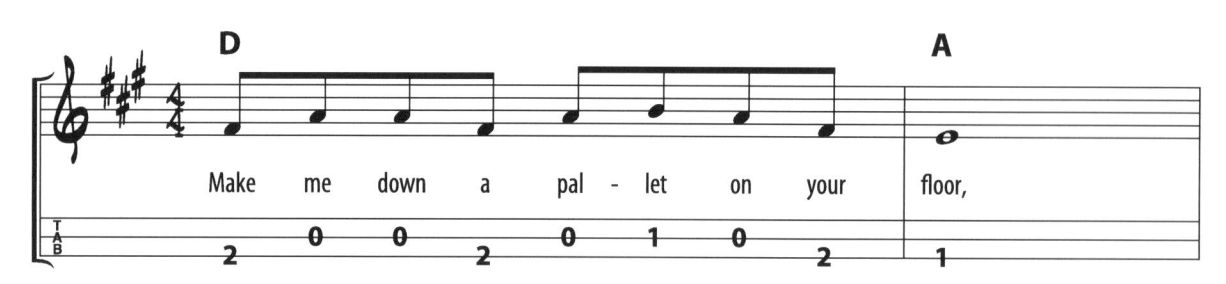

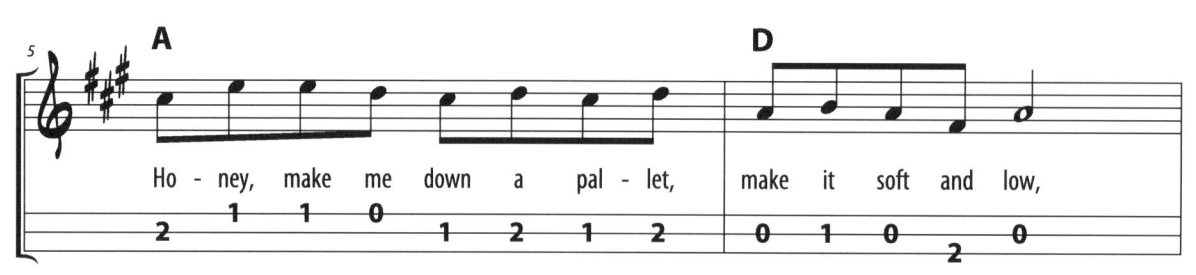

Make me down a pal-let on your floor,

make me down a pal-let on your floor.

Ho-ney, make me down a pal-let, make it soft and low,

then may-be my good girl, she won't know

2. Up the country, where there's sleet and snow,
   up the country where there's sleet and snow.
   I'm goin' up the country where there's sleet and snow,
   no tellin' how much further I may go.

3. Way of sleepin', my back and shoulders' tired,
   Way of sleepin', my back and shoulders' tired.
   This way of sleepin', my back and shoulders' tired,
   Goin' turn over and try it on the side.

4. Don't you let my good girl catch you here,
   please don't let my good girl catch you here.
   Or she might shoot you, might cut and stab you, too,
   ain't no tellin' just what she might do.

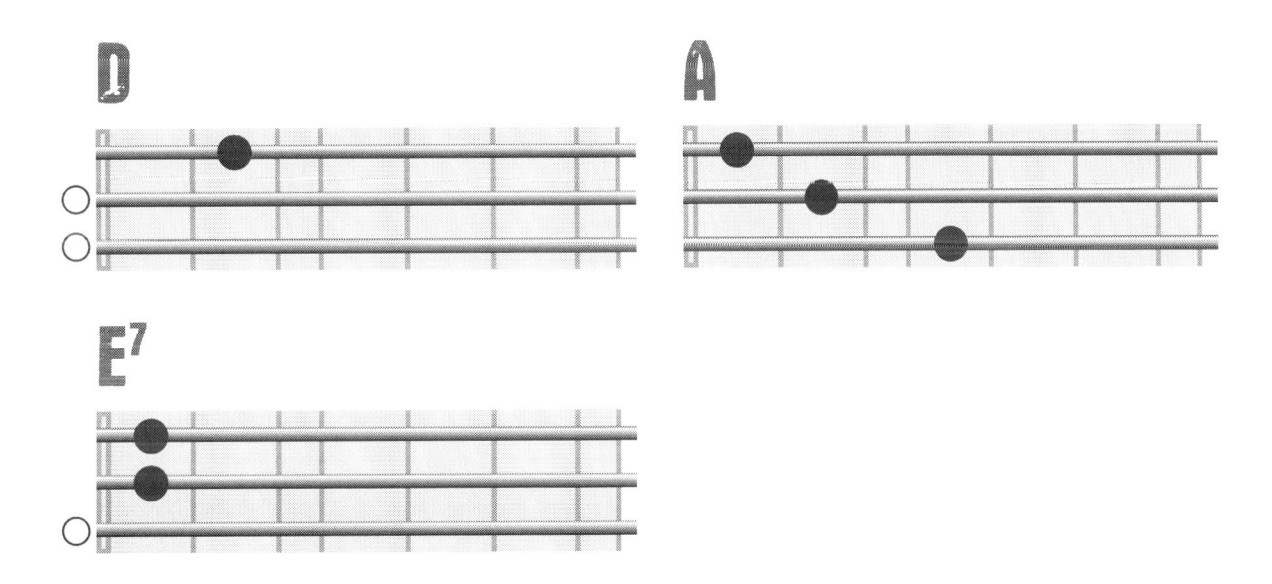

All creatures of our God and King

2. O rushing wind so wild and strong,
   white clouds that sail in heaven along,
   alleluia, alleluia!
   New rising dawn in praise rejoice;
   you lights of evening find a voice:
   O praise Him, O praise Him,
   alleluia, alleluia, alleluia!

3. Cool flowing water, pure and clear,
   make music for your Lord to hear:
   alleluia, alleluia!
   Fierce fire, so masterful and bright,
   providing us with warmth and light.
   O praise Him, O praise Him,
   alleluia, alleluia, alleluia!

4. Earth ever fertile, day by day
   bring forth your blessings on our way;
   alleluia, alleluia!
   All flowers and fruits that is you grow,
   let the His glory also show;
   O praise Him, O praise Him,
   alleluia, alleluia, alleluia!

5. All you who are of tender heart,
   forgiving others, take your part;
   alleluia, alleluia!
   All you who pain and sorrow bear,
   praise God and on Him cast your care;
   O praise Him, O praise Him,
   alleluia, alleluia, alleluia!

6. Let all things their Creator bless,
   and worship Him in humbleness,
   alleluia, alleluia!
   Praise, praise the Father, praise the Son,
   and praise the Spirit, Three in One:
   O praise Him, O praise Him,
   alleluia, alleluia, alleluia!

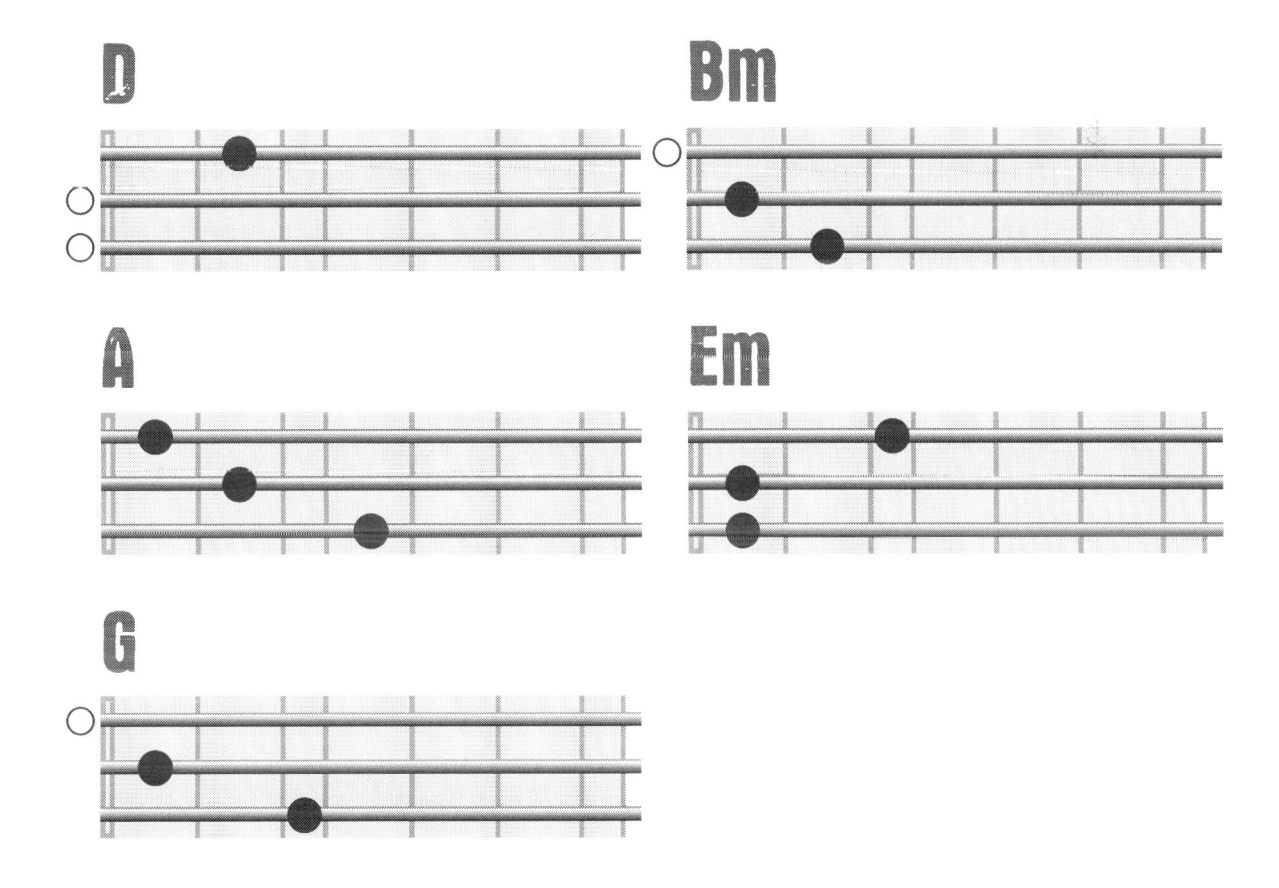

D

A

G

Bm

Em

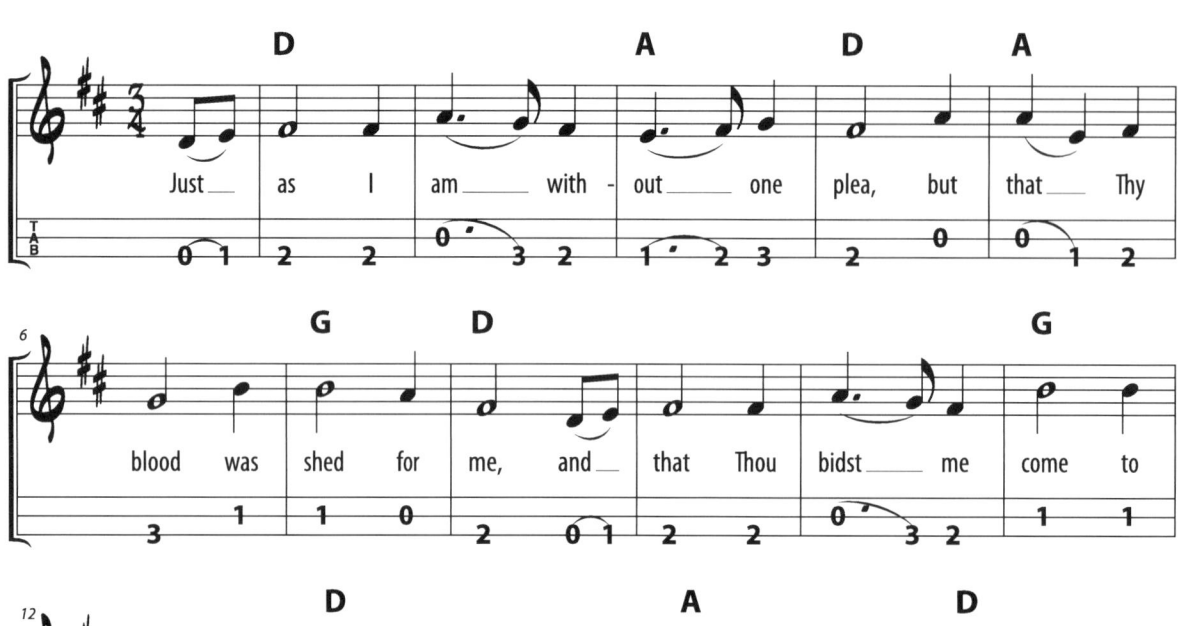

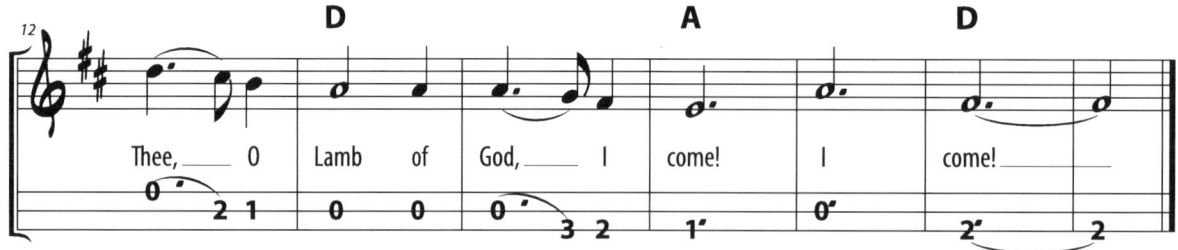

Just as I am

2. Just as I am - and waiting not
   to rid my soul of one dark blot,
   to Thee, whose blood can cleanse each spot,
   o Lamb of God, I come!

3. Just as I am - though toss'd about
   with many a conflict, many a doubt,
   fightings and fears within, without,
   o Lamb of God, I come!

4. Just as I am - poor, wretched, blind;
   Sight, riches, healing of the mind,
   yea, all I need, in Thee to find,
   o Lamb of God, I come!

5. Just as I am - Thou wilt receive,
   wilt welcome, pardon, cleanse, relieve;
   Because Thy promise I believe,
   o Lamb of God, I come!

6. Just as I am – Thy love unknown
   has broken every barrier down;
   Now to be Thine, yea, Thine alone,
   O Lamb of God, I come!

7. Just as I am - of that free love
   the breadth, length, depth, and height to prove,
   here for a season, then above,
   o Lamb of God, I come!

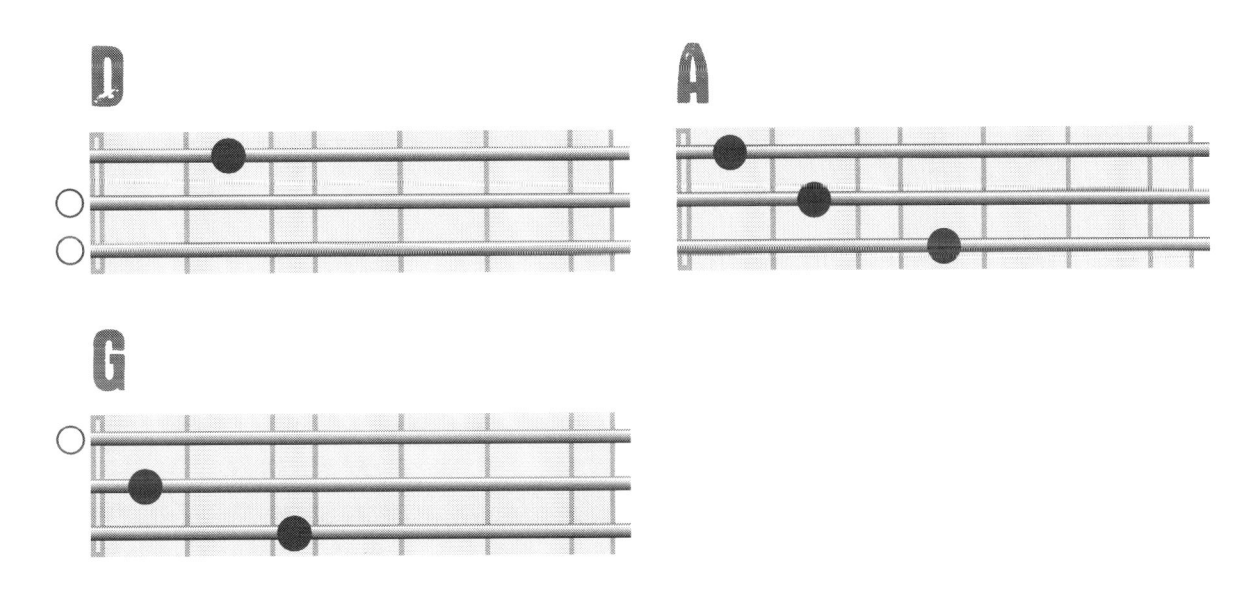

D

A

G

How firm a foundation

2. In ev'ry condition - in sickness in health,
   in poverty's vale, or abounding in wealth,
   at home and abroad, on the land, on the sea,
   as thy days may demand, so thy succor shall be.

3. "Fear not, I am with thee; O be not dismayed!
   For I am thy God, and will still give thee aid;
   I'll strengthen thee, help thee, and cause thee to stand,
   upheld by my righteous, omnipotent hand.

4. "When through the deep waters I call thee to go,
   the rivers of sorrow shall not thee o'erflow;
   For I will be with thee, thy troubles to bless,
   and sanctify to thee thy deepest distress.

5. "When through fiery trials thy pathway shall lie,
   my grace all-sufficient shall be thy supply;
   The flame shall not hurt thee; I only design,
   Thy dross to consume, and thy gold to refine.

6. "E'en down to old age, all my people shall prove
   my sov'reign eternal, unchangeable love;
   And then, when grey hairs shall their temples adorn,
   like lambs they shall still in my bosom be borne.

7. "The soul that on Jesus hath leaned for repose,
   I will not, I cannot, desert to His foes:
   That soul, though all hell should endeavor to shake,
   I'll never - no, never, no, never forsake!"

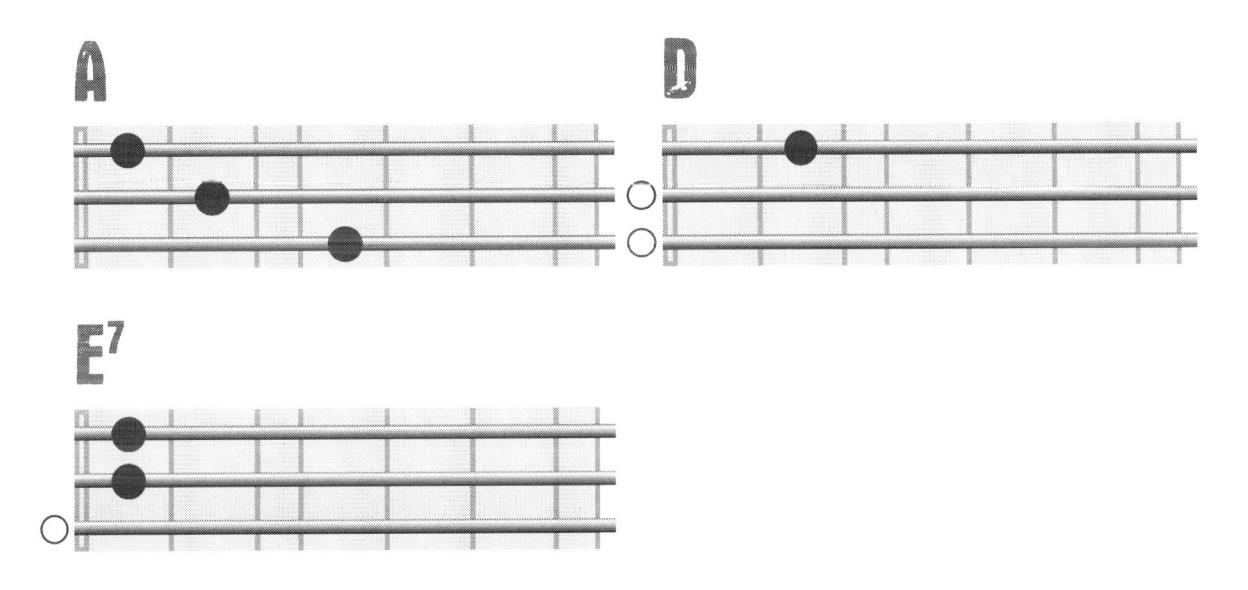

A

D

E⁷

Shall we gather at the river

Shall we gath-er at the ri - ver, where bright an - gel feet have trod;
with its crys-tal tide for - ev - er flow-ing by the throne of God?
Yes, we'll gath-er at the riv - er, the beau-ti-ful, the beau-ti-ful riv - er;
gath-er with the saints at the riv - er that flows by the throne of God.

2. On the margin of the river,
   washing up its silver spray,
   we will walk and worship ever,
   all the happy golden day.
   Yes, we'll gather at the river ...

3. Ere we reach the shining river,
   lay we ev'ry burden down;
   Grace our spirits will deliver,
   and provide a robe and crown.
   Yes, we'll gather at the river ...

4. Soon we'll reach the shining river,
   soon our pilgrimage will cease;
   Soon our happy hearts will quiver
   with the melody of peace.
   Yes, we'll gather at the river ...

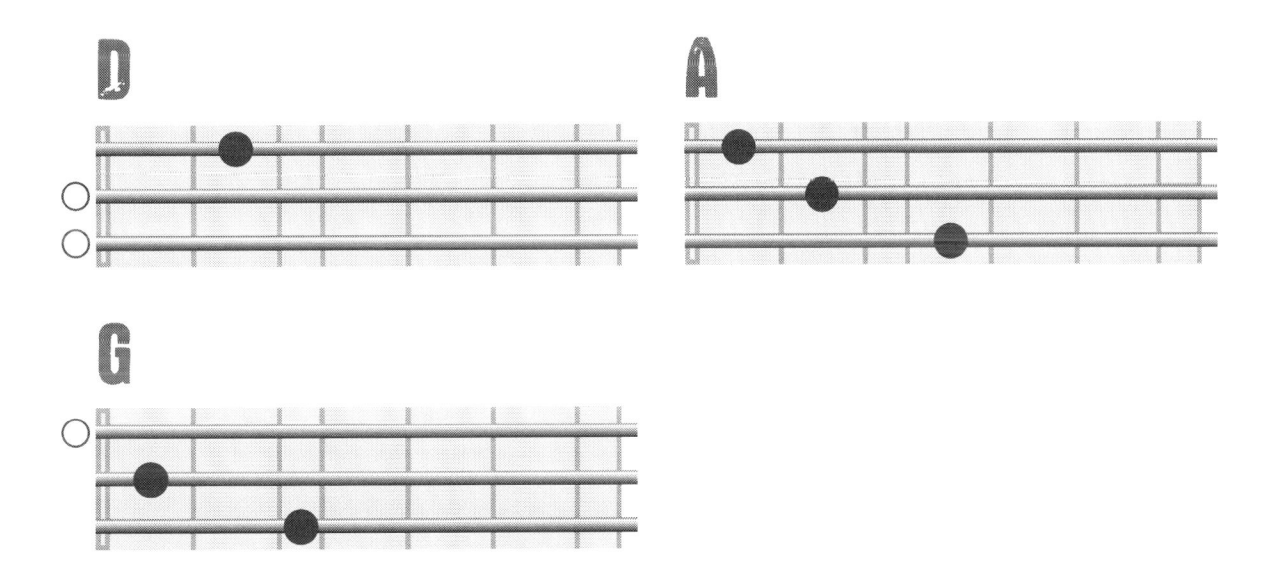

D

A

G

It is well with my soul

2. Though Satan should buffet, though trials should come,
   let this blest assurance control,
   that Christ has regarded my helpless estate,
   and hath shed His own blood for my soul.

3. My sin, oh, the bliss of this glorious thought!
   My sin, not in part but the whole,
   is nailed to the cross, and I bear it no more,
   praise the Lord, praise the Lord, O my soul!

4. For me, be it Christ, be it Christ hence to live:
   If Jordan above me shall roll,
   no pang shall be mine, for in death as in life,
   Thou wilt whisper Thy peace to my soul.

5. But Lord, ,tis for Thee, for Thy coming we wait,
   the sky, not the grave, is our goal;
   Oh, trump of the angel! Oh, voice of the Lord!
   Blessed hope, blessed rest of my soul.

6. And Lord, haste the day when my faith shall be sight,
   the clouds be rolled back as a scroll;
   The trump shall resound, and the Lord shall descend,
   a song in the night, oh my soul!

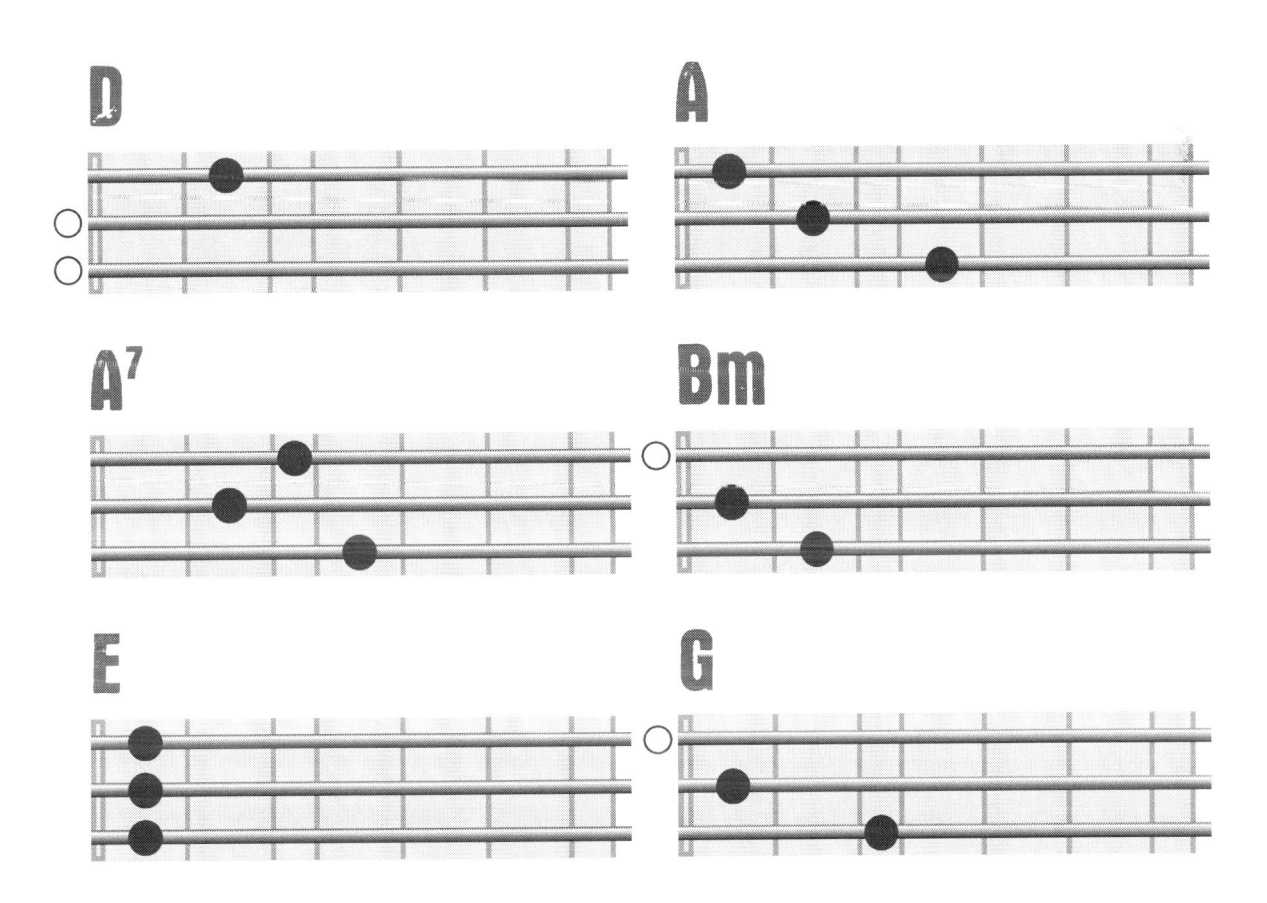

Come, Thou fount of every blessing

2. Here I raise my Ebenezer;
   hither by Thy help I'm come;
   and I hope, by Thy good pleasure,
   safely to arrive at home.
   Jesus sought me when a stranger,
   wandering from the fold of God;
   He, to rescue me from danger,
   interposed His precious blood.

3. O to grace how great a debtor
   daily I'm constrained to be!
   Let that grace now like a fetter,
   bind my wandering heart to Thee.
   Prone to wander, Lord, I feel it,
   prone to leave the God I love;
   here's my heart, O take and seal it,
   seal it for Thy courts above.

Text: Robert Robinson (1726-1791)
Music: „Nettleton", John Wyeth (17. Century)

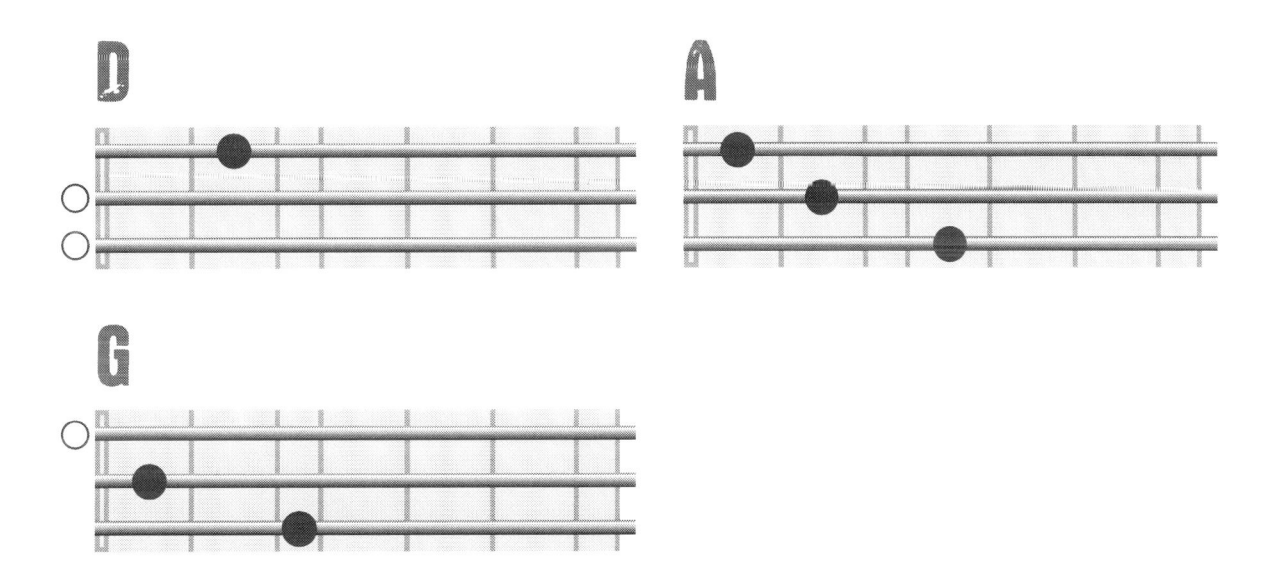

D

A

G

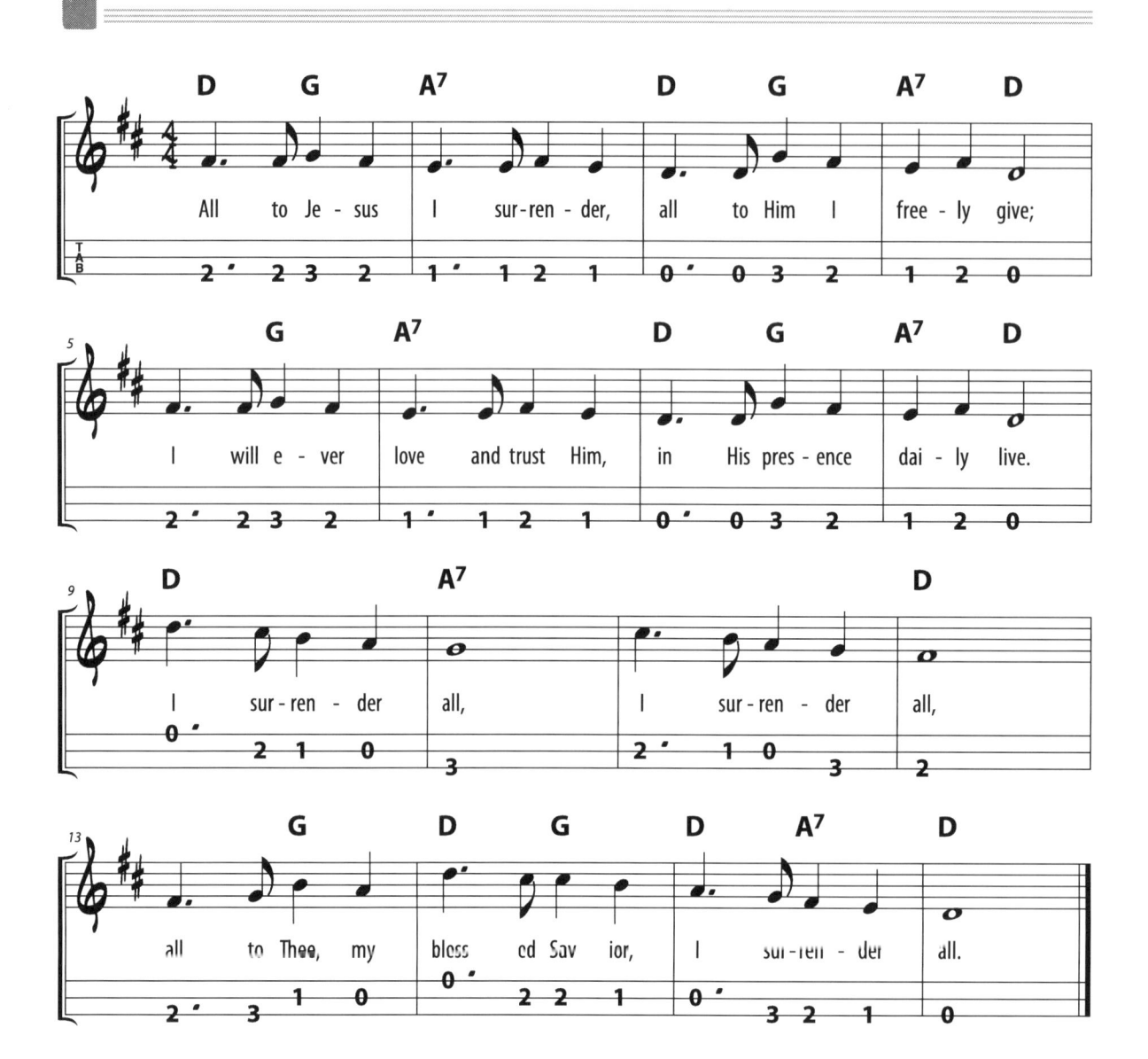

surrender all

All to Jesus I surrender, all to Him I freely give;
I will ever love and trust Him, in His presence daily live.
I surrender all, I surrender all,
all to Thee, my blessed Savior, I surrender all.

2. All to Jesus I surrender,
   humbly at His feet I bow,
   worldly pleasures all forsaken,
   take me, Jesus, take me now.
   I surrender all ...

3. All to Jesus I surrender;
   Make me, Savior, wholly thine;
   Let me feel the Holy Spirit,
   truly know that thou art mine.
   I surrender all ...

4. All to Jesus I surrender,
   Lord, I give myself to thee,
   fill me with thy love and power,
   let thy blessing fall on me.
   I surrender all ...

5. All to Jesus I surrender;
   Now I feel the sacred flame.
   Oh, the joy of full salvation!
   Glory, glory, to His name!
   I surrender all ...

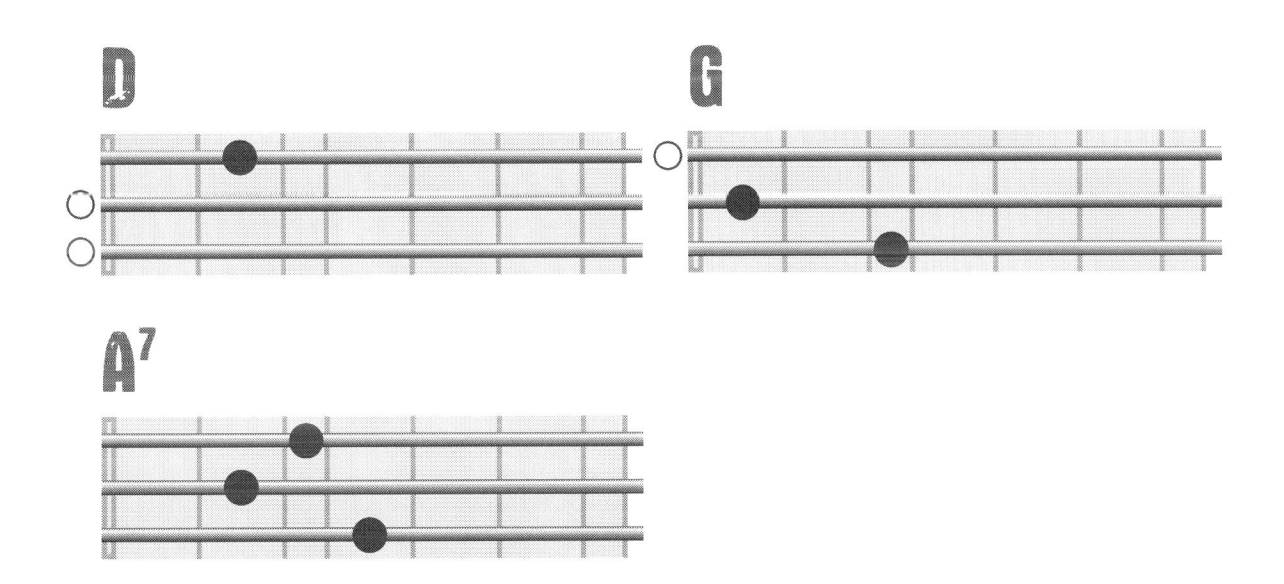

D

G

A⁷

My faith looks up to Thee

My faith looks up to Thee, Thou Lamb of Cal-va-ry, Sav-ior di-vine! Now hear me while I pray; take all my guilt a-way. O let me from this day be whol-ly thine!

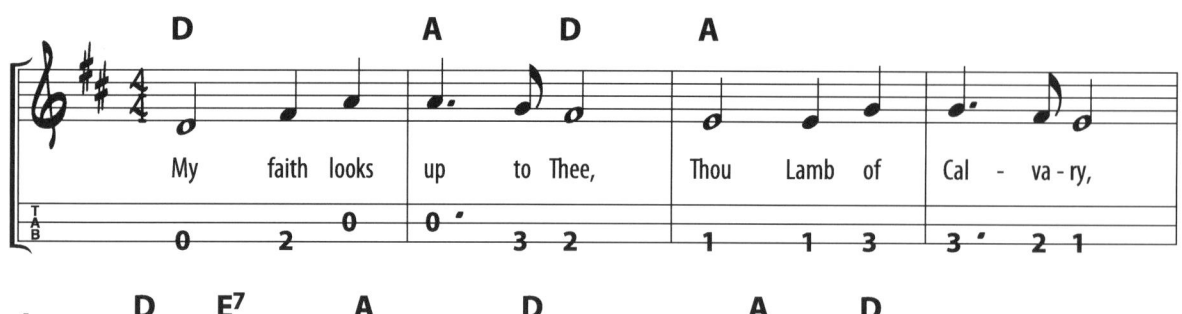

2. May thy rich grace impart
   strength to my fainting heart,
   my zeal inspire.
   As thou hast died for me,
   O may my love to thee
   pure, warm, and changeless be,
   a living fire!

3. While life's dark maze I tread
   and griefs around me spread,
   be thou my guide;
   bid darkness turn to day,
   wipe sorrow's tears away,
   nor let me ever stray
   from thee aside.

4. When life's swift race is run,
   death's cold work almost done,
   be near to me.
   Blest Savior, then, in love
   fear and distrust remove.
   O bear me safe above,
   redeemed and free!

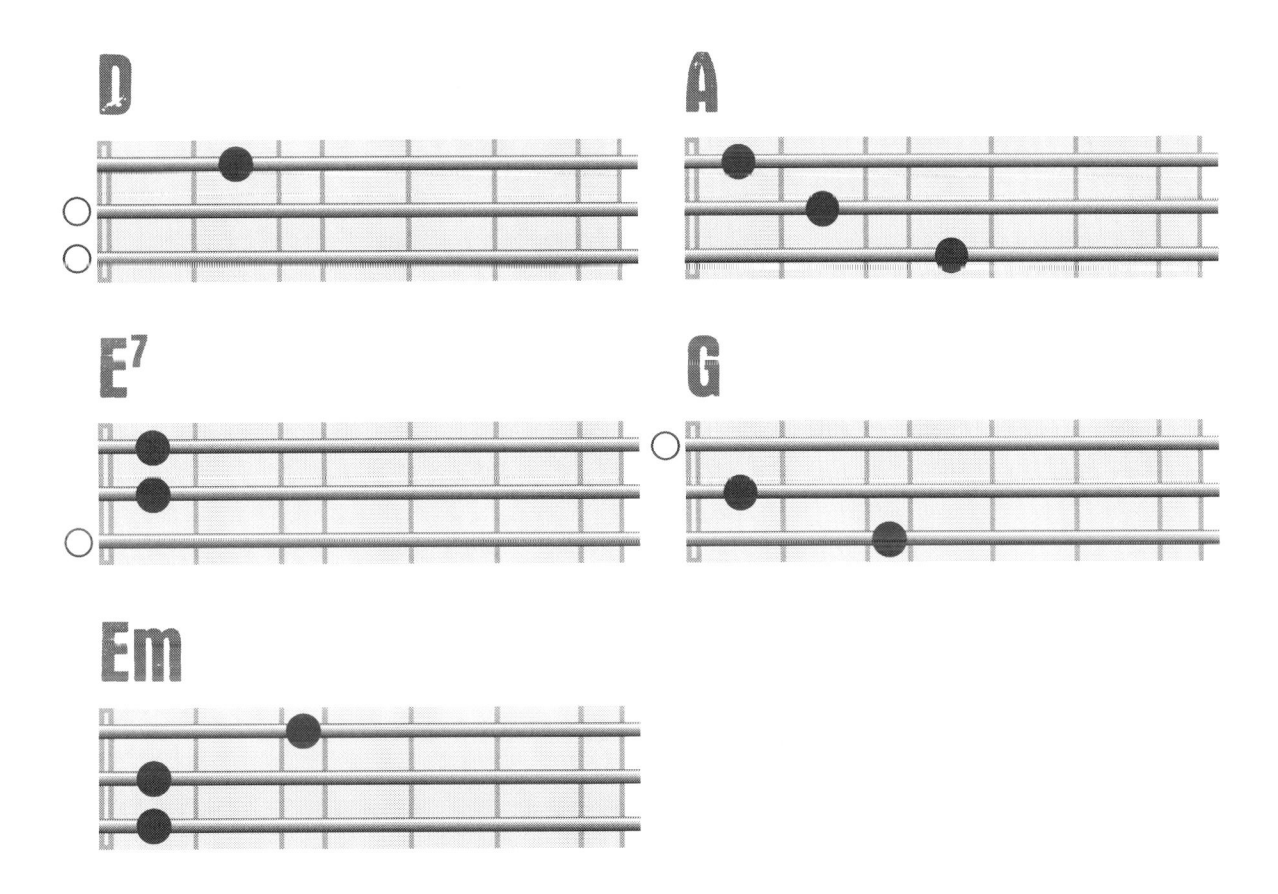

D

A

E⁷

G

Em

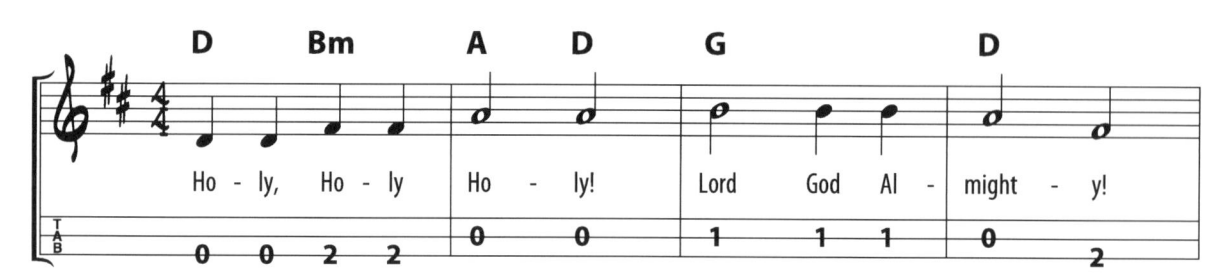

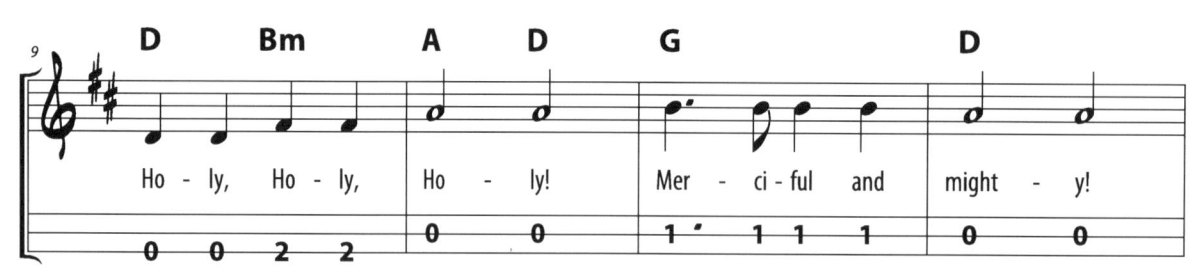

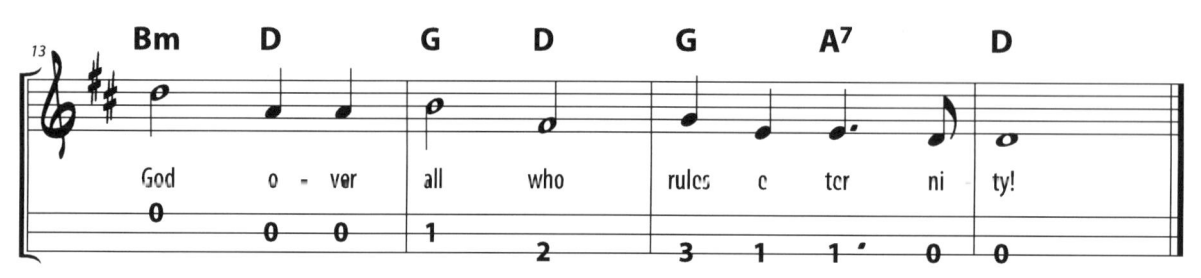

Holy, holy, holy

2. Holy, Holy, Holy! All the saints adore Thee,
    casting down their golden crowns around the glassy sea;
    Cherubim and Seraphim falling down before Thee,
    which wert, and art,and evermore shalt be.

3. Holy, Holy, Holy! though the darkness hide Thee,
    though the eye of sinful man Thy glory may not see:
    Only Thou art holy, there is none beside Thee,
    perfect in power in love,and purity.

4. Holy, Holy, Holy! Lord God Almighty!
    All Thy works shall praise thy name in earth and sky and sea;
    Holy, Holy, Holy! Merciful and Mighty!
    God in Three Persons, blessed Trinity!

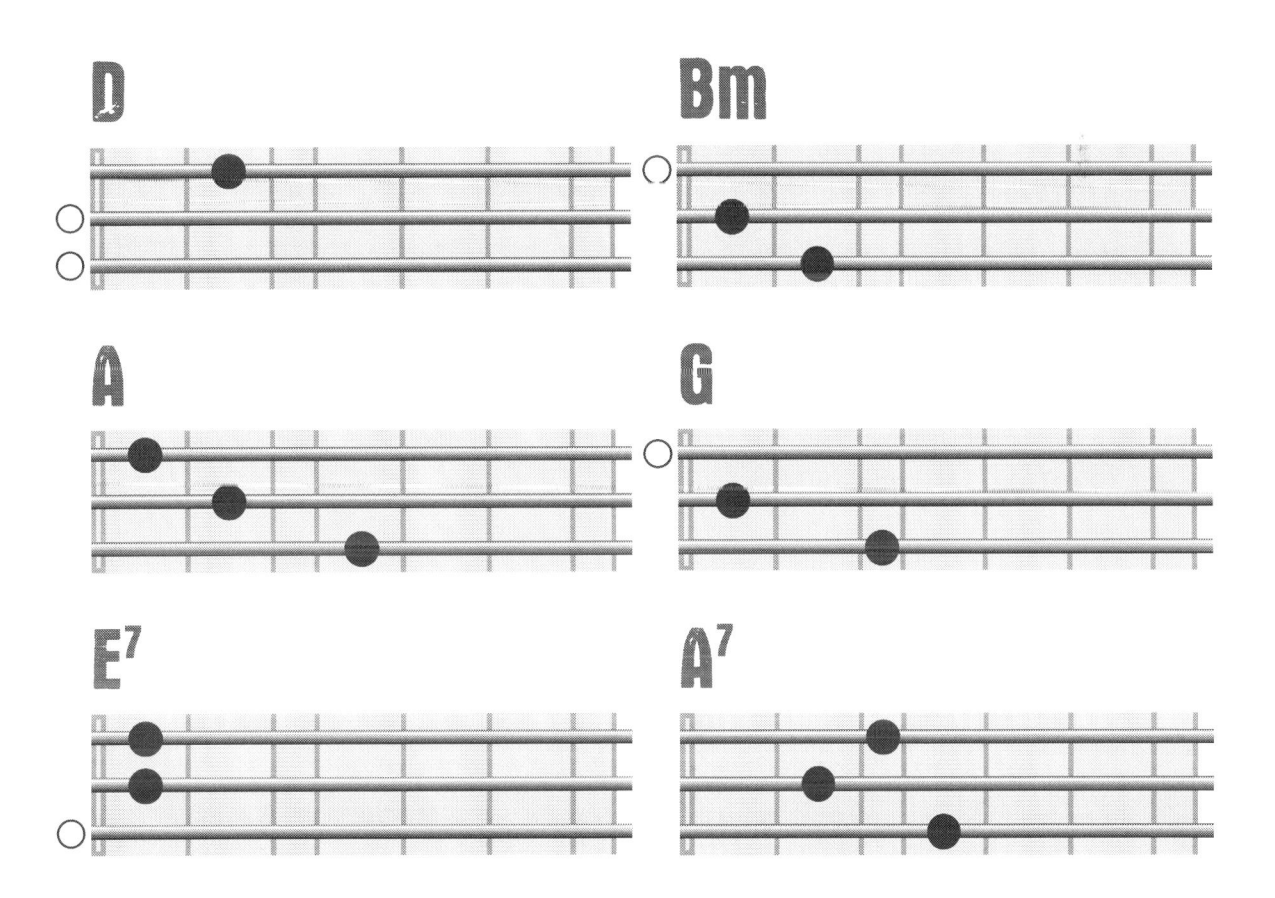

Jesus paid it all

I hear the Savior say, "Thy strength indeed is small. Child of weakness, watch and pray, find in Me thine all in all." Jesus paid it all, all to Him I owe; sin had left a crimson stain, He washed it white as snow.

2. Lord, now indeed I find
   Thy pow'r and Thine alone,
   can change the leper's spots
   and melt the heart of stone.
   Jesus paid it all ...

3. For nothing good have I
   where-by Thy grace to claim;
   I'll wash my garments white
   in the blood of Calv'ry's Lamb.
   Jesus paid it all ...

4. And when, before the throne,
   I stand in Him complete,
   "Jesus died my soul to save,"
   my lips shall still repeat.
   Jesus paid it all ...

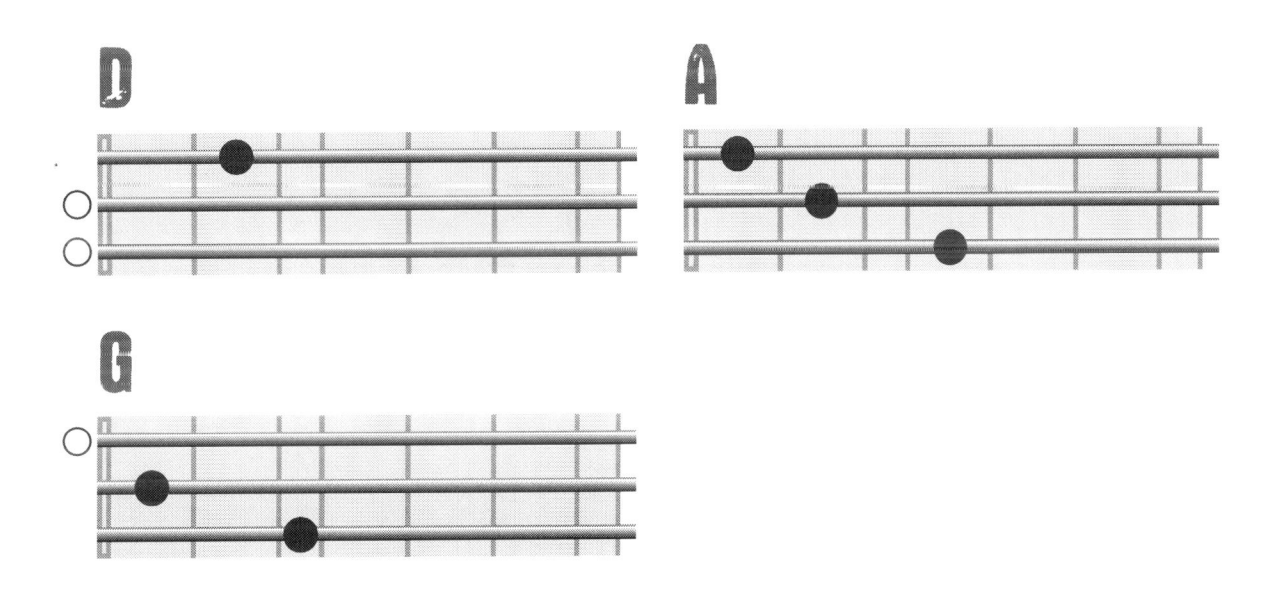

Nothing but the blood

What can wash a-way my sin? Nothing but the blood of Jesus. What can make me whole a-gain? Nothing but the blood of Jesus. O precious is the flow that makes me white as snow; no other fount I know, nothing but the blood of Jesus.

2. For my pardon this I see:
   nothing but the blood of Jesus.
   For my cleansing this my plea:
   nothing but the blood of Jesus.
   O precious is the flow . . .

3. Nothing can for sin atone:
   nothing but the blood of Jesus.
   Naught of good that I have done:
   nothing but the blood of Jesus.
   O precious is the flow . . .

4. This is all my hope and peace:
   nothing but the blood of Jesus.
   This is all my righteousness:
   nothing but the blood of Jesus.
   O precious is the flow . . .

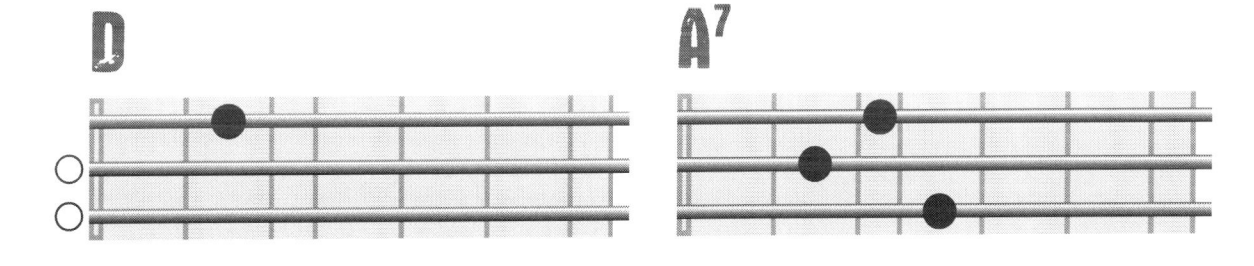

Saviour, like a shepherd lead us

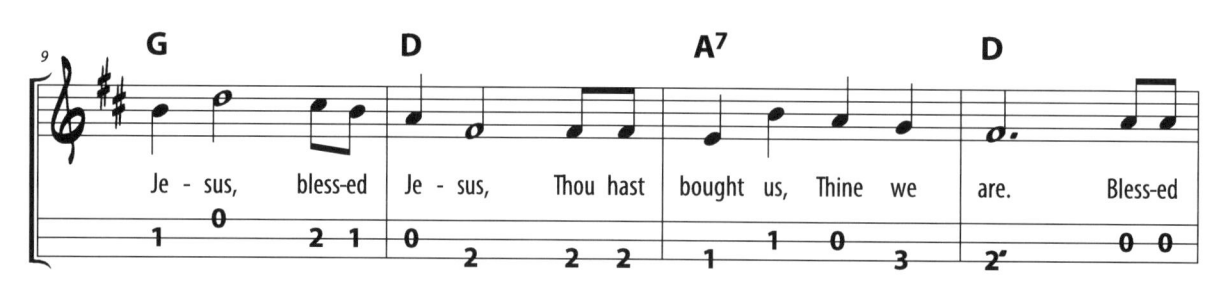

2. We are Thine, do Thou befriend us,
   be the guardian of our way;
   Keep Thy flock, from sin defend us,
   seek us when we go astray:
   Blessed Jesus, blessed Jesus,
   hear, O hear us when we pray;
   Blessed Jesus, blessed Jesus,
   hear, O hear us when we pray.

3. Thou hast promised to receive us,
   poor and sinful though we be;
   Thou hast mercy to relieve us,
   grace to cleanse, and pow'r to free:
   Blessed Jesus, blessed Jesus,
   early let us turn to Thee;
   Blessed Jesus, blessed Jesus,
   early let us turn to Thee.

4. Early let us seek Thy favor,
   early let us do Thy will;
   Blessed Lord and only Savior,
   with Thy love our bosoms fill:
   Blessed Jesus, blessed Jesus,
   Thou hast loved us, love us still;
   Blessed Jesus, blessed Jesus,
   Thou hast loved us, love us still.

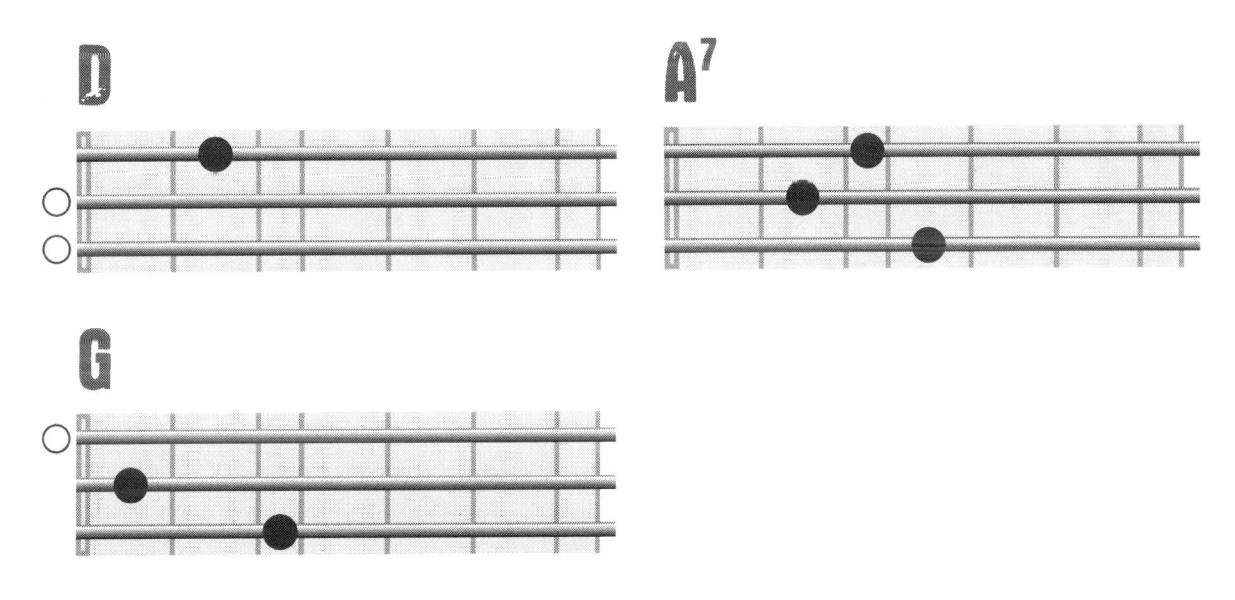

The minstrel boy

The min-strel boy to the war is gone, in the ranks of death you'll find him. His fath-er's sword he has gird-ed on, and his wild harp slung be-hind him. "Oh land of Song!" said the war-rior bard, "Though all the world be-tray thee, one sword at least thy rights shall guard, one faith-ful harp shall praise thee!"

2. The minstrel fell! But the foeman's chain
   could not bring his proud soul under;
   the harp he loved ne'er spoke again,
   for he tore its chords asunder;
   and said "No chains shall sully thee,
   thou soul of love and bravery!
   Thy songs were made for the pure and free
   they shall never sound in slavery!"

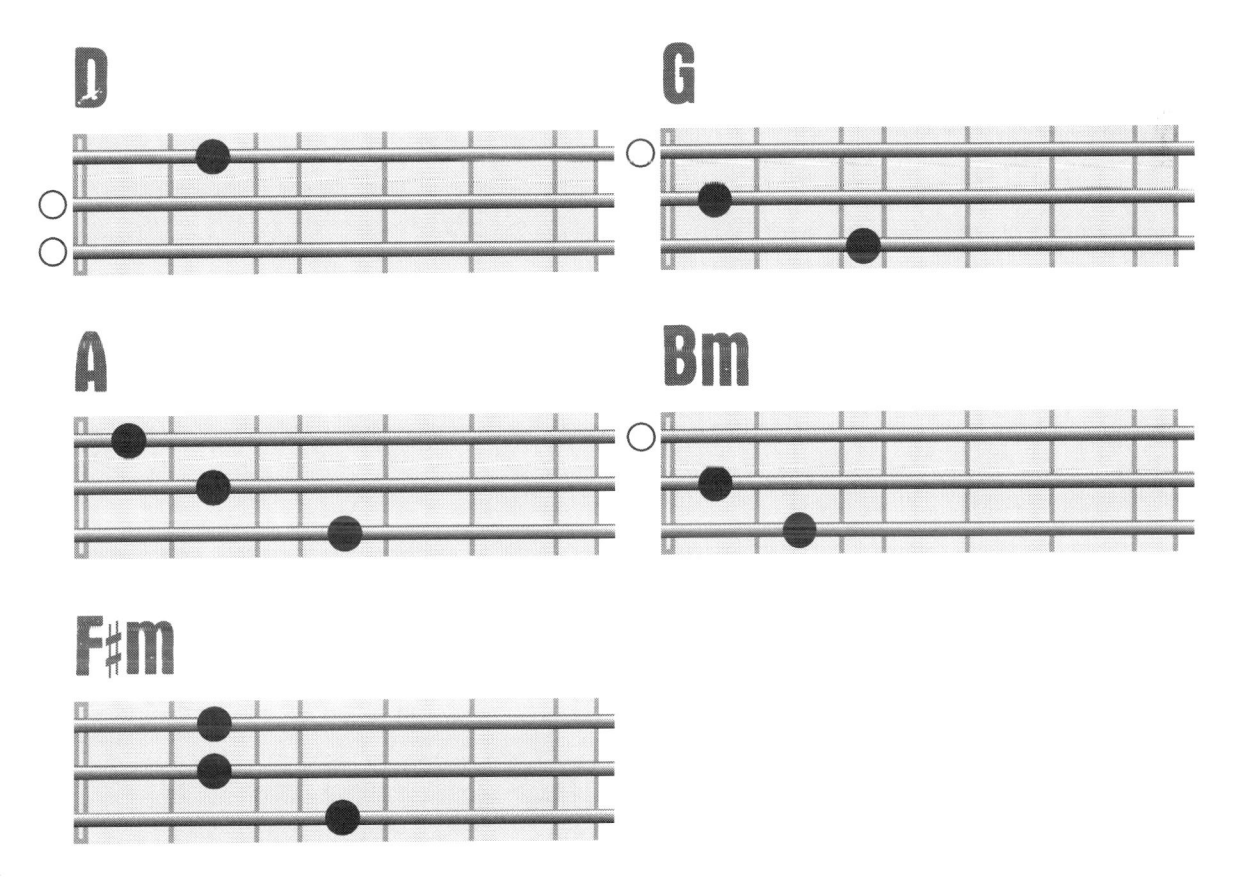

D

G

A

Bm

F♯m

The Sally Gardens

It was down by the Sally Gardens, my love and I did meet. She crossed the Sally Gardens with little snow-white feet. She bid me take love easy, as the leaves grow on the tree, but I was young and foolish, and with her did not agree.

2. In a field down by the river, my love and I did stand,
   and on my leaning shoulder, she laid her snow-white hand.
   She bid me take life easy, as the grass grows on the weirs
   but I was young and foolish, and now am full of tears.

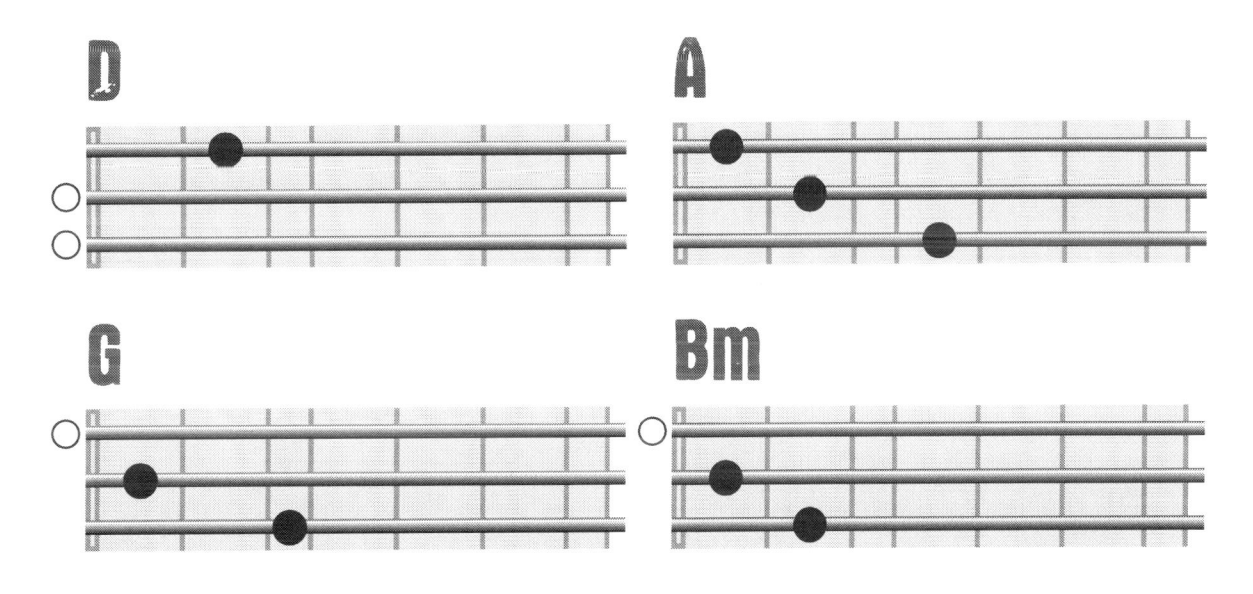

D

A

G

Bm

Carrickfergus

1. I wish I was in Carrickfergus only for nights in Ballygrand.
   I would swim over the deepest ocean the deepest ocean for my love to find.
   But the sea is wide and I cannot swim over and neither have I wings to fly.
   If I could find me a handsome boatsman to ferry me over to my love and die.

2. My childhood days bring back sad reflections of happy times spent so long ago.
   My childhood friends and my own relations have all passed on now like melting snow.
   But I'll spend my days in endless roaming, soft is the grass, my bed is free.
   Ah, to be back now in Carrickfergus, on that long road down to the sea.

3. But in Kilkenny, it is reported, there are marble stones as black as ink.
   With gold and silver I would support her, but I'll sing no more now 'til I get a drink.
   I'm drunk today and I'm seldom sober, a handsome rover from town to town
   But I am sick now, and my days are numbered, come all you young men and lay me down.

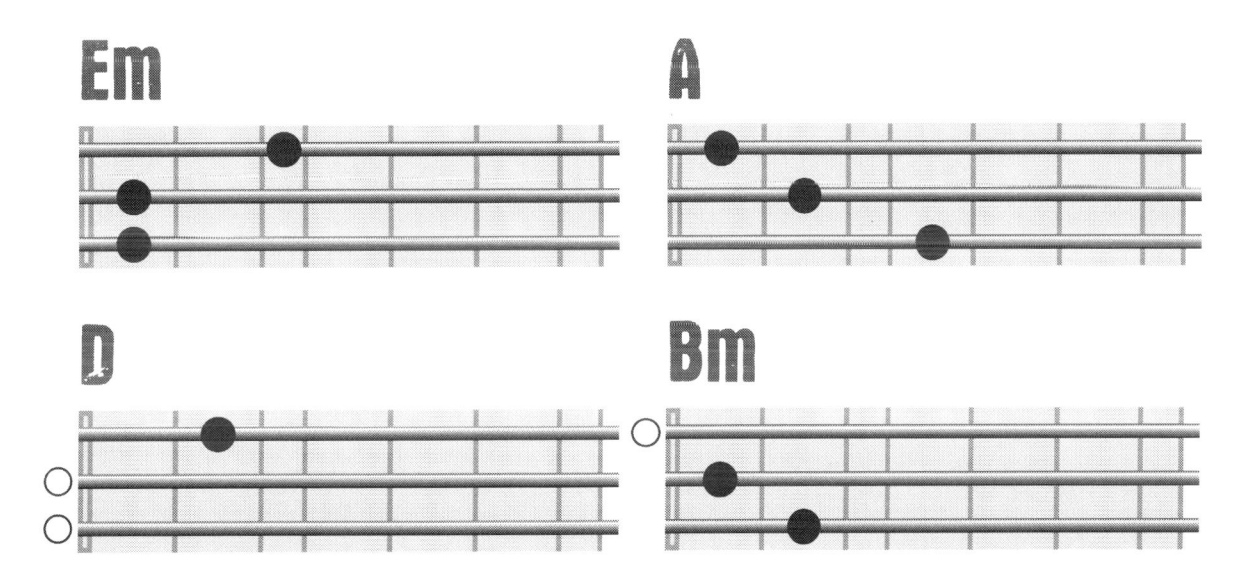

She moved through the fair

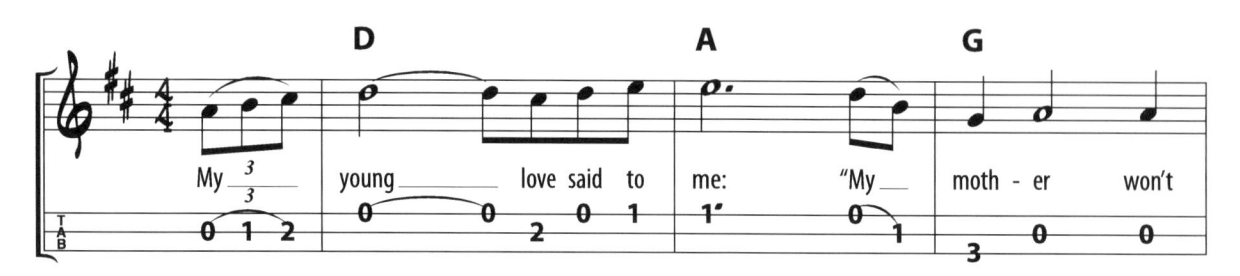

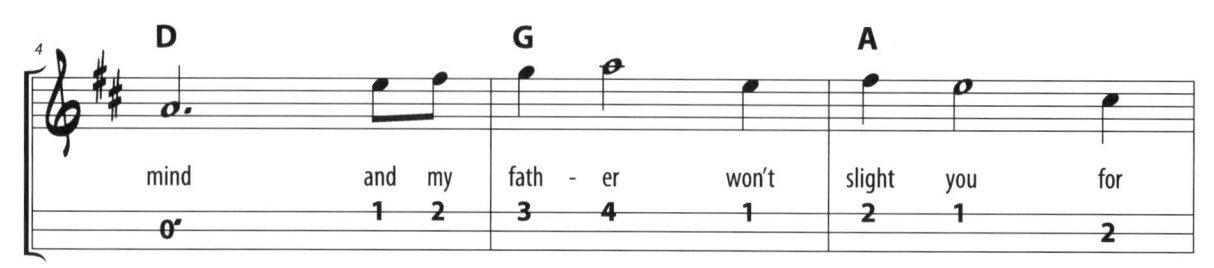

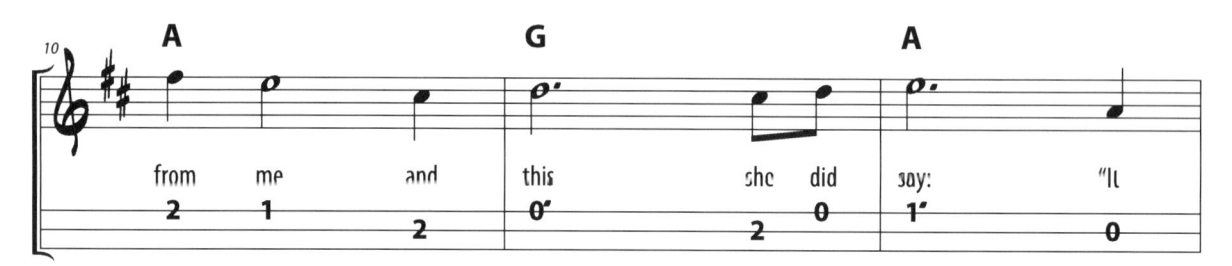

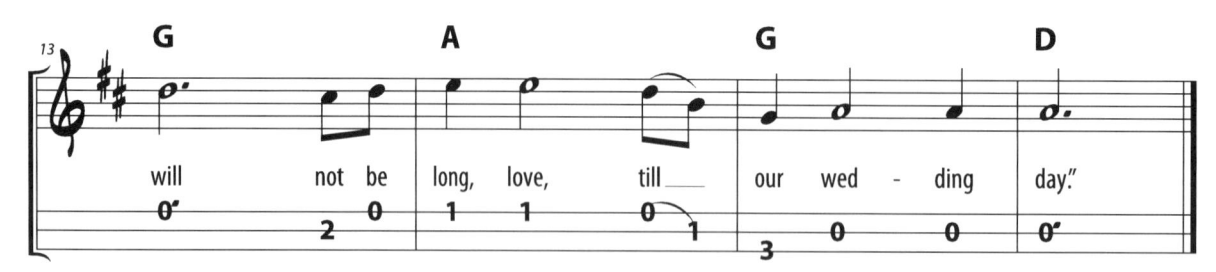

2. She stepped away from me
   and she moved through the fair
   and fondly I watched her
   move here and move there.
   And then she made her way homeward,
   with one star awake,
   as the swan in the evening
   moved over the lake.

3. The people were saying,
   no two e'er were wed
   but one had a sorrow
   that never was said.
   And I smiled as she passed
   with her goods and her gear,
   and that was the last
   that I saw of my dear

4. Last night she came to me,
   my dead love came in.
   So softly she came
   that her feet made no din.
   As she laid her hand on me,
   and this she did say:
   It will not be long, love,
   'til our wedding day.

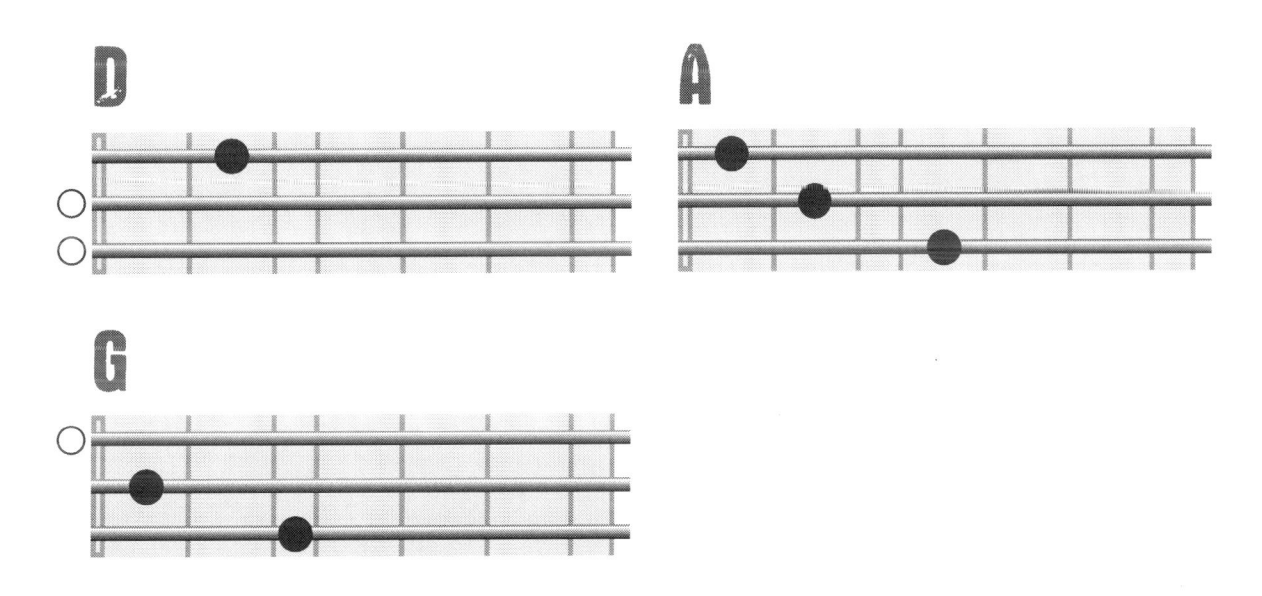

Three score and ten

And it's three score and ten boys and men were lost from Grims-by Town. From Yar-mouth down to Scar-bo-rough, man-y hun-dreds more were drowned. Their her-ring craft, their traw-lers their fish-ing smacks as well, a-lone they fight the bit-ter night and bat-tle with the swell.

2. Me thinks I see a host of craft spreading their sails a-lee,
    as down the Humber they do steer bound for the great North Sea.
    Me thinks I see a wee small craft and crew with hearts so brave,
    they go to earn their daily bread upon the restless waves.
    And it's three score and ten boys ...

3. Me thinks I see them yet again as they leave this land behind,
    casting their nets into the sea the herring shoals to find.
    Me thinks I see them yet again and they're safe on board alright,
    with their sails close reefed their decks washed clean and their sidelights burning bright.
    And it's three score and ten boys ...

4. October's night brought such a sight 'twas never seen before,
    There were yards of masts and broken spars washed up upon the shore.
    There was many a heart of sorrow there was many a heart so brave,
    There was many a true and noble lad to find a watery grave.
    And it's three score and ten boys ...

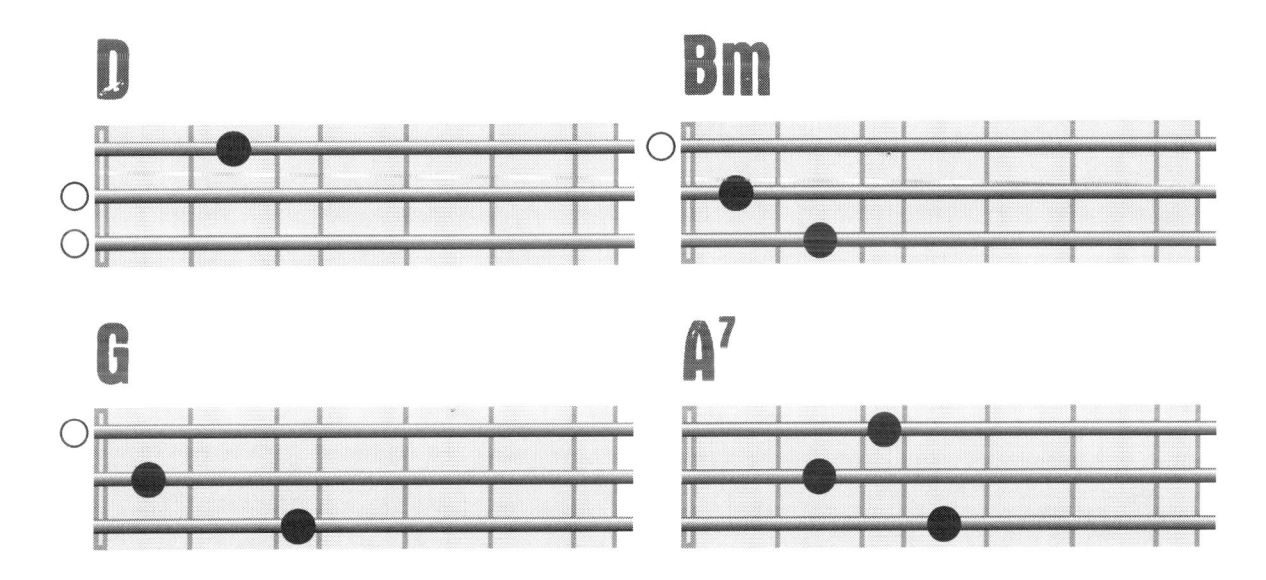

D

Bm

G

A⁷

Botany Bay

Farewell to old England forever, farewell to my rum culls as well. Farewell to the well-known Old Bailey, where I used for to cut such a swell.

Chorus

Singing tooral-li, ooral-li, addity, singing tooral-li, ooral-li, ay. Singing tooral-li, ooral-li, addity, and we're bound for Botany Bay.

110

2. There's the captain as is our commander,
   there's the bo'sun and all the ship's crew,
   there's the first- and the second-class passengers,
   knows what we poor convicts go through.

3. 'Taint leaving old England we cares about,
   'taint cos we mis-spells what we knows.
   But because all we light-fingered gentry,
   hops around with a log on our toes.

4. For seven long years I'll be staying here,
   for seven long years and a day.
   Just for meeting a bloke down our alley,
   and taking his ticker away.

5. Oh, had I the wings of a turtle-dove,
   I'd soar on my pinions so high,
   slap bang to the arms of my Polly love,
   and in her sweet presence I'd die.

6. Now all my young Dookies and Duchesses,
   take warning from what I've to say:
   Mind all is your own as you toucheses,
   or you'll find us in Botany Bay.

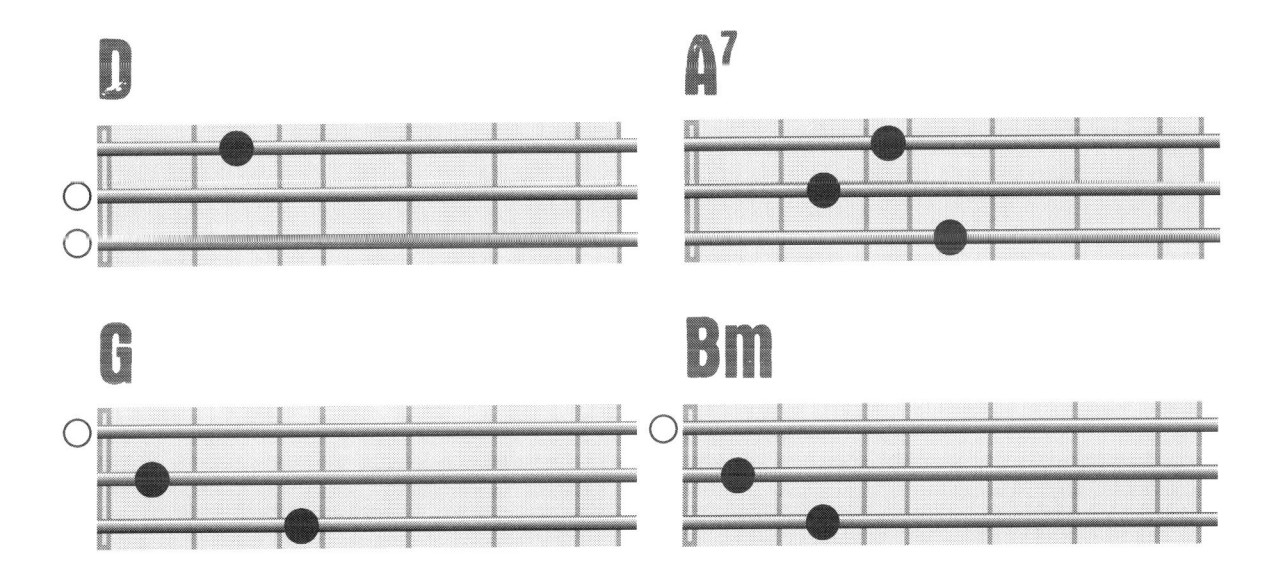

Finnegan's wake

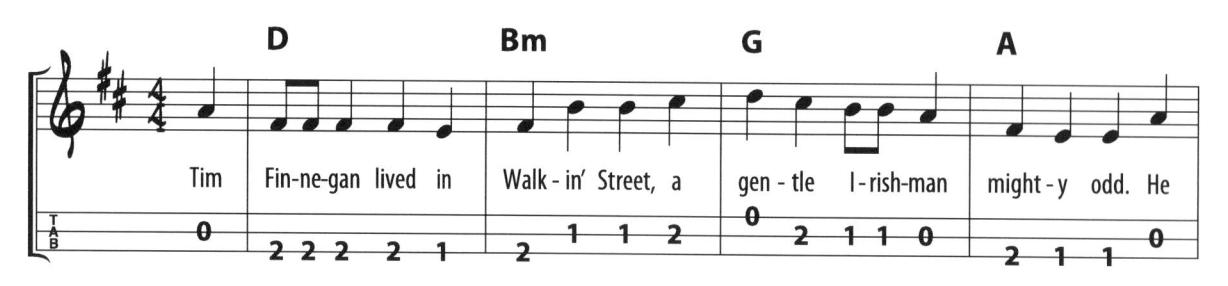

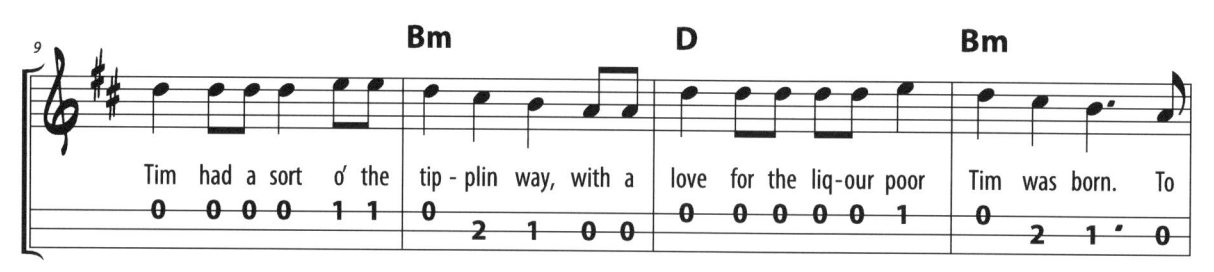

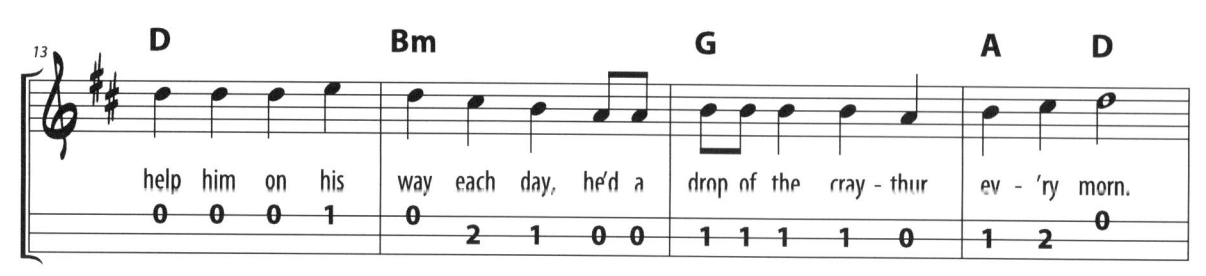

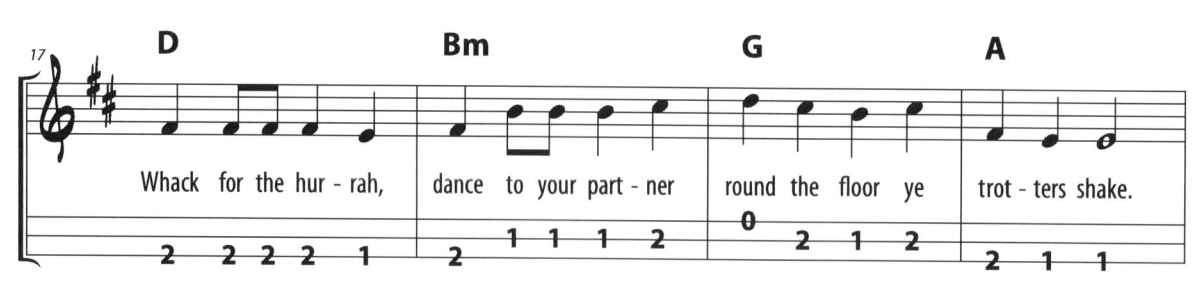

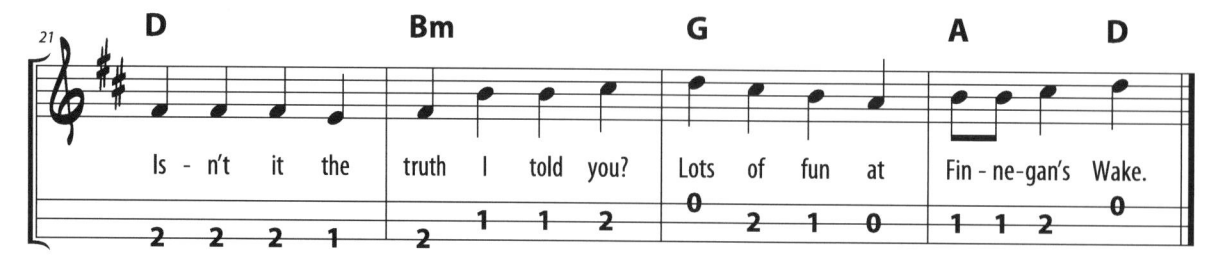

2. One morning Tim was rather full,
   his head felt heavy which made him shake.
   He fell from a ladder and he broke his skull,
   so they carried him home his corpse to wake.
   They rolled him up in a nice clean sheet,
   and laid him out upon the bed.
   A bottle of whiskey at his feet,
   and a barrel of porter at his head.
   Whack for the hurrah ...

3. His friends assembled at the wake,
   and Missus Finnegan called for lunch.
   First she brought out tay and cake,
   then pipes, tobacco and whiskey punch.
   Then Biddy O'Brien began to cry,
   "Such a nice clean corpse, did you ever see,
   Tim, mavourneen! Why did you die?".
   "Will ye hould your gob?" said Paddy McGee.
   Whack for the hurrah ...

4. Then Maggie O'Connor took up the cry,
   "O Biddy" says she "you're wrong, I'm sure".
   Biddy, she gave her a belt in the gob,
   and sent her sprawling on the floor.
   And then the war did soon engage,
   t'was woman to woman and man to man.
   Shillelaigh law was all the rage,
   and a row and a ruction soon began.
   Whack for the hurrah ...

5. Mickey Maloney ducked his head,
   when a bucket of whiskey flew at him.
   It missed, and falling on the bed,
   the liquor scattered over Tim.
   Now the spirits new life gave the corpse, my joy!
   Bedad he revives, see how he rises!
   Cryin while he ran around like blazes,
   „Thunderin' blazes, do ye think I'm dead?"

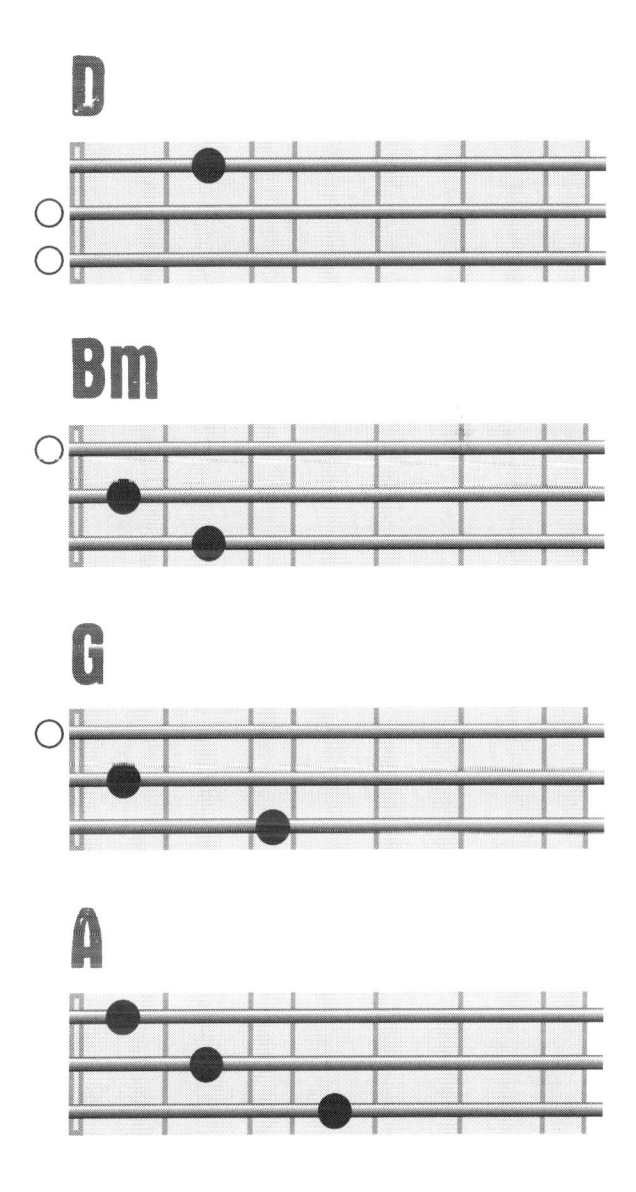

The jolly beggarman

It's of a jolly beggarman came tripping o'er the plains, he came unto a farmer's door a lodging for to gain. The farmer's daughter she came down and viewed him cheek and chin, she says: "He is a handsome man, I pray you take him in." We'll go no more a-roving, a-roving in the night. We'll go no more a-roving, less the moon shines so bright. We'll go no more a-roving.

2. He would not lie within the barn nor yet within the byre,
   but he would in the corner lie down by the kitchen fire.
   Oh then the beggar's bed was made of good clean sheets and hay,
   and down beside the kitchen fire the jolly beggar lay.
   We'll go no more a-roving ...

3. The farmer's daughter she got up to bolt the kitchen door,
   and there she saw the beggar standing naked on the floor.
   He took the daughter in his arms and to the bed he ran,
   "Kind sir' she says "Be easy now, you'll waken our good man."
   We'll go no more a-roving ...

4. "Now you are no beggar, you are some gentleman,
   for you have stolen my maidenhead and I am quite undone."
   "I am no lord, I am no squire, of beggars I be one,
   and beggars they be robbers all, so you are quite undone."
   We'll go no more a-roving ...

   She took her bed in both her hands and threw it at the wall
   says "Go ye with the beggarman, my maidenhead and all!"

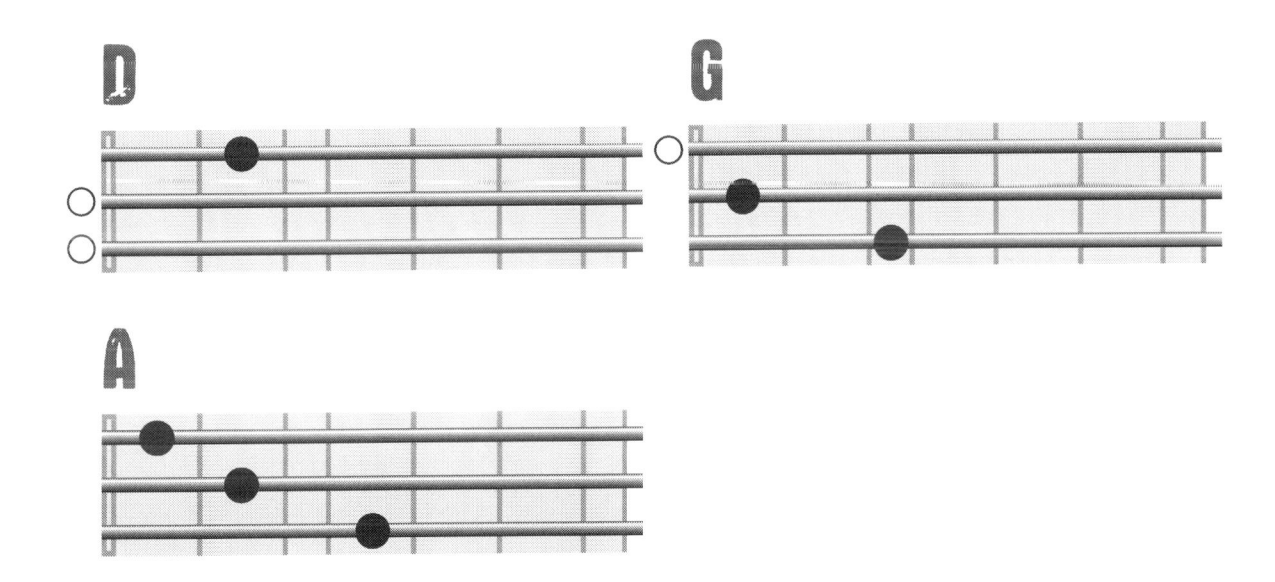

James Connolly

A great crowd had gathered outside of Kilmainhaim, with their heads all uncovered they knelt on the ground. For inside that grim prison lay a brave Irish soldier, his life for his country about to lay down.

2. He went to his death like a true son of Ireland,
   the firing party he bravely did face.
   Then the order rang out: "Present arms, fire!",
   James Connolly fell into a ready-made grave.

3. The black flag they hoisted, the cruel deed was over,
   gone was a man who loved Ireland so well.
   There was many a sad heart in Dublin that morning,
   when they murdered James Connolly, the Irish rebel.

4. Many years have rolled by since that Irish rebellion,
   when the guns of Britannia they loudly did speak.
   The bold I.R.A. they stood shoulder to shoulder,
   and the blood from their bodies flowed down Sackville Street.

5. The Four Courts of Dublin the English bombarded,
   the spirit of freedom they tried hard to quell.
   But above all the din came the cry "No Surrender",
   'twas the voice of James Connolly, the Irish rebel.

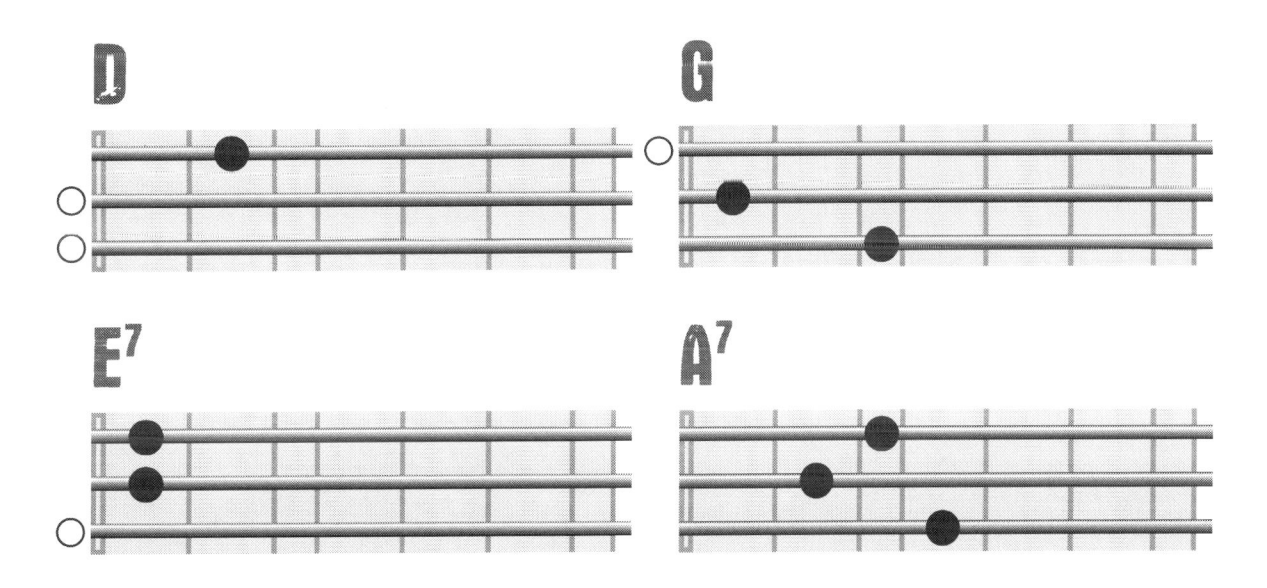

The rising of the moon

Oh, then tell me Sean O'Farrell, tell me why you hurry so. Hush me Buchall hush and listen, and his cheeks were all a-glow. I bear orders from the captain, get you ready quick and soon, for the pikes must be together by the rising of the moon. By the rising of the moon, by the rising of the moon. For the pikes must be together by the rising of the moon.

2. Oh, then tell me Sean O'Farrell, where the gathering is to be.
   In the old spot by the river, right well known to you and me.
   One more word for signal token, whistle up the marching tune.
   With your pike upon your shoulder by the rising of the moon.
   By the rising of the moon ...

3. Out of many a mud wall cabin, eyes were watching thru' the night.
   Many a manly heart was throbbing for the coming morning light.
   Murmurs ran along the valley, like the banshee's lonely croon,
   and a thousand pikes were flashing by the rising of the moon.
   By the rising of the moon ...

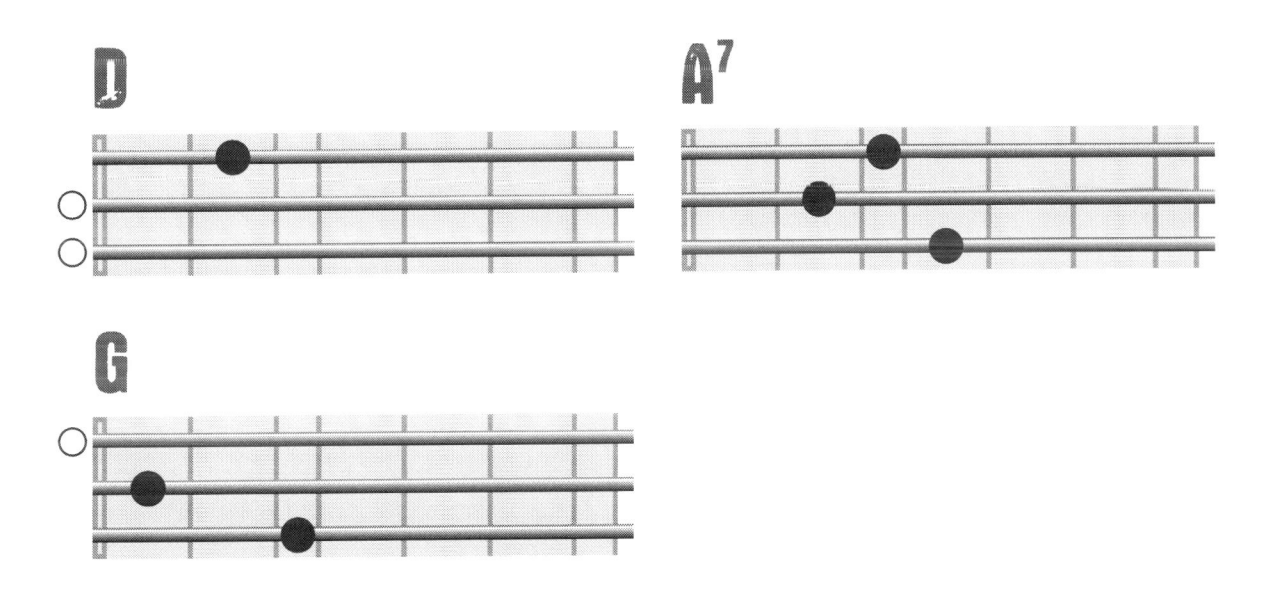

The star of the County Down

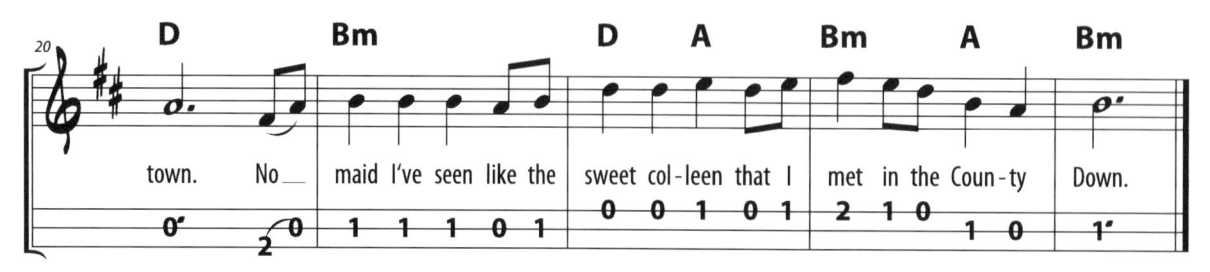

Near Banbridge town, in the County Down, one morning in July, down a boreen green came a sweet colleen, and she smiled as she passed me by. She looked so sweet from her two white feet to the sheen of her nut-brown hair, such a coaxing elf, I'd to shake myself to make sure I was standing there. From Bantry Bay up to Derry Quay and from Galway to Dublin town, no maid I've seen like the sweet colleen that I met in the County Down.

2. As she onward sped I shook my head,
   and I gazed with a feeling rare.
   And I said, says I, to a passerby,
   "Who's the maid with the nut-brown hair?"
   He smiled at me, and with pride says he,
   "That's the gem of Ireland's crown.
   She's young Rosie McCann from the banks of the Bann,
   She's the star of the County Down."
   From Bantry Bay ...

3. She'd a soft brown eye and a look so sly,
   and a smile like the rose in June.
   And you hung on each note from her lily-white throat,
   as she lilted an Irish tune.
   At the pattern dance you were held in trance,
   as she tripped through a reel or jig.
   And when her eyes she'd roll, she'd coax upon my soul,
   a spud from a hungry pig.
   From Bantry Bay ...

4. I've travelled a bit, but never was hit,
   since my roving career began.
   But fair and square I surrendered there,
   to the charms of young Rose McCann.
   From Bantry Bay ...

5. With a heart to let and no tenant yet,
   did I meet with in shawl or gown.
   But in she went and I asked no rent,
   from the star of the County Down.
   From Bantry Bay ...

6. At the harvest fair I'll be surely there,
   And I'll dress in my Sunday clothes.
   And I'll try sheep's eyes, and deludhering lies,
   on the heart of the nut-brown rose.
   No pipe I'll smoke, no horse I'll yoke,
   though with rust my plow turns brown.
   Till a smiling bride by my own fireside,
   sits the star of the County Down.
   From Bantry Bay ...

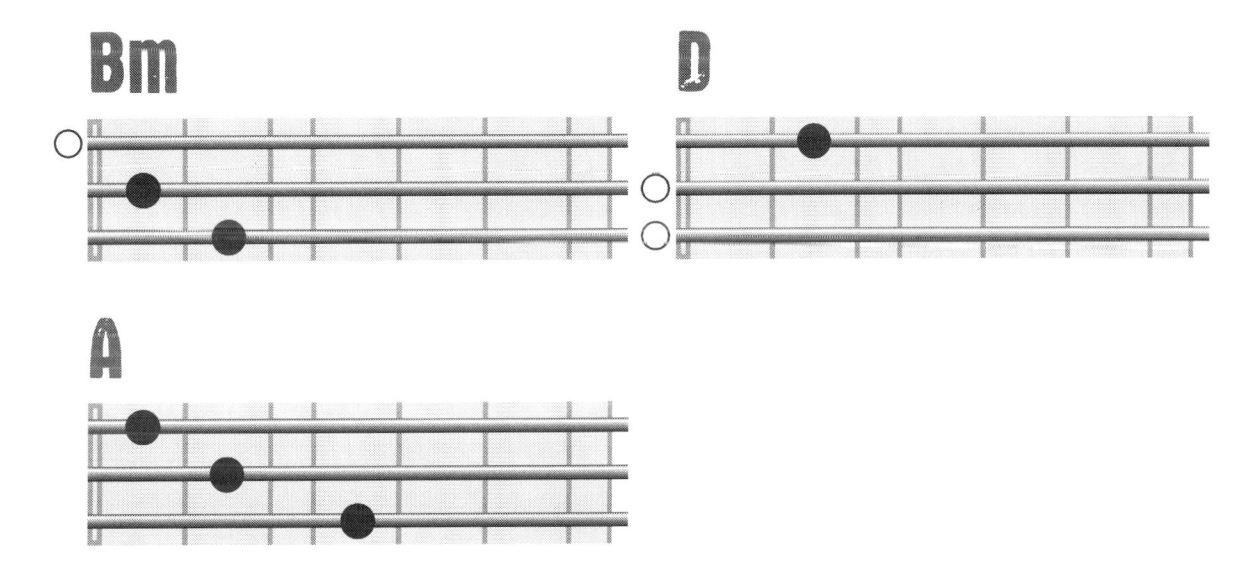

Bm

D

A

Brennan on the moor

2. One day upon the highway as Willie he went down,
   he met the Mayor of Cashiell, a mile outside of town.
   The mayor he knew his features and he said, "Young man", said he,
   "Your name is Willie Brennan, you must come along with me."

3. Now Brennan's wife had gone to town, provisions for to buy,
   and when she saw her Willie she commenced to weep and cry.
   She said, "Hand to me that tenpenny", as soon as Willie spoke,
   she handed him a blunderbuss from underneath her cloak.

4. Now with this loaded blunderbuss – the truth I will unfold –
   he made the mayor tremble and he robbed him of his gold.
   One hundred pounds was offered for his apprehension there,
   so he, with horse and saddle to the mountains did repair.

5. Now Brennan being an outlaw upon the mountains high
   with cavalry and infantry to take him they did try
   he laughed at them with scorn until at last 'twas said
   by a false-hearted woman he was cruelly betrayed.
   Brennan on the moor ...

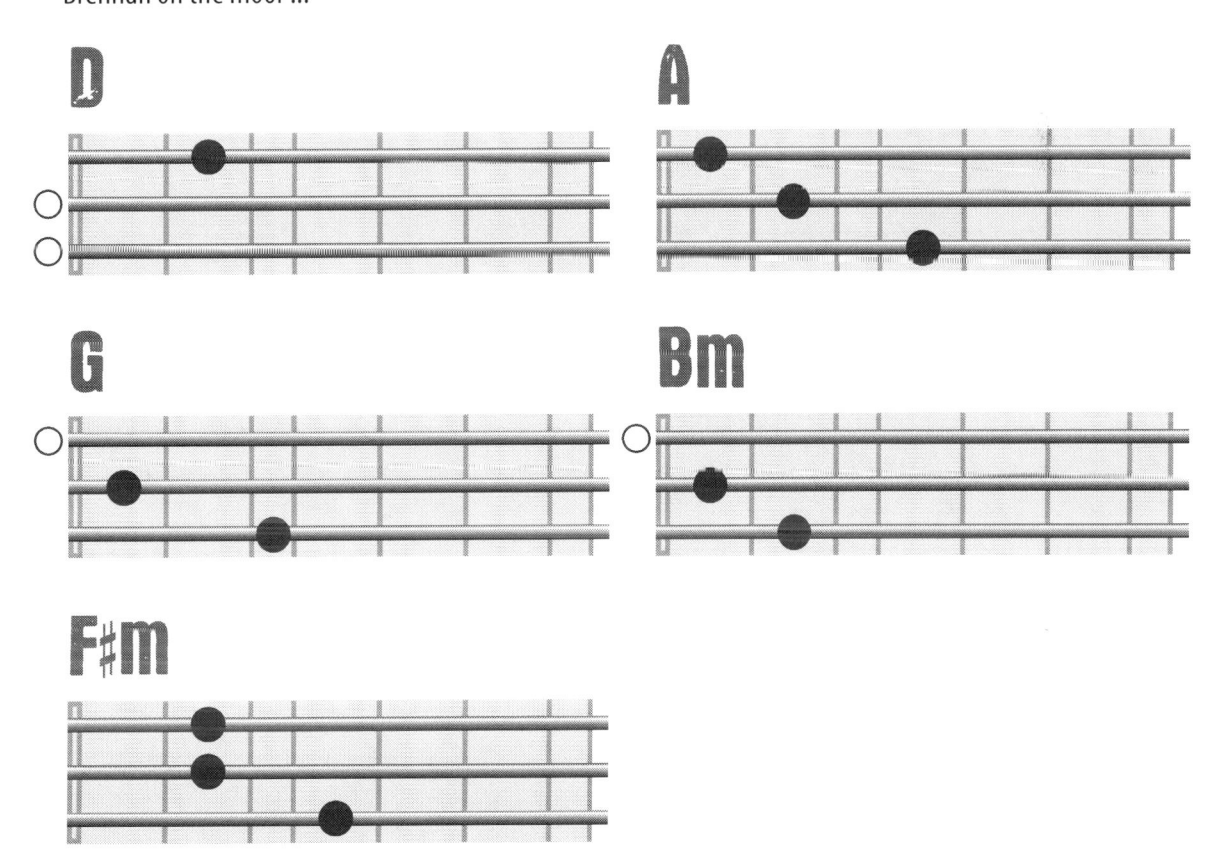

D

A

G

Bm

F♯m

The auld orange flute

In the coun-ty Ty-rone, near the town of Dun-gan-non, there were many a ruc-tion me-self had a hand in. Bob Will-iams who lived there, a wea-ver by trade, and all of us thought him a stout Or-ange blade. On the twelfth of Ju-ly as it year-ly did come, Bob played on his flute to the sound of the drum. You may talk of your fid-dle, your harp or your lute, but no-thing could sound like the auld or-ange flute.

2. But the treacherous scoundrel, he took us all in,
   for he married a Papish named Bridget McGinn.
   Turned Papish himself and forsook the Old Cause,
   that gave us our freedom, religion and laws.
   And the boys in the county made noise upon it,
   they forced Bob to flee to the province of Connaught;
   Took with him his wife and his fixins, to boot,
   and along with the rest went the auld orange flute.

3. Each Sunday at mass, to atone for past deeds,
   Bob said Paters and Aves and counted his beads.
   Till one Sunday morn, at the priest´s own require,
   he went for to play with the flutes in the choir.
   He went with the old flute to play in the loft,
   but the instrument shivered and sighed and then coughed.
   When he blew it and fingered it, it made a strange noise,
   for the flute would play only "The Protestant Boys".

4. Bob jumped up and started, and got in a flutter,
   he pitched the old flute in the best holy water;
   He thought that this charm would bring some other sound,
   when he tried it again, it played "Croppies Lie Down!"
   And all he did whistle, and finger and blow,
   for to play Papish music, the flute would not go;
   "Kick the Pope", "The Boyne Water", and such like 'twould sound
   not one Papish bleat in it could e'er be found.

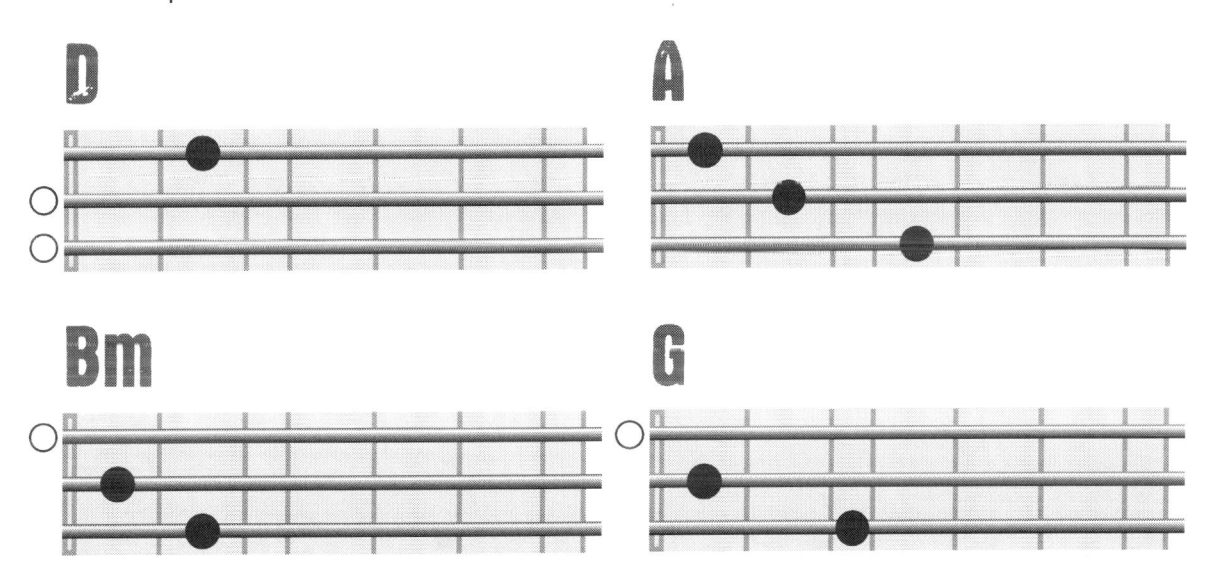

The moonshiner

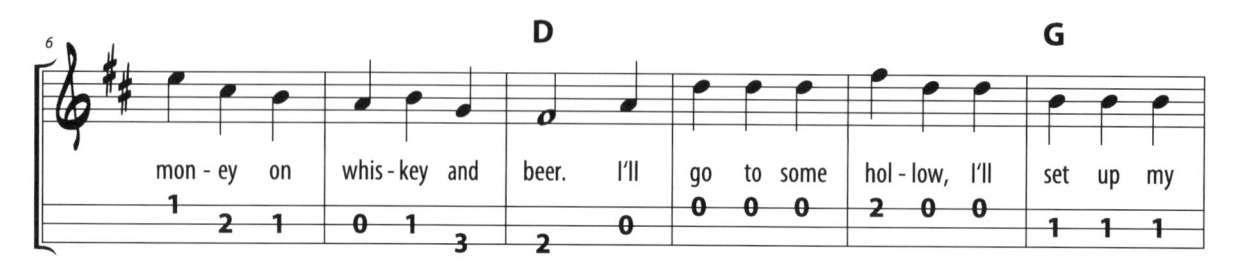

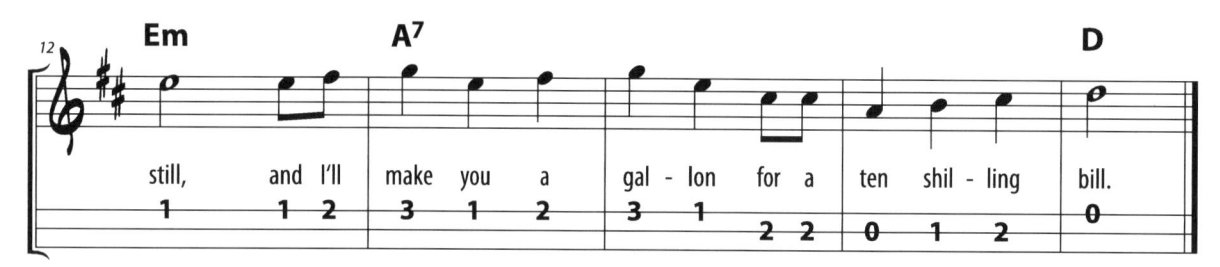

I've been a moon-shin-er for man-y a year, I've spent all me mon-ey on whis-key and beer. I'll go to some hol-low, I'll set up my still, and I'll make you a gal-lon for a ten shil-ling bill.

2. I'll go to some hollow in this counterie,
   ten gallons of wash I can go on a spree.
   No women to follow, the world is all mine,
   I love none so well as I love the moonshine.
   I'm a rambler, I'm a gambler ...

3. Oh, moonshine, dear moonshine, oh, how I love thee,
   you killed me old father, but dare you try me.
   Now bless all moonshiners and bless all moonshine,
   their breath smells as sweet as the dew on the vine.
   I'm a rambler, I'm a gambler ...

126

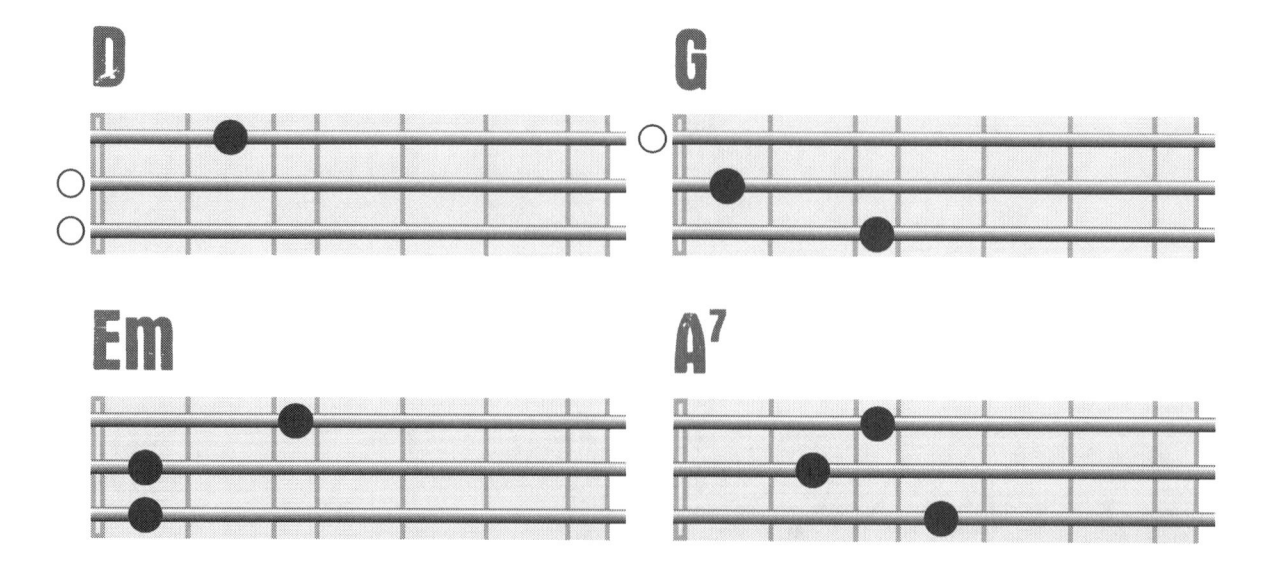

The hills of Connemara

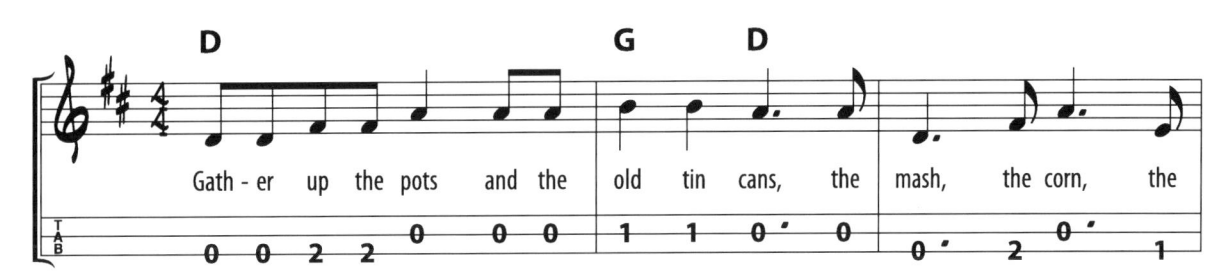

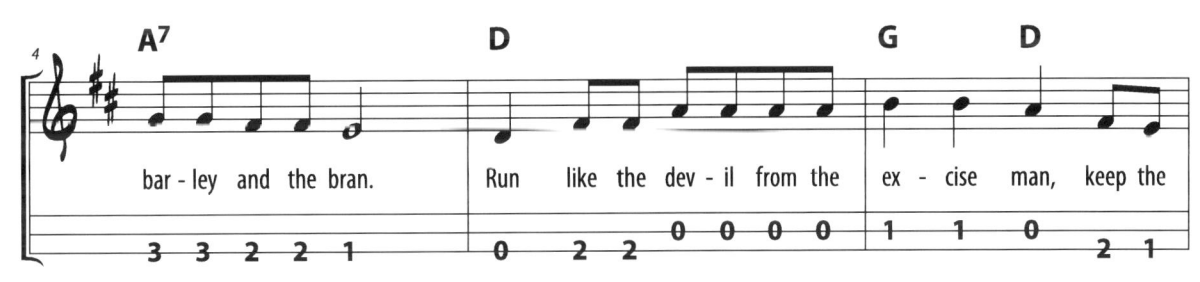

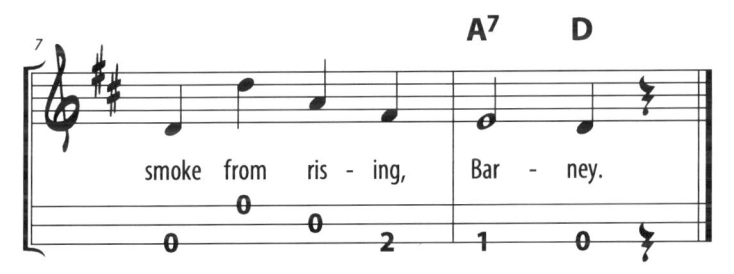

Gath-er up the pots and the old tin cans, the mash, the corn, the bar-ley and the bran. Run like the dev-il from the ex-cise man, keep the smoke from ris - ing, Bar - ney.

2. Keep your eyes well peeled today,
   the excise men are on their way.
   Searching for the mountain tay,
   in the hills of Connemara.

3. Swinging to the left, swinging to the right,
   the excise men will dance all night.
   Drinkin' up the tay till the broad daylight,
   in the hills of Connemara.

4. A gallon for the butcher and a quart for John,
   and a bottle for poor old Father Tom.
   Just to help the poor old dear along,
   in the hills of Connemara.

5. Stand your ground, for it's too late,
   the excise men are at the gate.
   Glory be to Paddy, but they're drinkin' it straight,
   in the hills of Connemara.

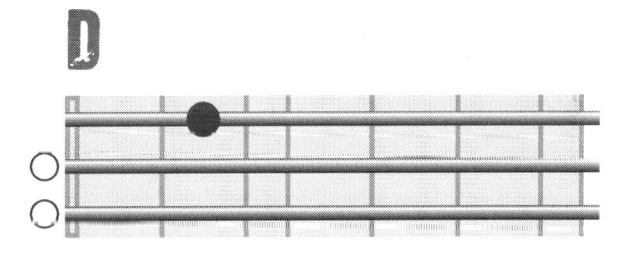

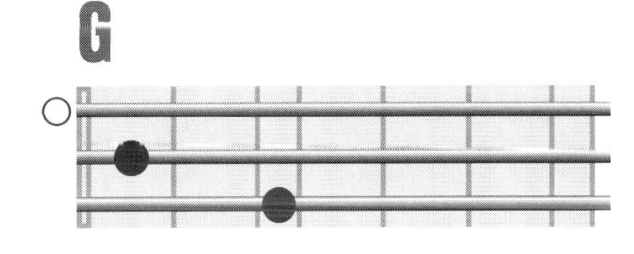

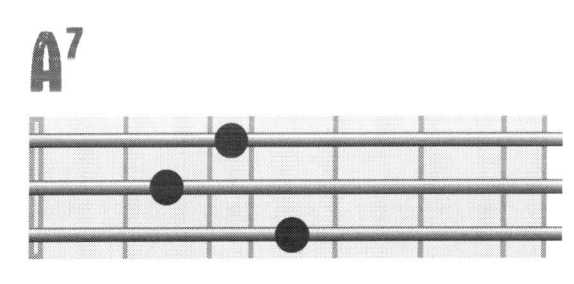

127

The rose of Mooncoin

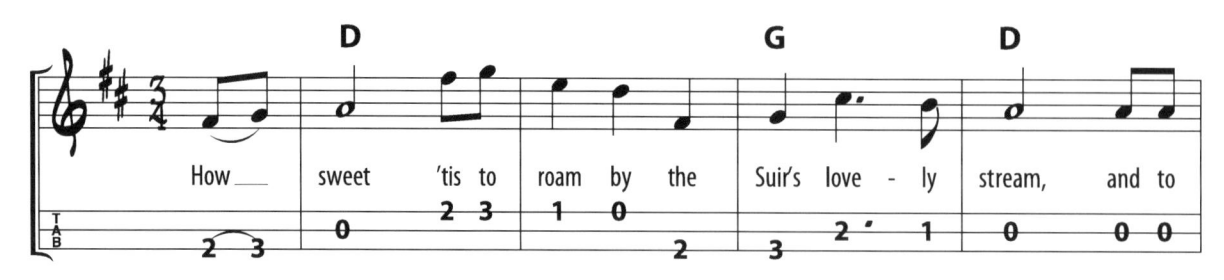

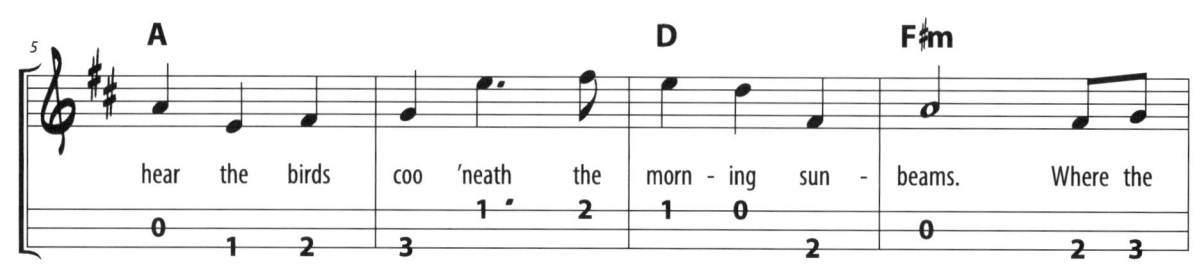

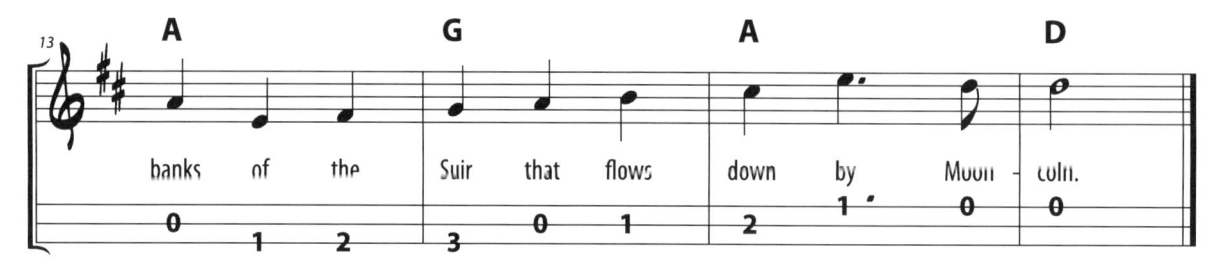

Chorus:
    Flow on lovely river flow gently along,
    by your waters so sweet sounds the Lark's merry song,
    on your green banks I'll wander, where first I did join,
    with you lovely Molly, the rose of Mooncoin.

2. Oh Molly dear Molly it breaks my fond heart,
    to know that we two for each must part.
    I'll think of you Molly while sun and moon shine,
    on the banks of the Suir that flows down by Mooncoin.

3. She has sailed far away o're the dark rolling foam,
    far away from the hills of her dear Irish home.
    Where the fisherman sports with his small boat and line,
    on the banks of the Suir that flows down by Mooncoin.

4. Then here's to the Suir with it's valleys so fair,
    as oft times we wandered in the cool morning air.
    Where the roses are blooming and lillies entwine,
    on the banks of the Suir that flows down by Mooncoin.

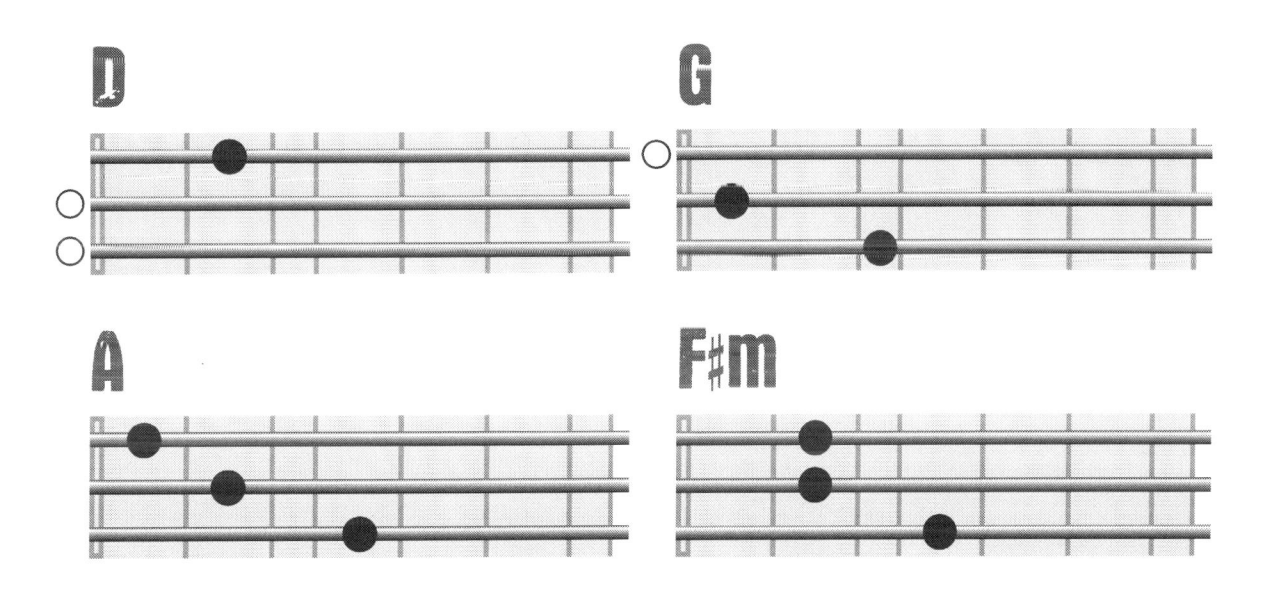

The last rose of summer

'Tis the last rose of summer, left blooming all alone; all her lovely companions are faded and gone. No flower of her kindred, no rosebud is nigh, to reflect back her blushes and give sigh for sigh.

2. I'll not leave thee, thou lone one!
    To pine on the stem;
    Since the lovely are sleeping,
    go, sleep thou with them.
    Thus kindly I scatter,
    thy leaves o'er the bed,
    where thy mates of the garden
    lie scentless and dead.

3. So soon may I follow,
    when friendships decay,
    and from Love's shining circle
    the gems drop away.
    When true hearts lie withered,
    and fond ones are flown.
    Oh! who would inhabit
    this bleak world alone?

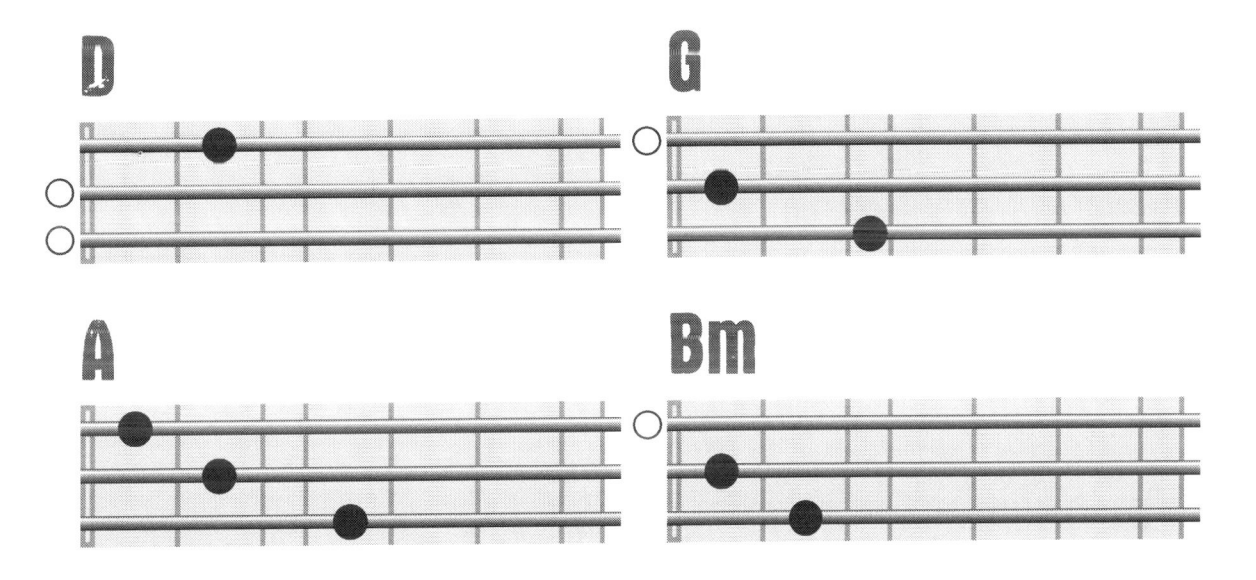

D

G

A

Bm

The merry ploughboy

Well, I am a merry plough-boy, and I plough the fields all day. Till a sudden thought came to my mind, that I should run a-way. For I'm sick and tired of slav-'ry, since the day that I was born. So I'm off to join the I.R.A., and im off to mor row morn. And we're off to Dub-lin in the green in the green, where the hel-mets glist-en in the sun. Where the bayo-nets flash and the rif-les crash, to the ech-o of a Thomp-son gun.

2. I'll leave aside my pick and spade I'll leave aside my plough,
   and I'll leave aside my old grey mare for no more I'll need them now.
   I'll leave aside my Mary, she's the girl I do adore,
   and I wonder if she'll think of me when she hears the cannon roar.
   And we're off to Dublin ...

3. And when the war is over and dear old Ireland's free,
   I will take her to the church to wed and a rebel's wife she'll be.
   Well some men fight for silver and some men fight for gold,
   but the I.R.A. are fighting for the land the Saxon's stole.
   And we're off to Dublin ...

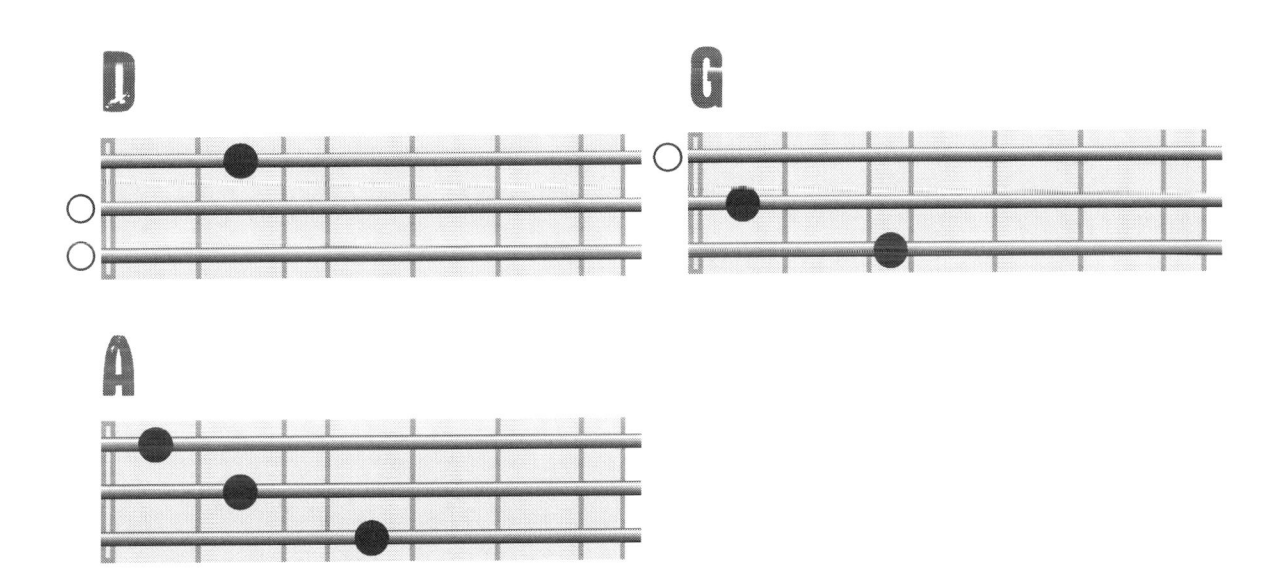

Humpty Dumpty

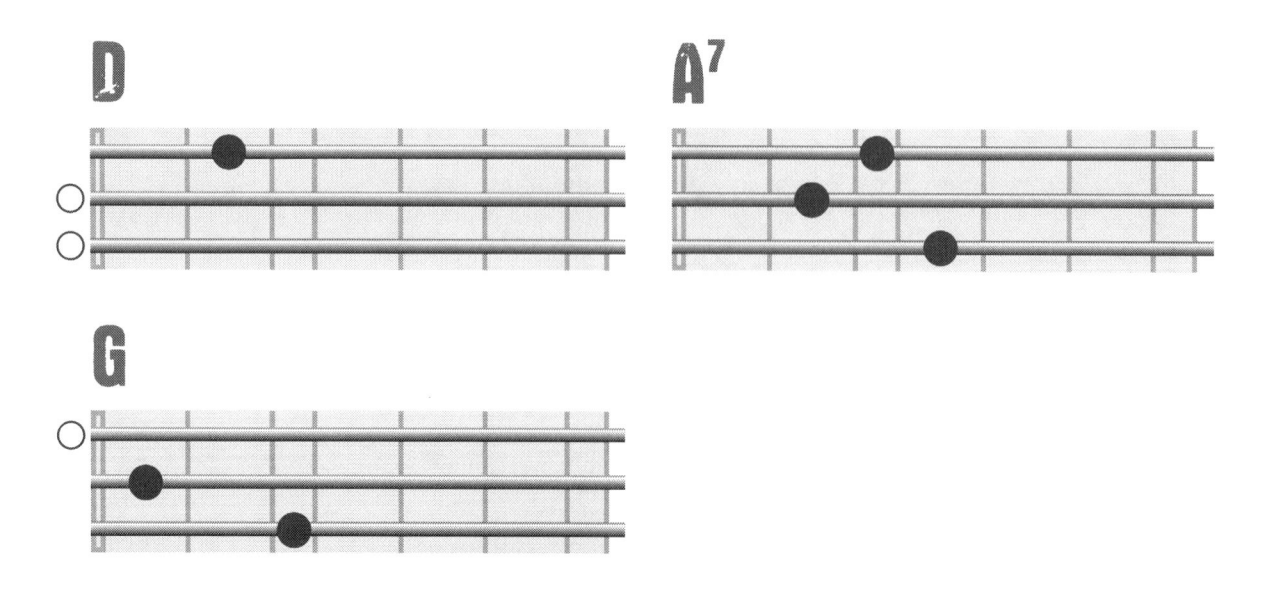

Humpty Dumpty sat on a wall, Humpty Dumpty had a great fall. All the king's horses and all the king's men couldn't put Humpty together again.

D

A7

G

134

Row, row, row

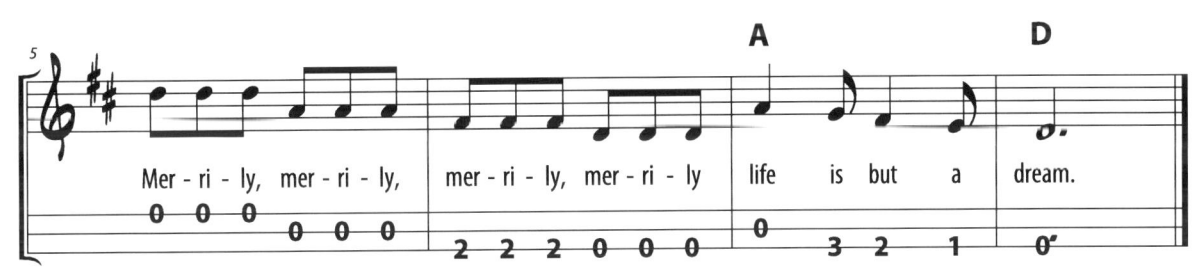

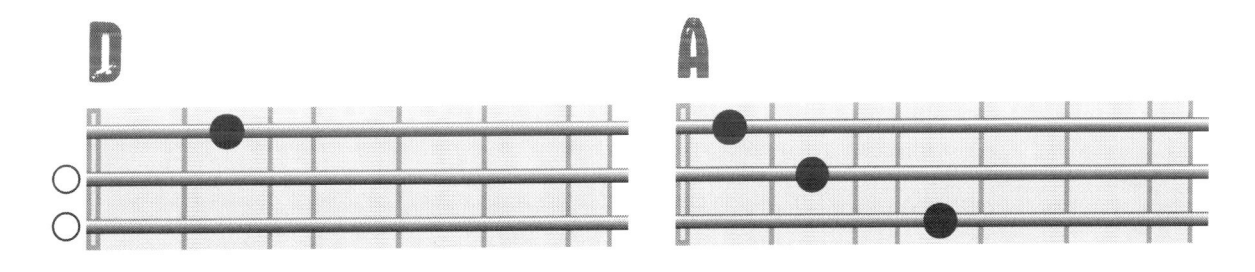

Lavender's blue

La-ven-der's blue, dil-ly, dil-ly, la-ven-der's green,

when I am king, dil-ly, dil-ly, you shall be queen.

Who told you so, dil-ly, dil-ly, who told you so?

'Twas my own heart, dil-ly, dil-ly, that told me so.

2. Call up your men, dilly, dilly, set them to work,
   some to the plough, dilly, dilly, some to the fork,
   some to make hay, dilly, dilly, some to cut corn,
   while you and I, dilly, dilly, keep ourselves warm.

3. Lavender's green, dilly, dilly, Lavender's blue,
   if you love me, dilly, dilly, I will love you.
   Let the birds sing, dilly, dilly, and the lambs play;
   we shall be safe, dilly, dilly, out of harm's way.

4. I love to dance, dilly, dilly, I love to sing;
   when I am queen, dilly, dilly, you'll be my king.
   Who told me so, dilly, dilly, who told me so?
   I told myself, dilly, dilly, I told me so.

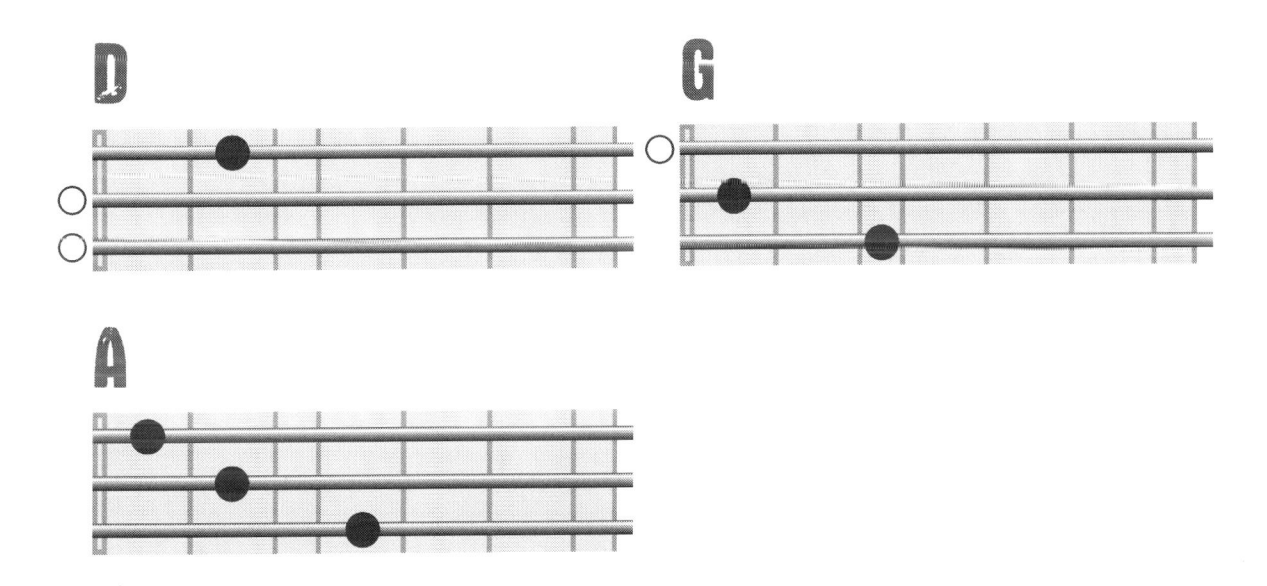

Brahms' lullaby

2. Lullaby, and good night, your mother's delight,
   shining angels beside my darling abide.
   Soft and warm is your bed,
   close your eyes and rest your head.
   Soft and warm is your bed,
   close your eyes and rest your head.

3. Sleepyhead, close your eyes,
   mother's right here beside you.
   I'll protect you from harm,
   you will wake in my arms.
   Guardian angels are near,
   so sleep on, with no fear.
   Guardian angels are near,
   so sleep on, with no fear.

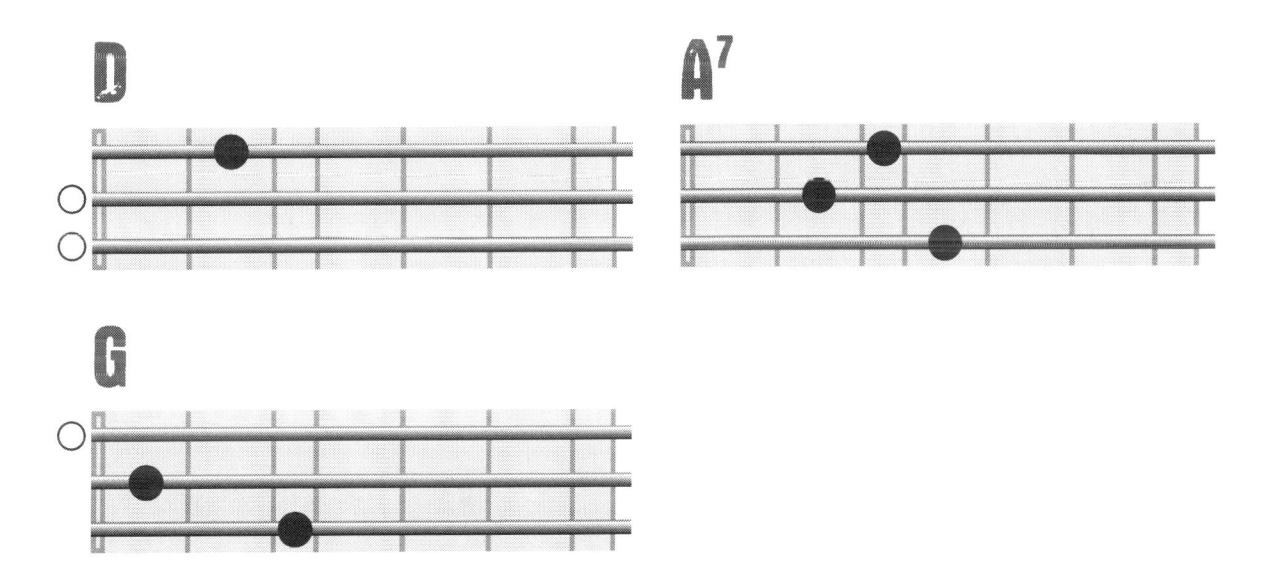

Mary had a little lamb

2. And everywhere that Mary went,
   Mary went, Mary went,
   everywhere that Mary went
   the lamb was sure to go.

3. It followed her to school one day,
   school one day, school one day,
   it followed her to school one day
   which was against the rule.

4. It made the children laugh and play,
   laugh and play, laugh and play,
   it made the children laugh and play
   to see a lamb at school.

5. And so the teacher turned it out,
   turned it out, turned it out,
   and so the teacher turned it out
   but still it lingered near.

6. And waited patiently about,
   patiently, patiently,
   and waited patiently about
   till Mary did appear.

7. "Why does the lamb love Mary so,
   Mary so, Mary so?"
   "Why does the lamb love Mary so?"
   the eager children cry.

8. "Because the lamb loves Mary so,
   Mary so, Mary so",
   "Because the lamb loves Mary so",
   the teacher did reply.

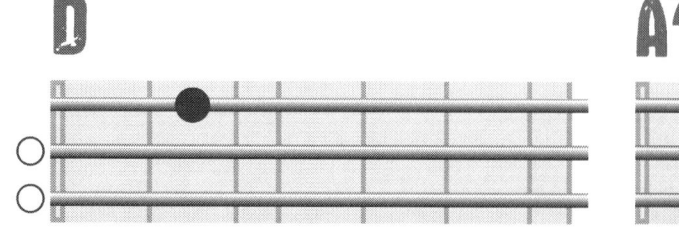

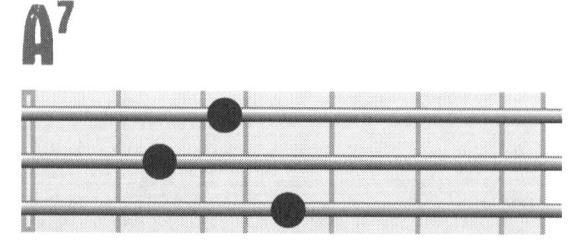

140

The farmer in the dell

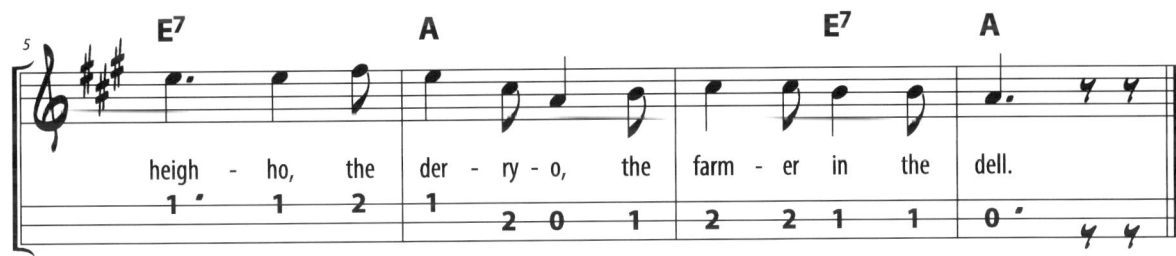

2. The farmer takes the wife, (2x)
   heigh-ho, the derry-o,
   the farmer takes the wife.

3. The wife takes the child, (2x)
   heigh-ho, the derry-o,
   the wife takes the child,

4. The child takes the nurse (2x)
   Heigh-ho, the derry-o ...
   The child takes the nurse

5. The nurse takes the cow, (2x)
   heigh-ho, the derry-o,
   the nurse takes the cow.

6. The cow takes the dog, (2x)
   heigh-ho, the derry-o,
   the cow takes the dog.

7. The dog takes the cat, (2x)
   heigh-ho, the derry-o,
   the dog takes the cat.

8. The cat takes the mouse, (2x)
   heigh-ho, the derry-o,
   the cat takes the mouse.

9. The mouse takes the cheese, (2x)
   heigh-ho, the derry-o,
   the mouse takes the cheese.

10. The cheese stands alone, (2x)
    heigh-ho, the derry-o,
    the cheese stands alone.

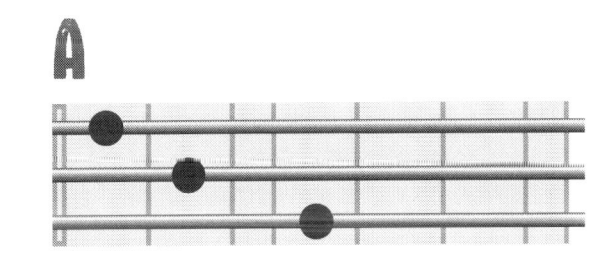

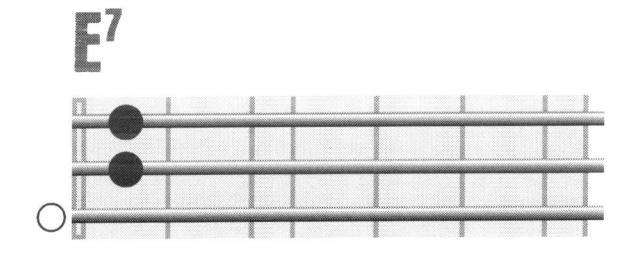

Crawdad song

You get a line and I'll get a pole, Hon - ey.

You get a line and I'll get a pole, Ba - by.

You get a line and I'll get a pole, and we'll go down to the craw - dad hole, Hon - ey, Ba - by mine.

2. Sittin' on the bank 'til my feet get cold, Honey.
   Sittin' on the bank 'til my feet get cold, Baby.
   Sittin' on the bank 'til my feet get cold,
   lookin' down that crawdad hole, Honey, Baby mine.

3. Yonder comes a man with a sack on his back, Honey.
   Yonder comes a man with a sack on his Baby.
   Yonder comes a man with a sack on his back,
   packin' all the crawdads he can pack, Honey, Baby mine.

4. The man fell down and he broke that sack, Honey.
   The man fell down and he broke that sack, Baby.
   The man fell down and he broke that sack,
   see those crawdads backing back, Honey, Baby mine.

5. I heard the duck say to the drake, honey, honey.
   I heard the duck say to the drake, baby, baby.
   I heard the duck say to the drake,
   there ain't no crawdads in this lake, Honey, Baby mine.

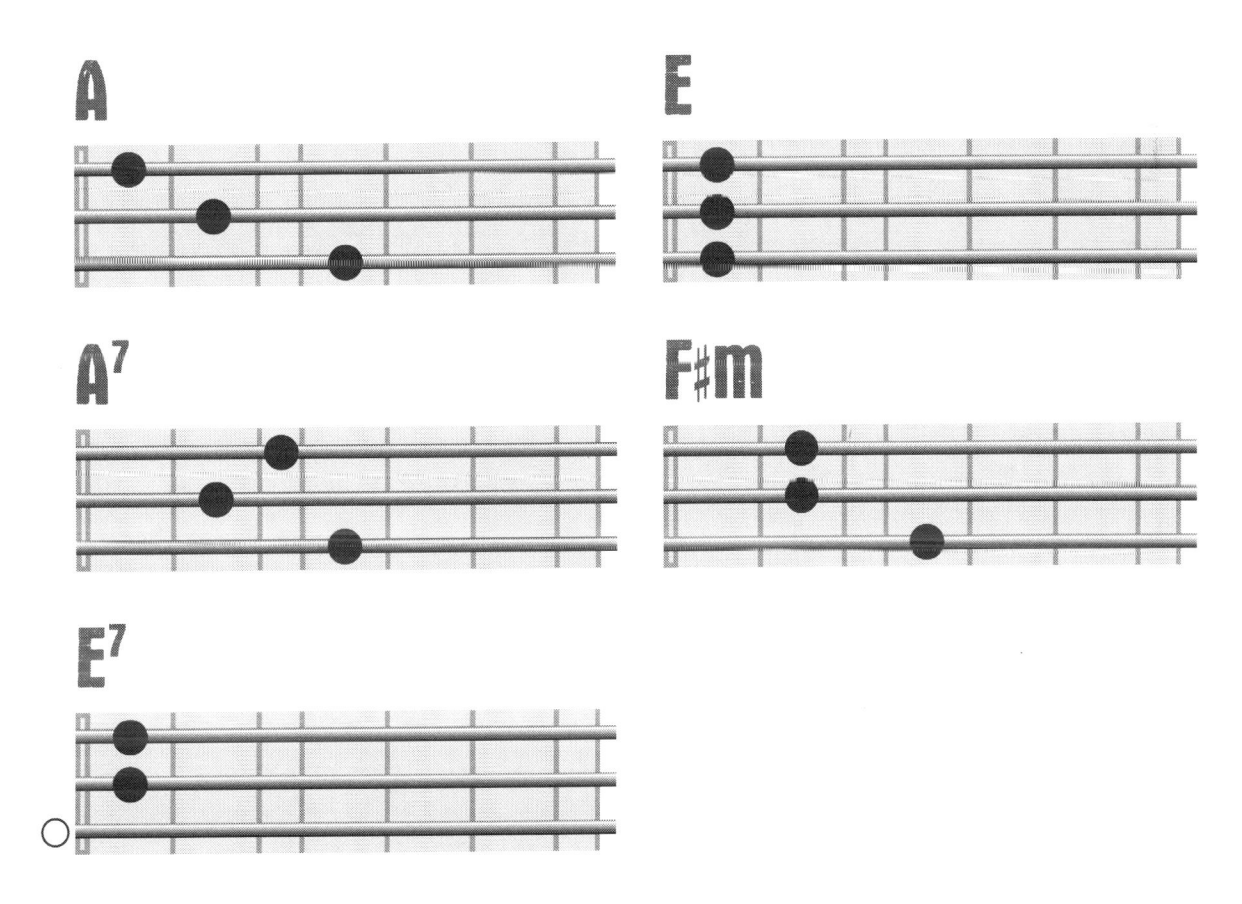

Pop! Goes the weasel

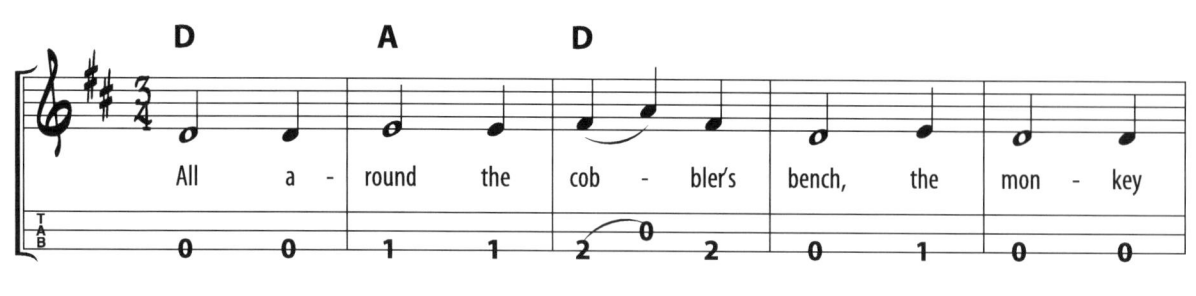

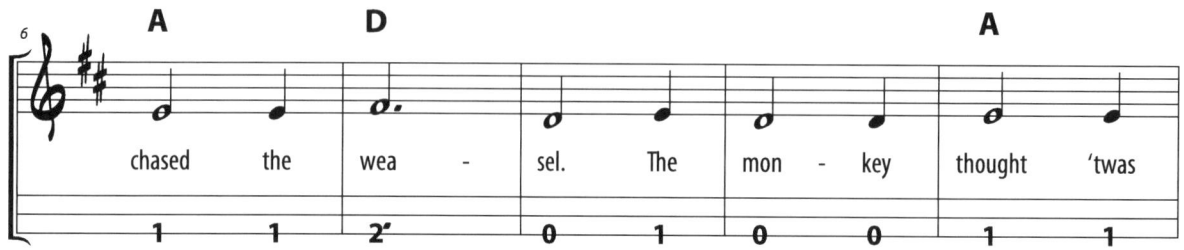

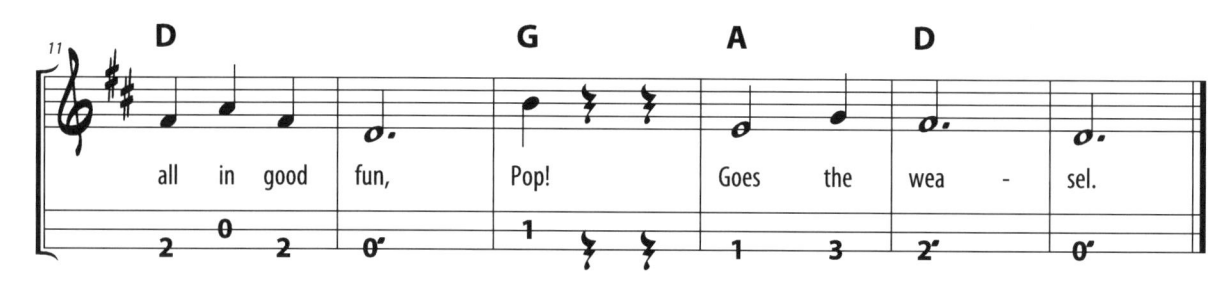

[Sheet music with chords D, A, D, A, D, A, D, G, A, D]

All a-round the cob-bler's bench, the mon-key chased the wea-sel. The mon-key thought 'twas all in good fun, Pop! Goes the wea-sel.

2. A penny for a spool of thread,
   a penny for a needle.
   That's the way the money goes,
   Pop! Goes the weasel.

3. Jimmy's got the whooping cough
   and Timmy's got the measles.
   That's the way the story goes
   Pop! Goes the weasel.

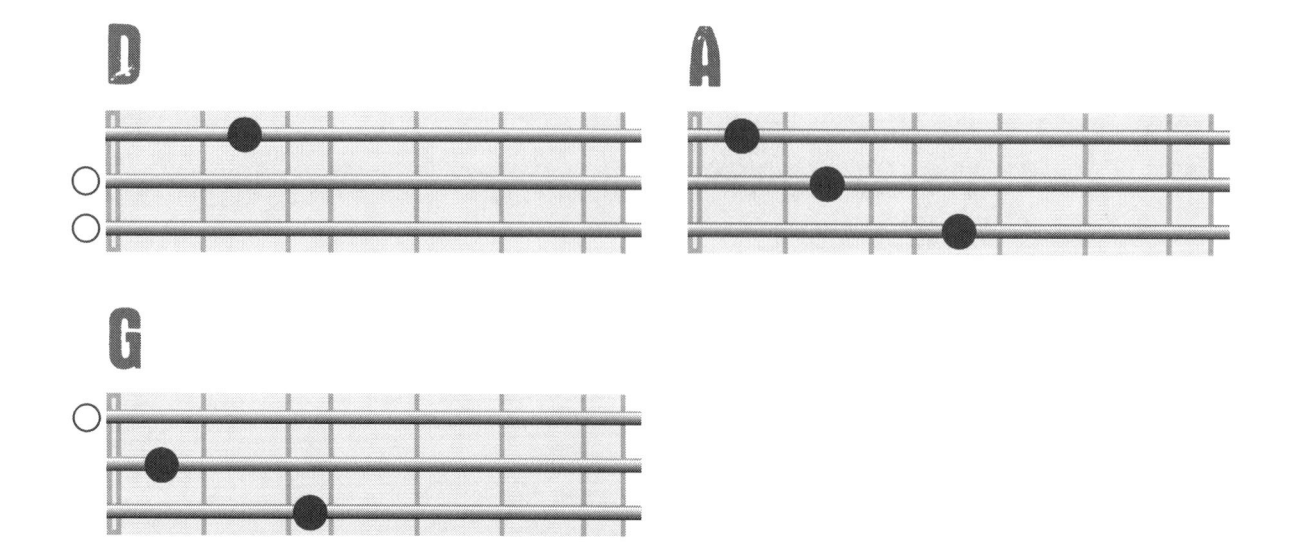

[Chord diagrams for D, A, and G]

Itsy bitsy spider

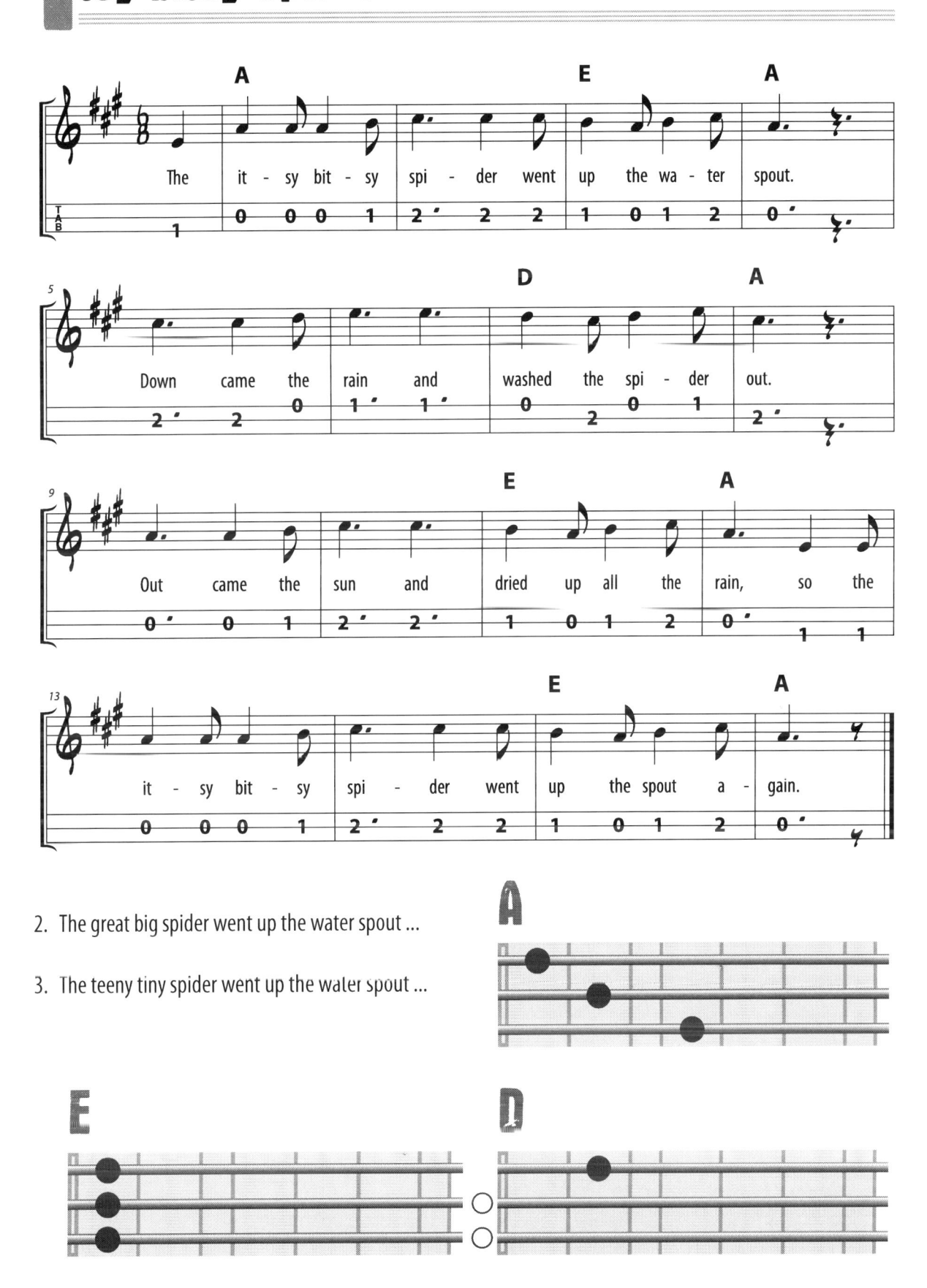

The it-sy bit-sy spi-der went up the wa-ter spout.

Down came the rain and washed the spi-der out.

Out came the sun and dried up all the rain, so the

it-sy bit-sy spi-der went up the spout a-gain.

2. The great big spider went up the water spout ...

3. The teeny tiny spider went up the water spout ...

145

Rain, rain, go away

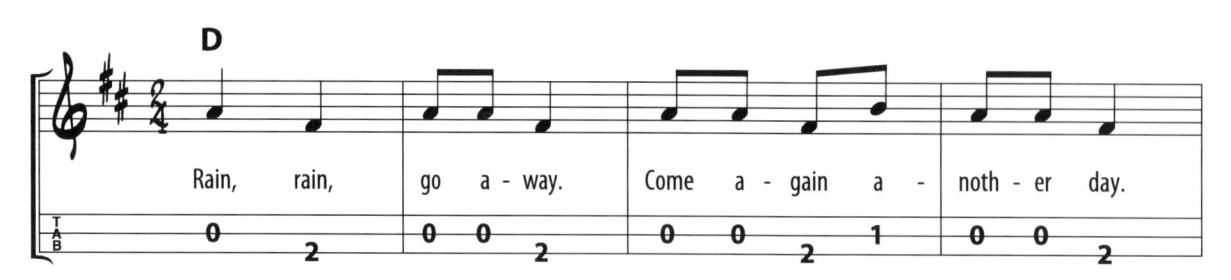

2. Rain, rain, go away.
   Come again another day.
   Daddy wants to play.
   Rain, rain, go away.

3. Rain, rain, go away.
   Come again another day.
   Mommy wants to play.
   Rain, rain, go away.

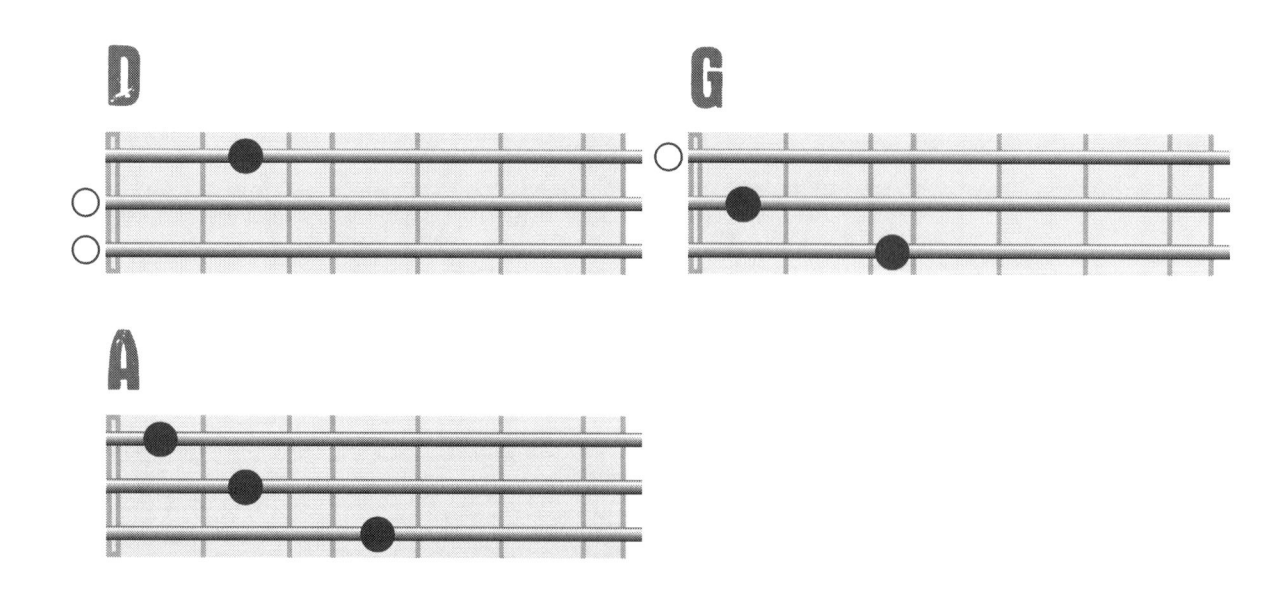

5. Rain, rain, go away.
   Come again another day.
   Brother wants to play.
   Rain, rain, go away.

6. Rain, rain, go away.
   Come again another day.
   Sister wants to play.
   Rain, rain, go away.

7. Rain, rain, go away.
   Come again another day.
   Baby wants to play.
   Rain, rain, go away.

8. Rain, Rain, go away.
   Come again another day.
   All the family wants to play.
   Rain, rain, go away.

Pease porridge hot

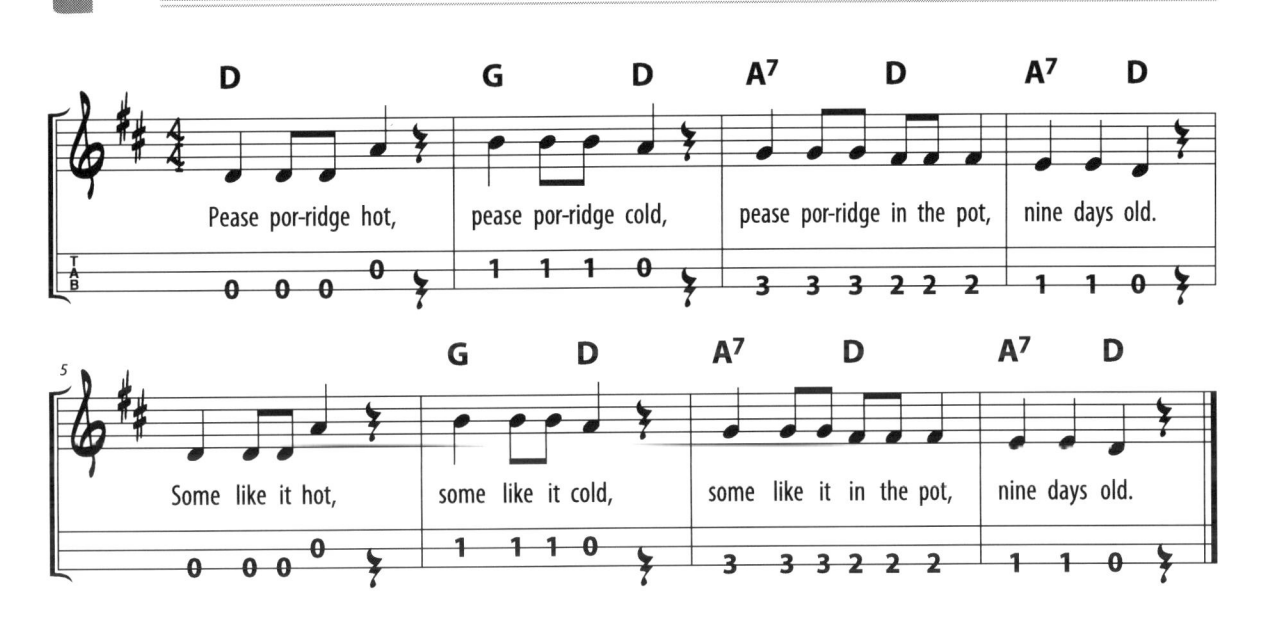

Pease por-ridge hot, pease por-ridge cold, pease por-ridge in the pot, nine days old.

Some like it hot, some like it cold, some like it in the pot, nine days old.

D

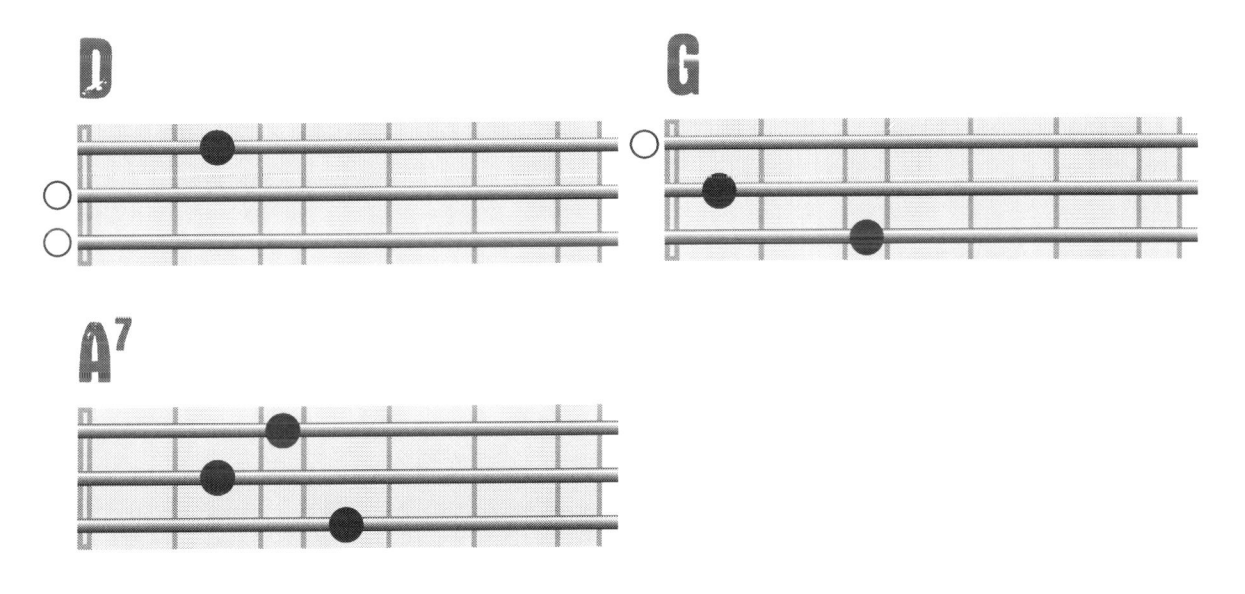

G

A⁷

147

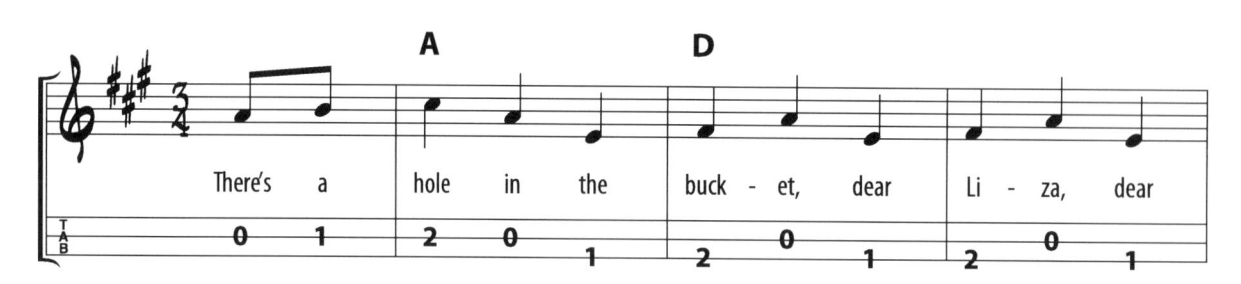

There's a hole in the bucket

There's a hole in the buck-et, dear Li-za, dear Li-za, there's a hole in the buck-et, dear Li-za, a hole.

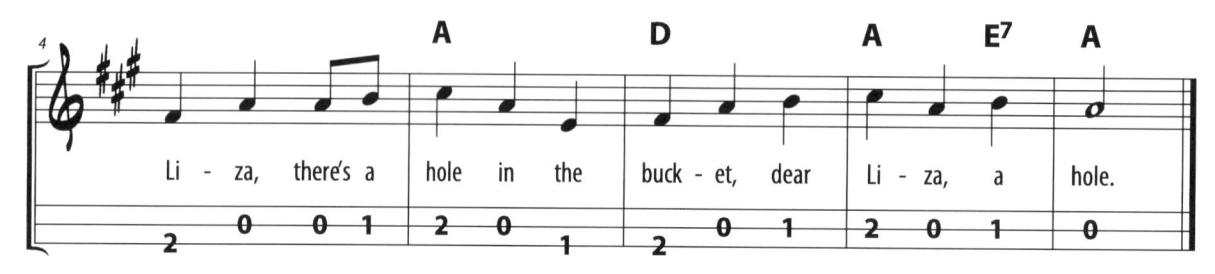

2. Then fix it, dear Henry, dear Henry, dear Henry, then fix it, dear Henry, dear Henry, fix it.

3. With what shall I fix it, dear Liza, dear Liza? with what shall I fix it, dear Liza, with what?

4. With straw, dear Henry, dear Henry, dear Henry, With straw, dear Henry, dear Henry, with straw.

5. The straw is too long, dear Liza, dear Liza, the straw is too long, dear Liza, too long.

6. Then cut it, dear Henry, dear Henry, dear Henry, then cut it, dear Henry, dear Henry, cut it.

7. With what shall I cut it, dear Liza, dear Liza? With what shall I cut it, dear Liza, with what?

8. With a knife, dear Henry, dear Henry, dear Henry, with a knife, dear Henry, dear Henry, with a knife.

9. The knife is too dull, dear Liza, dear Liza, the knife is too dull, dear Liza, too dull.

10. Then sharpen it, dear Henry, dear Henry, dear Henry, then sharpen it, dear Henry, dear Henry, sharpen it.

11. On what shall I sharpen it, dear Liza, dear Liza? On what shall I sharpen it, dear Liza, on what?

12. On a stone, dear Henry, dear Henry, dear Henry, on a stone, dear Henry, dear Henry, a stone.

13. The stone is too dry, dear Liza, dear Liza, the stone is too dry, dear Liza, too dry.

14. Then wet it, dear Henry, dear Henry, dear Henry,
then wet it, dear Henry, dear Henry, wet it.

15. With what shall I wet it, dear Liza, dear Liza?
With what shall I wet it, dear Liza, with what?

16. Try water, dear Henry, dear Henry, dear Henry,
try water, dear Henry, dear Henry, water.

17. In what shall I fetch it, dear Liza, dear Liza?
In what shall I fetch it, dear Liza, in what?

18. In the bucket, dear Henry, dear Henry, dear Henry,
In the bucket, dear Henry, dear Henry, a bucket.

19. But there's a hole in my bucket, dear Liza, dear Liza,
there's a hole in my bucket, dear Liza, a hole.

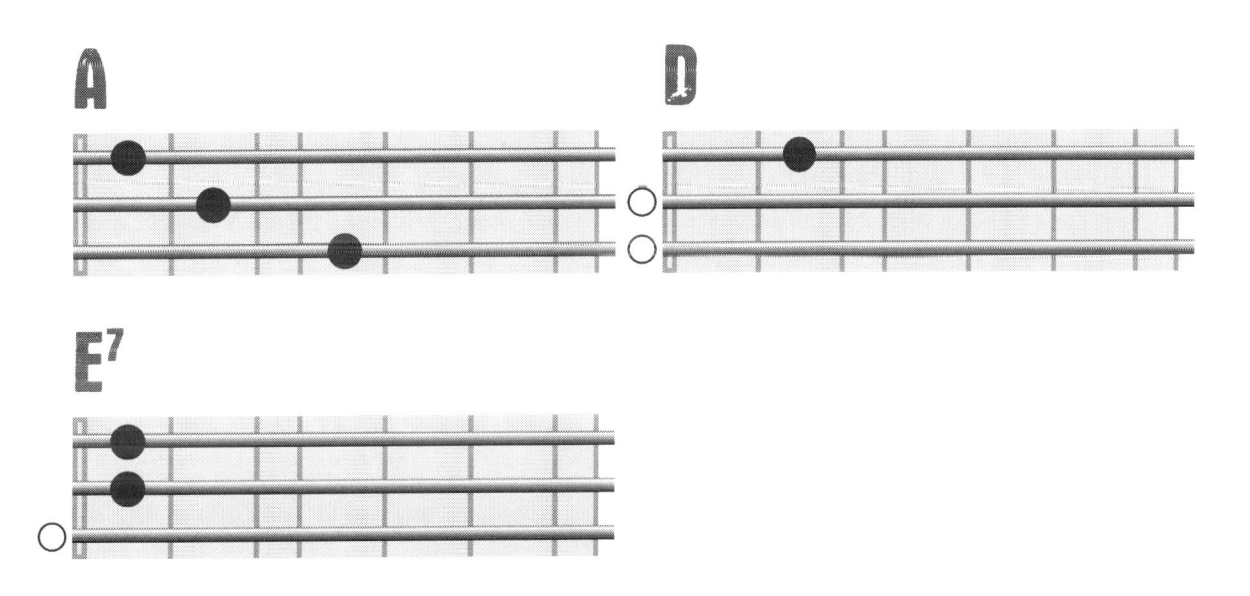

Jack and Jill

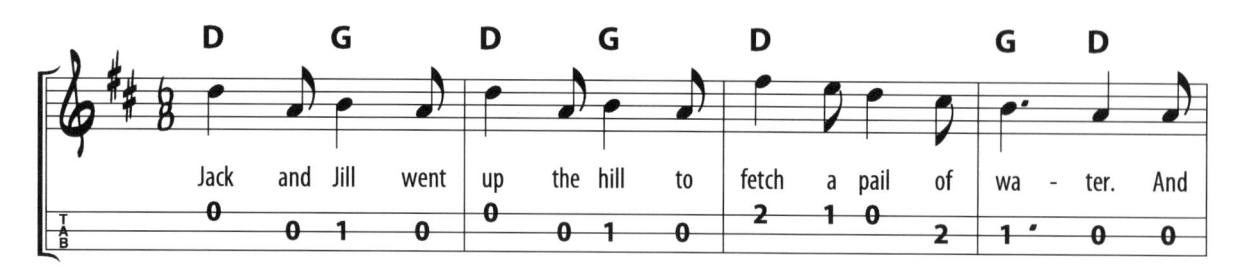

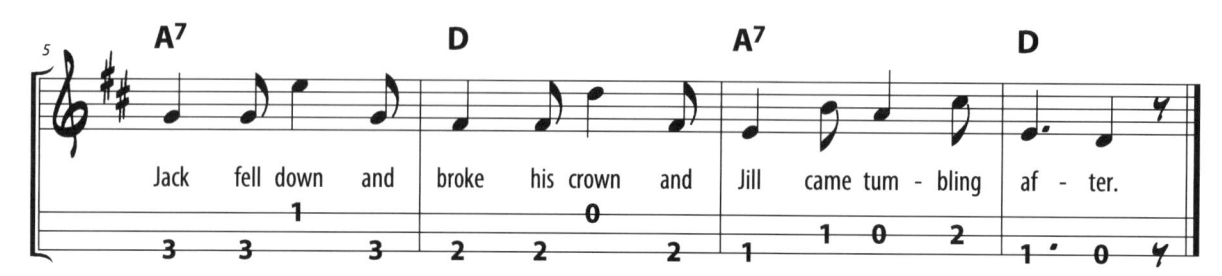

2. Up Jack got and home did trot,
   as fast as he could caper;
   and went to bed and bound his head
   with vinegar and brown paper.

3. When Jill came in how she did grin
   to see Jack's paper plaster;
   mother vexed did whip her next
   for causing Jack's disaster.

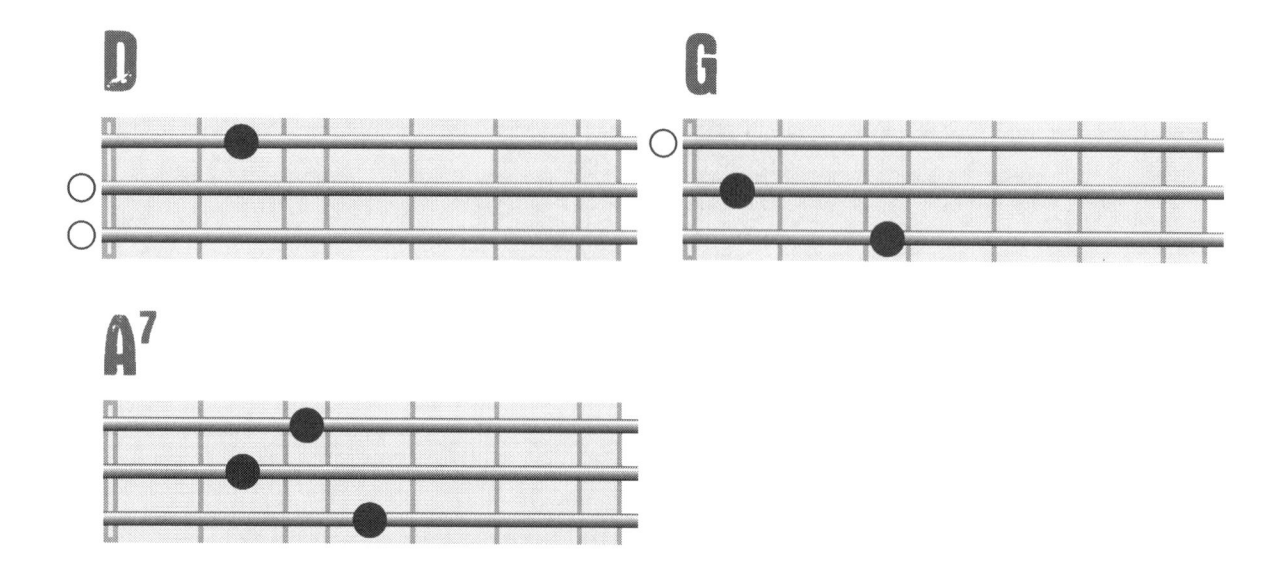

Amazing Grace

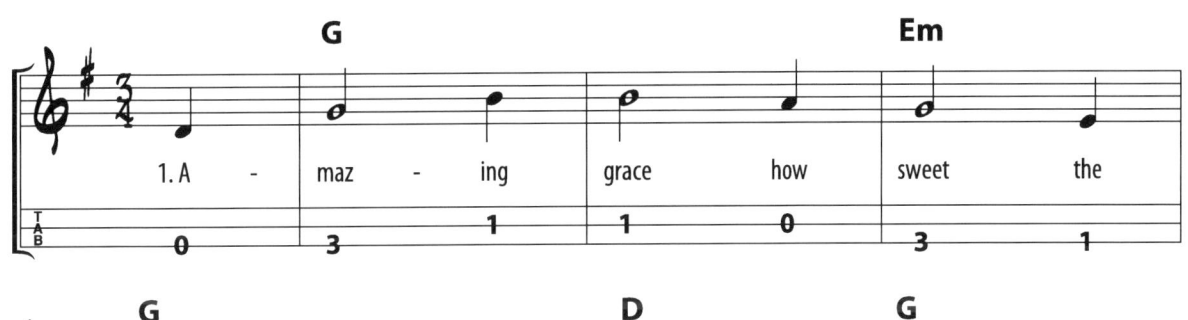

1. A-maz-ing grace how sweet the sounds, that saved a wretch like me. I once was lost, but now am found; was blind but now I see.

2. 'Twas grace that taught my heart to fear,
   and grace my fear relived.
   How precious did that grace appear,
   the hour I first believed.

3. When we've been there ten thousand years,
   bright shining as the sun.
   We've no less days to sing God's praise,
   than when we first begun.

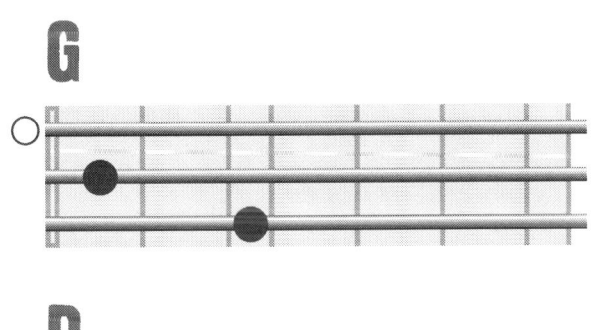

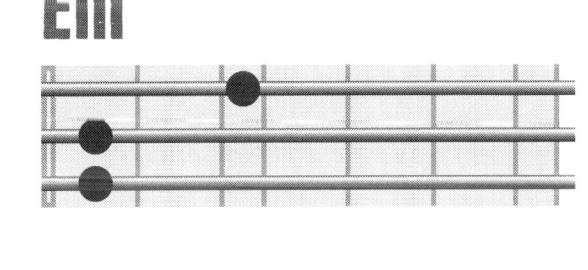

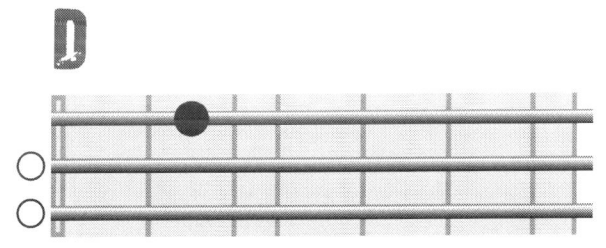

Rock-a-bye, baby

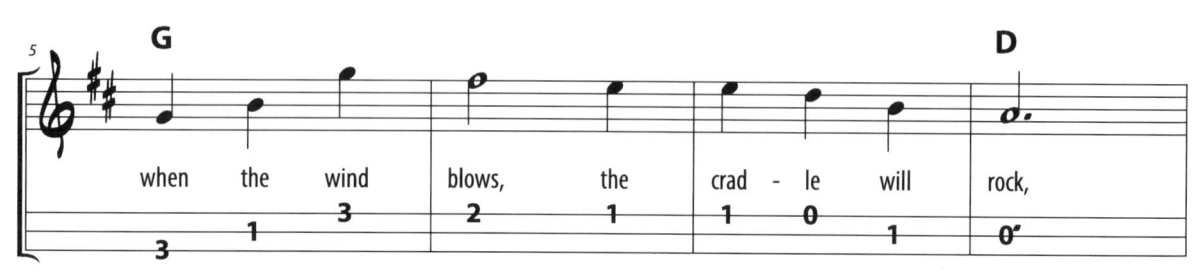

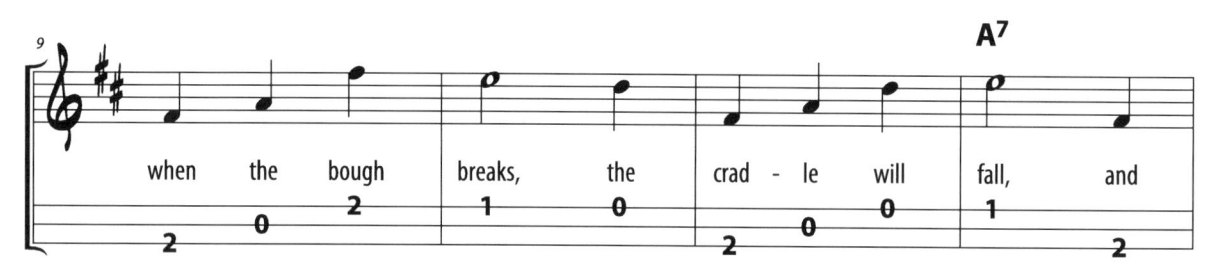

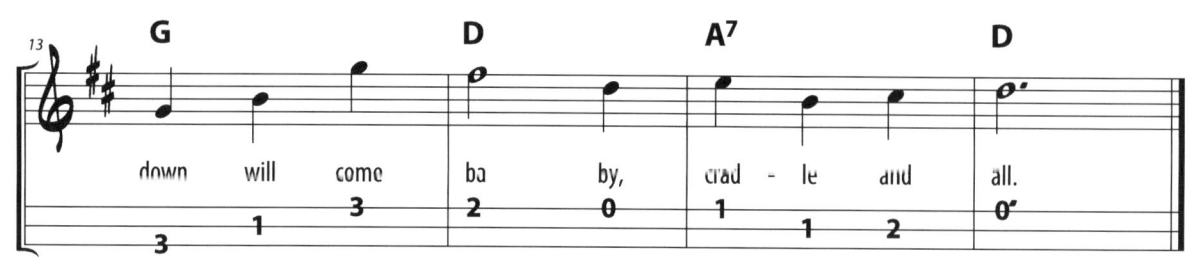

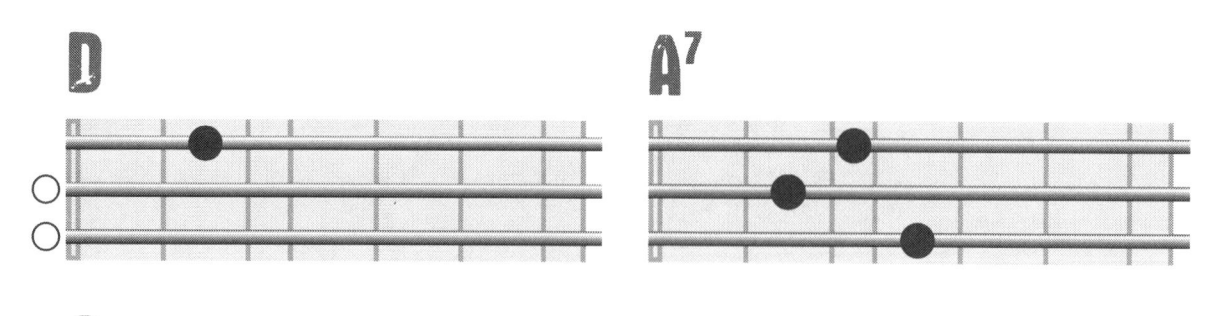

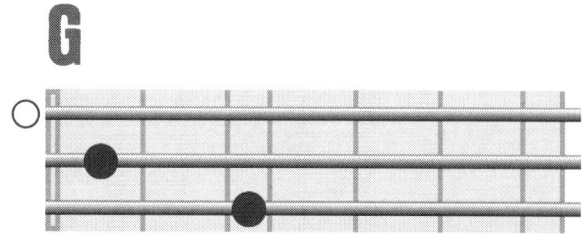

Animal fair

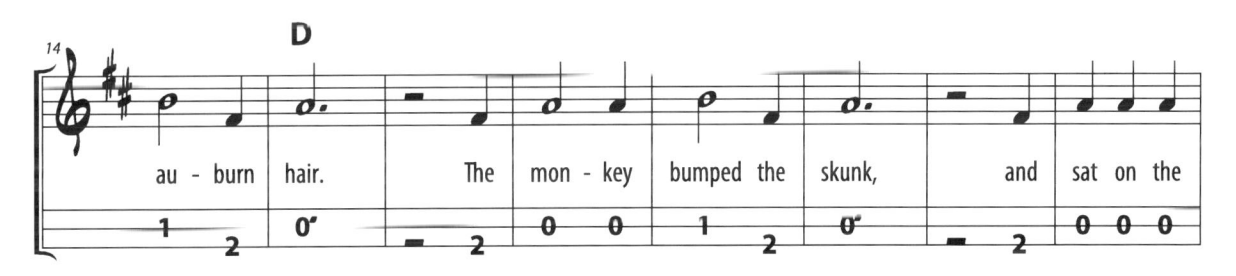

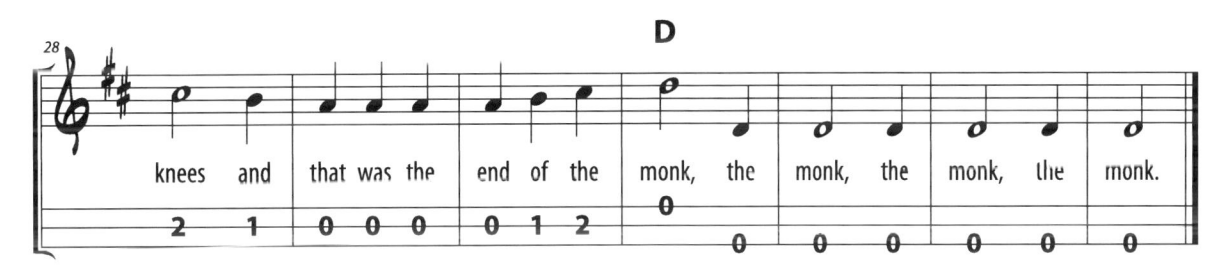

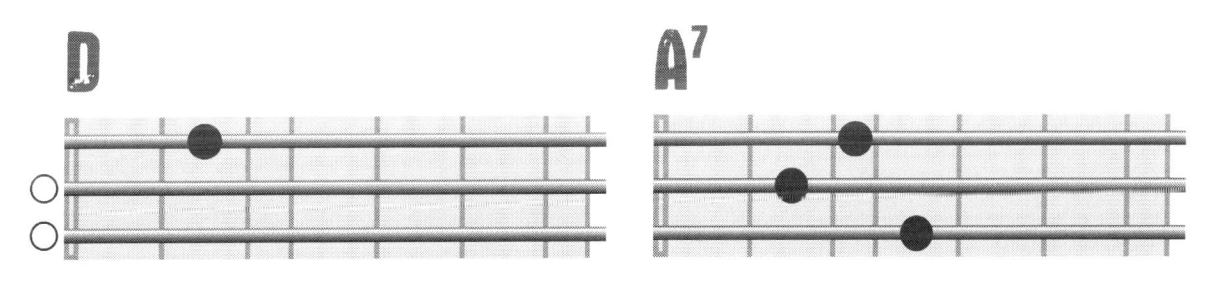

I went to the an-i-mal fair, the birds and beasts were there, the big ba-boon, by the light of the moon was comb-ing his au-burn hair. The mon-key bumped the skunk, and sat on the el-e-phant's trunk. The el-e-phant sneezed and fell to his knees and that was the end of the monk, the monk, the monk, the monk.

Hickory dickory dock

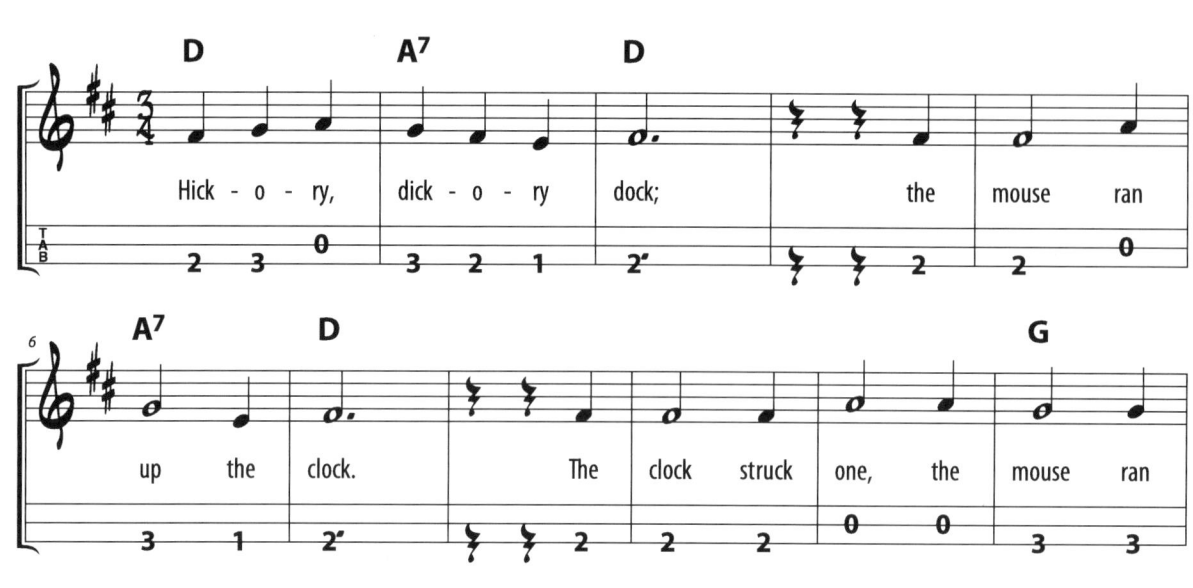

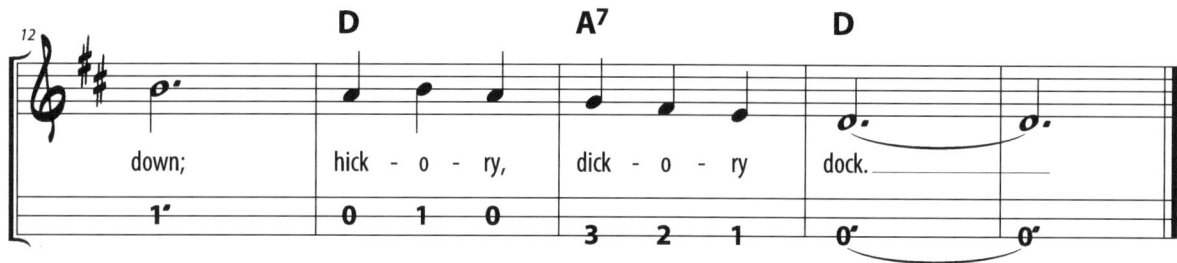

2. Hickory dickory dock,
   the mouse ran up the clock,
   the clock struck two
   and down he flew,
   hickory dickory dock.

3. Hickory dickory dock,
   the mouse ran up the clock,
   the clock struck three
   and he did flee,
   hickory dickory dock.

4. Hickory dickory dock,
   the mouse ran up the clock,
   the clock struck four,
   he hit the floor,
   hickory dickory dock.

5. Hickory dickory dock,
   the mouse ran up the clock,
   the clock struck five,
   the mouse took a dive,
   hickory dickory dock.

6. Hickory dickory dock,
   the mouse ran up the clock,
   the clock struck six,
   the mouse, he split,
   hickory dickory dock.

7. Hickory dickory dock,
   the mouse ran up the clock,
   the clock struck seven,
   8, 9, 10, 11,
   hickory dickory dock.

8. Hickory dickory dock,
   the mouse ran up the clock,
   as twelve bells rang,
   the mousie sprang,
   hickory dickory dock.

9. Hickory dickory dock,
   "Why scamper?" asked the clock,
   "You scare me so
   I have to go!"
   hickory dickory dock.

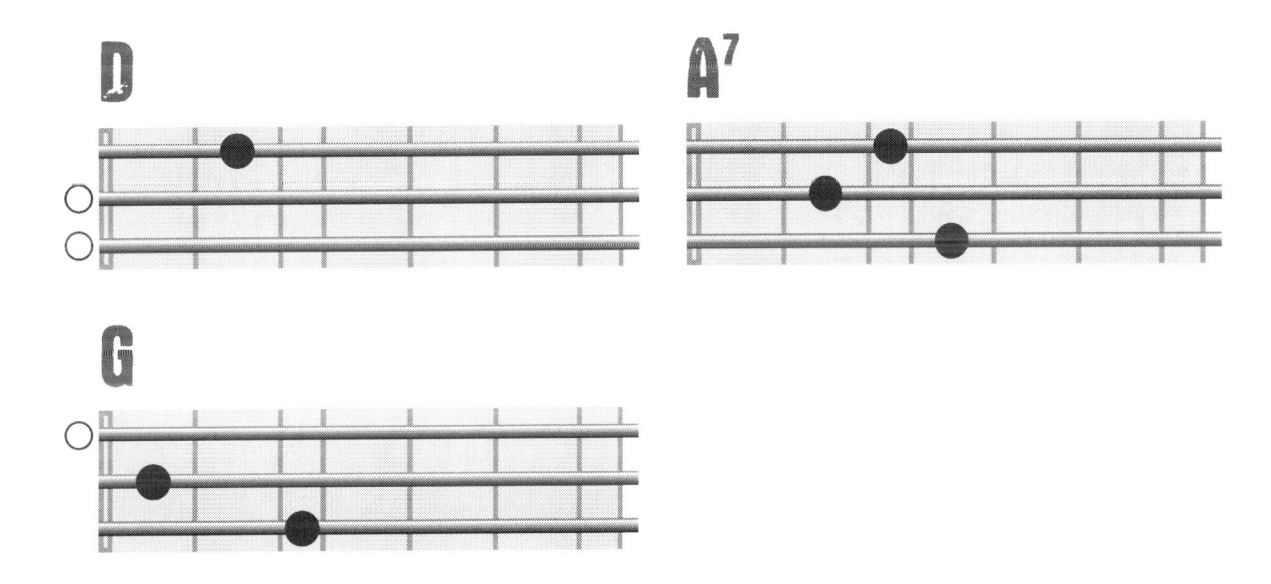

Jolly good fellow

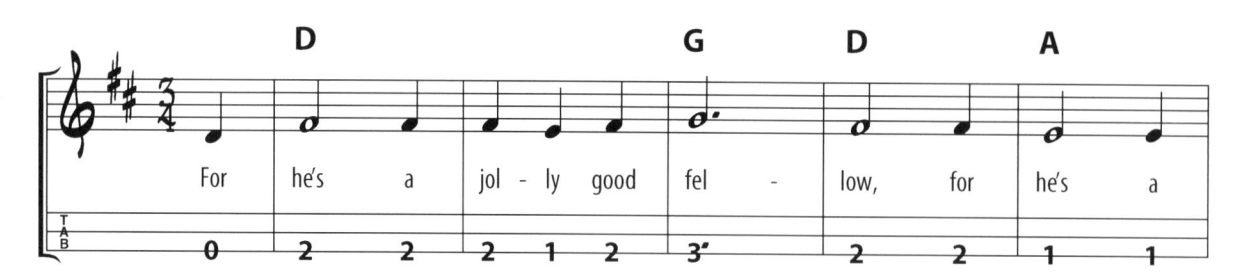

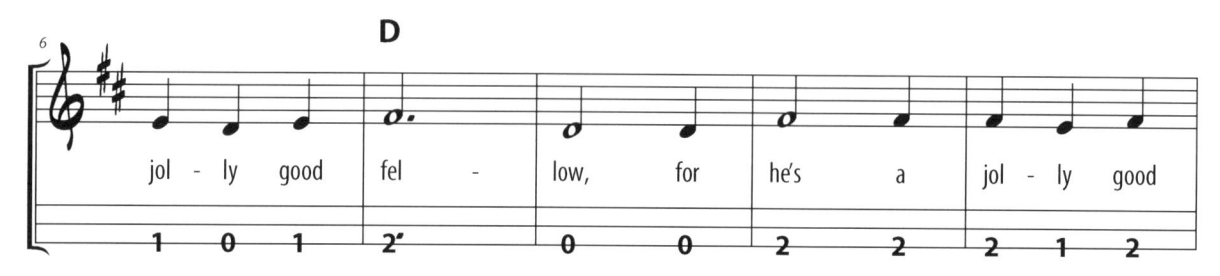

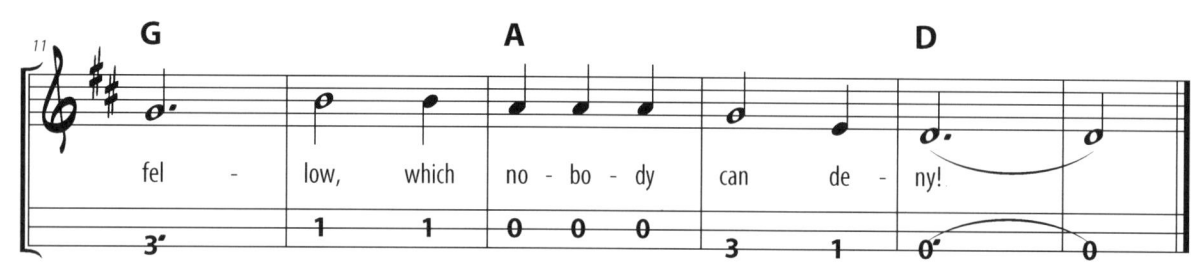

For he's a jol-ly good fel - low, for he's a jol-ly good fel - low, for he's a jol-ly good fel - low, which no-bo-dy can de - ny!

2. We won't go home until morning, (3x)
   'till daylight doth appear
   'Till daylight doth appear,

   'till daylight doth appear.
   We won't go home until morning, (3x)
   'till daylight doth appear.

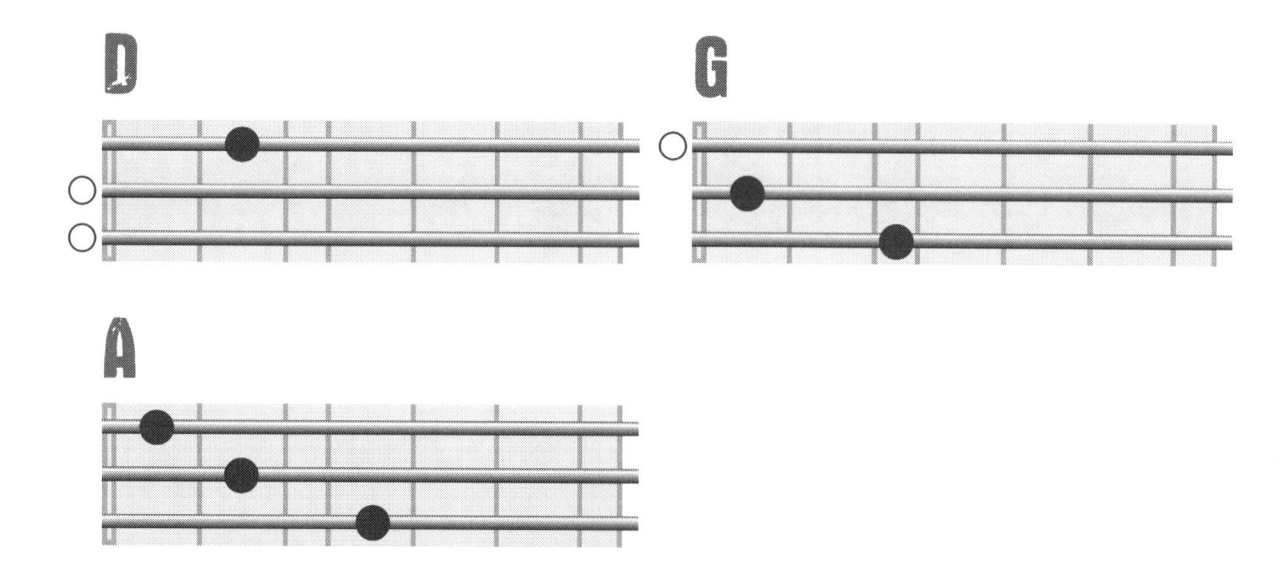

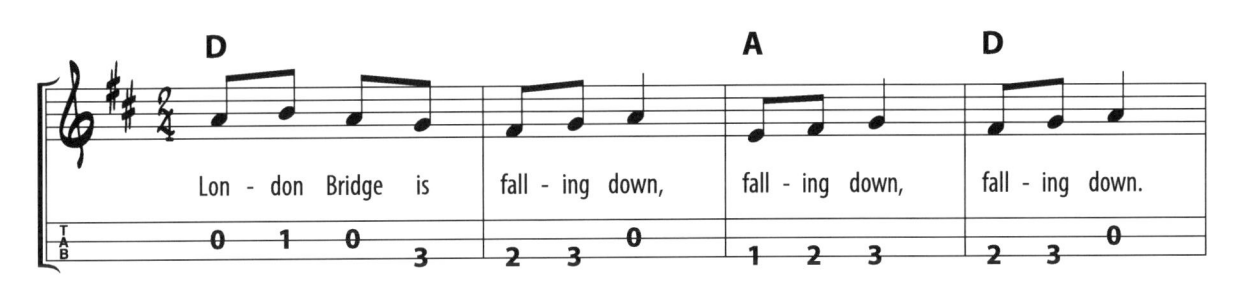

London Bridge is falling down

Lon - don Bridge is fall - ing down, fall - ing down, fall - ing down.

Lon - don Bridge is fall - ing down, my fair la - dy.

2. Take a key and lock her up,
lock her up, lock her up.
Take a key and lock her up,
my fair lady.

3. How will we build it up,
build it up, build it up?
How will we build it up,
my fair lady.

4. Build it up with gold and silver,
gold and silver, gold and silver.
Build it up with gold and silver,
my fair lady.

5. Gold and silver I have none,
I have none, I have none.
Gold and silver I have none,
my fair lady.

6. Build it up with needles and pins,
needles and pins, needles and pins.
Build it up with needles and pins,
my fair lady.

7. Pins and needles bend and break,
bend and break, bend and break.
Pins and needles bend and break,
my fair lady.

8. Build it up with wood and clay,
wood and clay, wood and clay.
Build it up with wood and clay,
my fair lady.

9. Wood and clay will wash away,
wash away, wash away.
Wood and clay will wash away,
my fair lady.

10. Build it up with stone so strong,
stone so strong, stone so strong.
Build it up with stone so strong,
my fair lady.

11. Stone so strong will last so long,
last so long, last so long.
Stone so strong will last so long,
my fair lady.

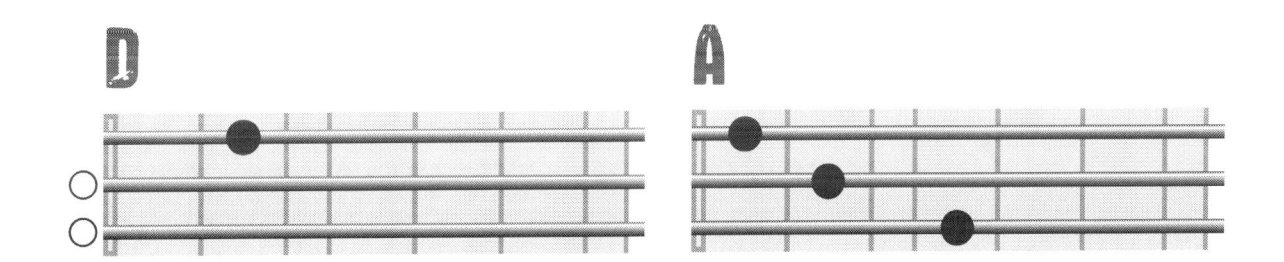

Yankee Doodle

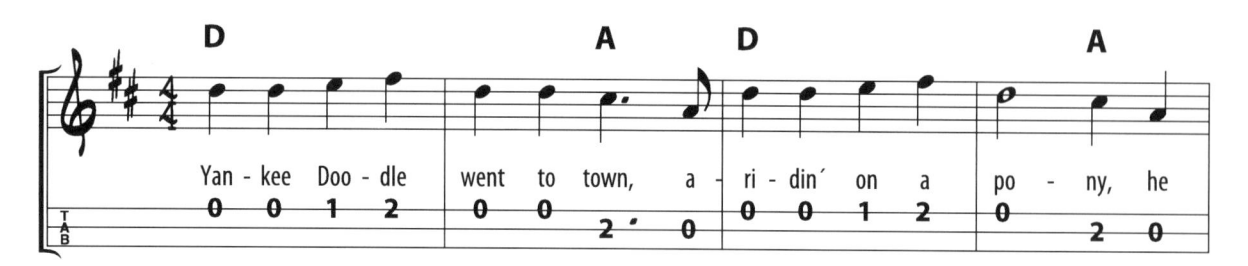

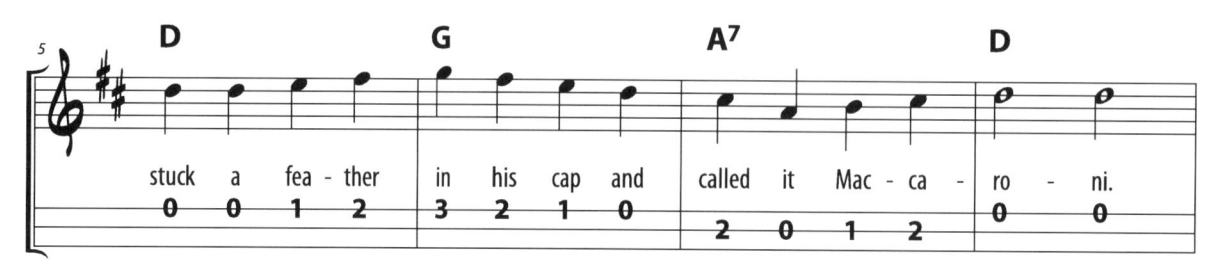

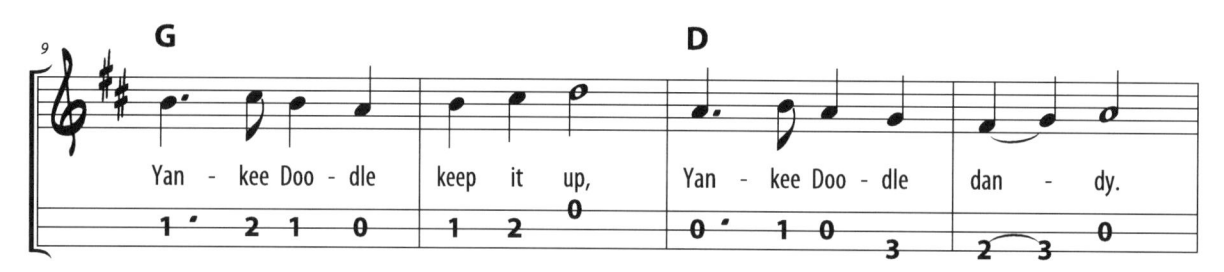

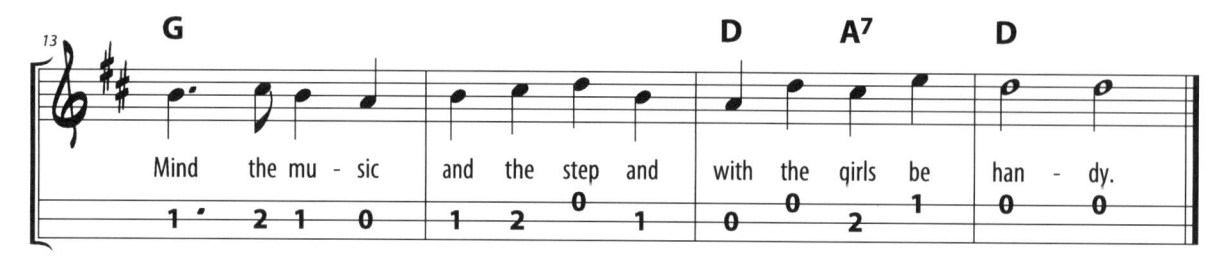

Yan-kee Doo-dle went to town, a-ri-din' on a po-ny, he stuck a fea-ther in his cap and called it Mac-ca-ro-ni. Yan-kee Doo-dle keep it up, Yan-kee Doo-dle dan-dy. Mind the mu-sic and the step and with the girls be han-dy.

2. Father and I went down to camp,
   along with Captain Gooding.
   And there we saw the men and boys,
   as thick as hasty pudding.
   Yankee Doodle, keep it up,
   Yankee Doodle dandy.
   Mind the music and the step,
   and with the girls be handy.

3. There was Captain Washington,
   upon a slapping stallion.
   A-giving orders to his men,
   I guess there was a million.
   Yankee Doodle, keep it up,
   Yankee Doodle dandy.
   Mind the music and the step,
   and with the girls be handy.

4. Yankee Doodle is a tune,
   that comes in mighty handy,
   The enemies all run away,
   at Yankee Doodle dandy!
   Yankee Doodle, keep it up,
   Yankee Doodle dandy.
   Mind the music and the step,
   and with the girls be handy.

D

A

G

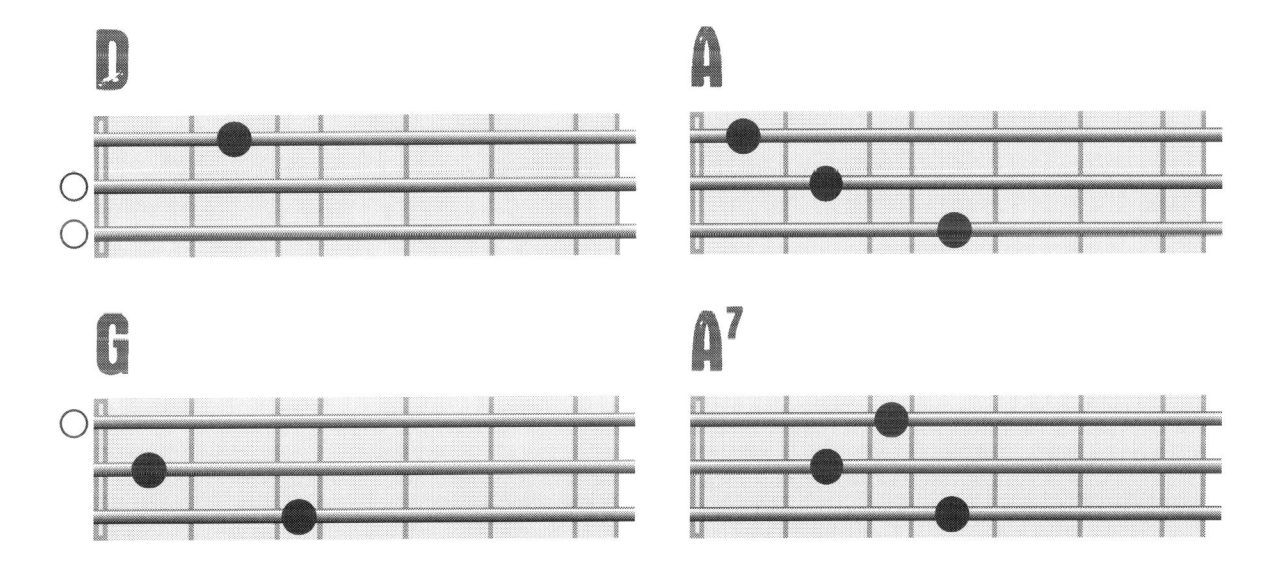

A7

This old man

2. This old man, he played two,
he played knick-knack on my shoe;
with a knick-knack paddywhack,
give the dog a bone,
this old man came rolling home.

3. This old man, he played three,
he played knick-knack on my knee;
with a knick-knack paddywhack,
give the dog a bone,
this old man came rolling home.

4. This old man, he played four,
he played knick-knack on my door;
with a knick-knack paddywhack,
give the dog a bone,
this old man came rolling home.

5. This old man, he played five,
he played knick-knack on my hive;
with a knick-knack paddywhack,
give the dog a bone,
this old man came rolling home.

6. This old man, he played six,
   he played knick-knack on my sticks;
   with a knick-knack paddywhack,
   give the dog a bone,
   this old man came rolling home.

7. This old man, he played seven,
   he played knick-knack up in heaven;
   with a knick-knack paddywhack,
   give the dog a bone,
   this old man came rolling home.

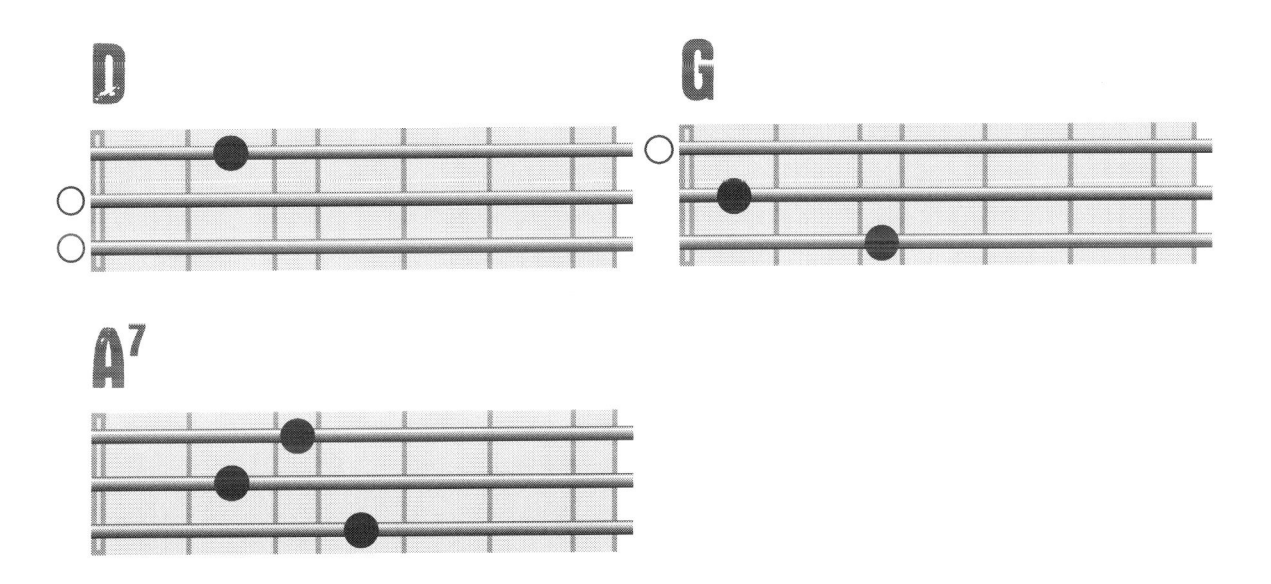

8. This old man, he played eight,
   he played knick-knack on my gate;
   with a knick-knack paddywhack,
   give the dog a bone,
   this old man came rolling home.

9. This old man, he played nine,
   he played knick-knack on my spine;
   with a knick-knack paddywhack,
   give the dog a bone,
   this old man came rolling home.

10. This old man, he played ten,
    he played knick-knack once again;
    with a knick-knack paddywhack,
    give the dog a bone,
    this old man came rolling home.

D

G

A⁷

Old Black Joe

Gone are the days when my heart was young and gay, gone are my friends from the cotton fields a-way. Gone from the earth to a better land I know, I hear their gent-le voi-ces call-ing, "Old Black Joe." I'm com-ing, I'm com-ing, for my head is bend-ing low. I hear those gent-le voi-ces call-ing "Old Black Joe."

2. Why do I weep when my heart should feel no pain?
   Why do I sigh that my friends come not again?
   Grieving for forms now departed long ago,
   I hear their gentle voices calling, "Old Black Joe."

3. Where are the hearts once so happy and so free?
   The children so dear that I held upon my knee?
   Gone to the shore where my soul has longed to go,
   I hear their gentle voices calling, "Old Black Joe."

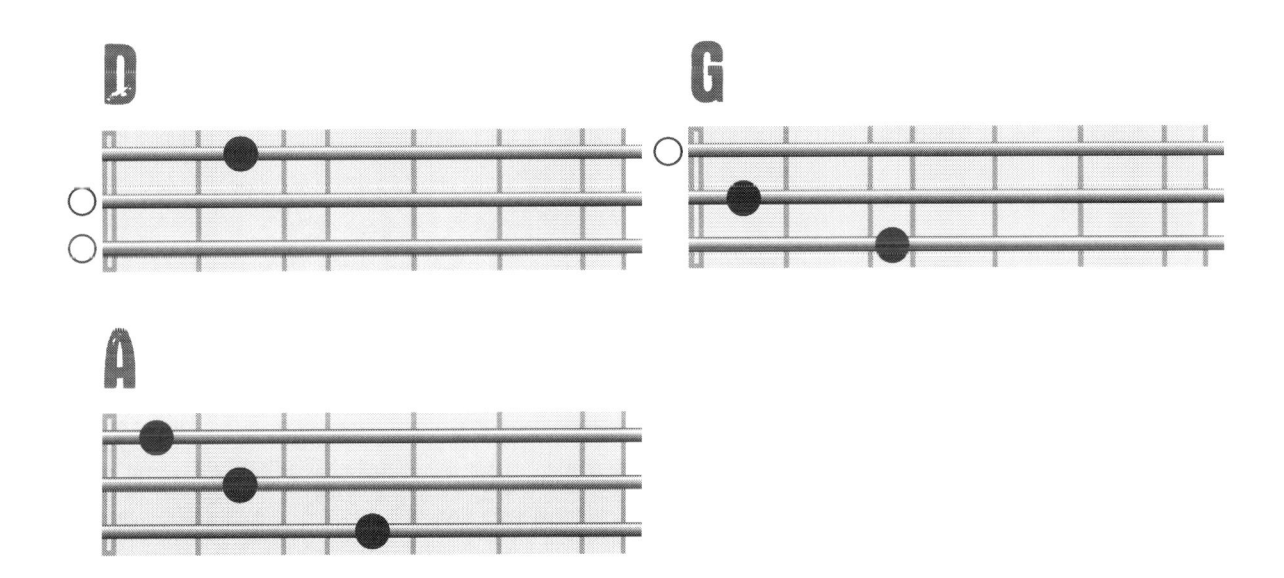

My home's across the smoky mountains

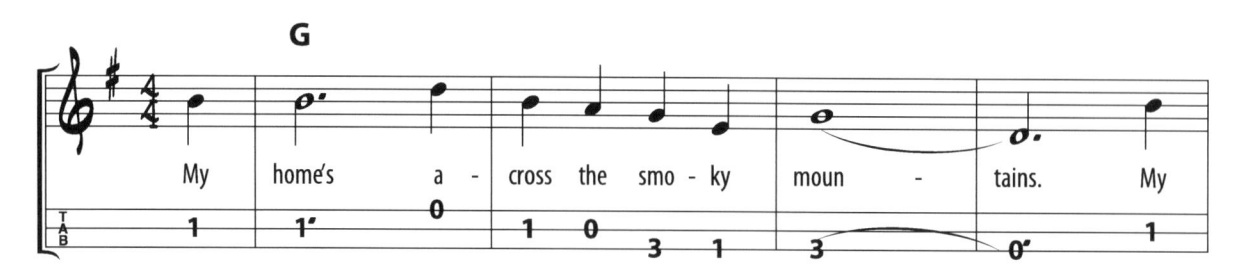

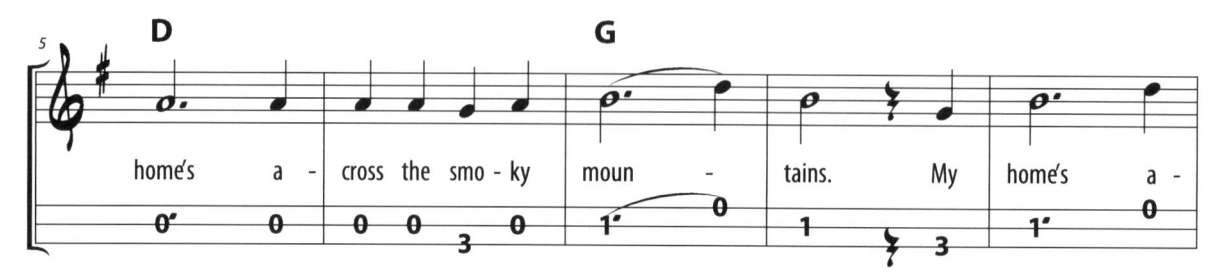

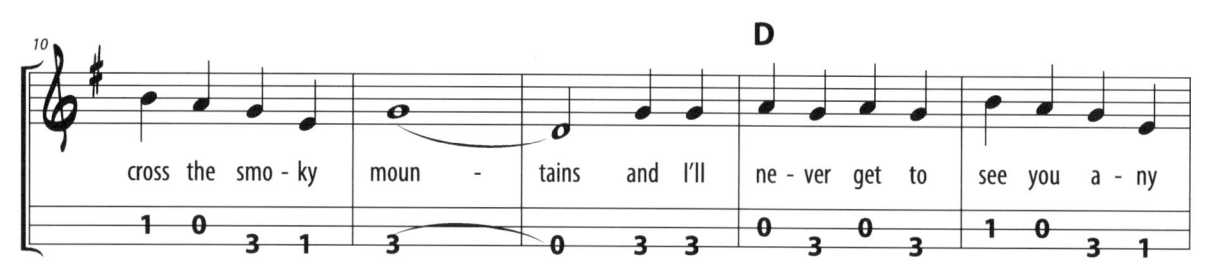

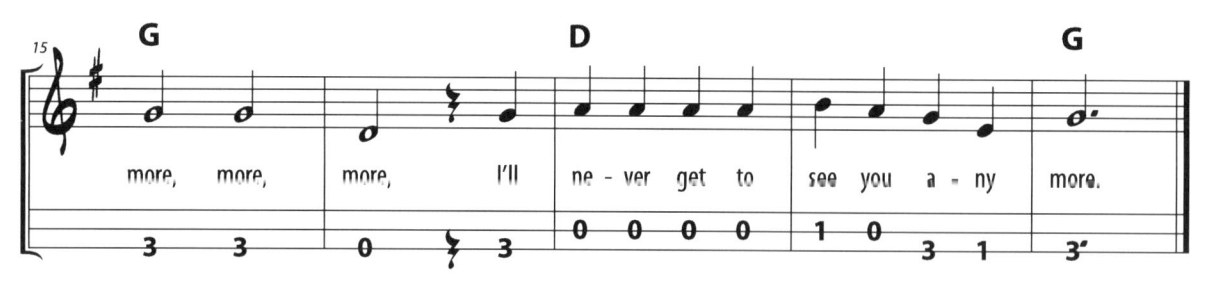

2. Goodbye honey, sugar darling.
   Goodbye honey, sugar darling.
   Goodbye honey, sugar darling,
   and I'll never get to see you any more, more, more,
   I'll never get to see you sny more.

3. Rock my baby, feed her candy.
   Rock my baby, feed her candy.
   Rock my baby, feed her candy,
   and I'll never get to see you any more, more, more,
   I'll never get to see you any more.

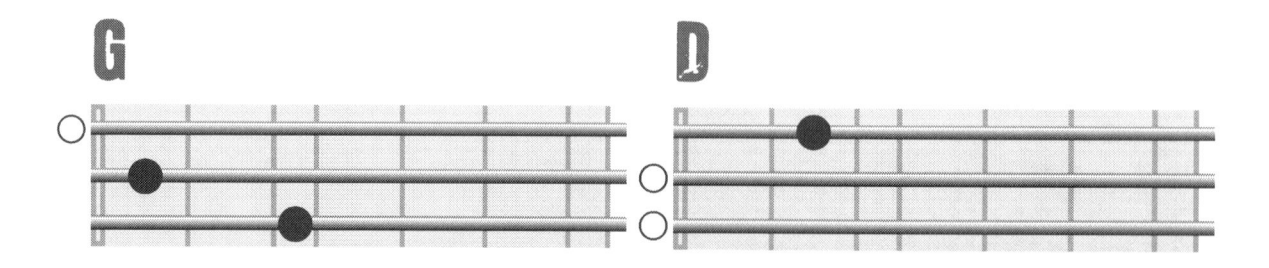

Bury me beneath the willow

Bury me beneath the willow, under the weeping willow tree.
When he finds where I am sleeping, maybe then he'll think of me.

2. My heart is sad I am lonely,
   for the only one I love.
   When shall I see her oh no never,
   'til we meet in heaven above.

3. She told me that she dearly loved me.
   How could I believe it untrue,
   until the angels softly whispered,
   she will prove untrue to you.

4. Tomorrow was to be our wedding,
   God, oh God, where can she be.
   She's out a courting with another,
   and no longer cares for me

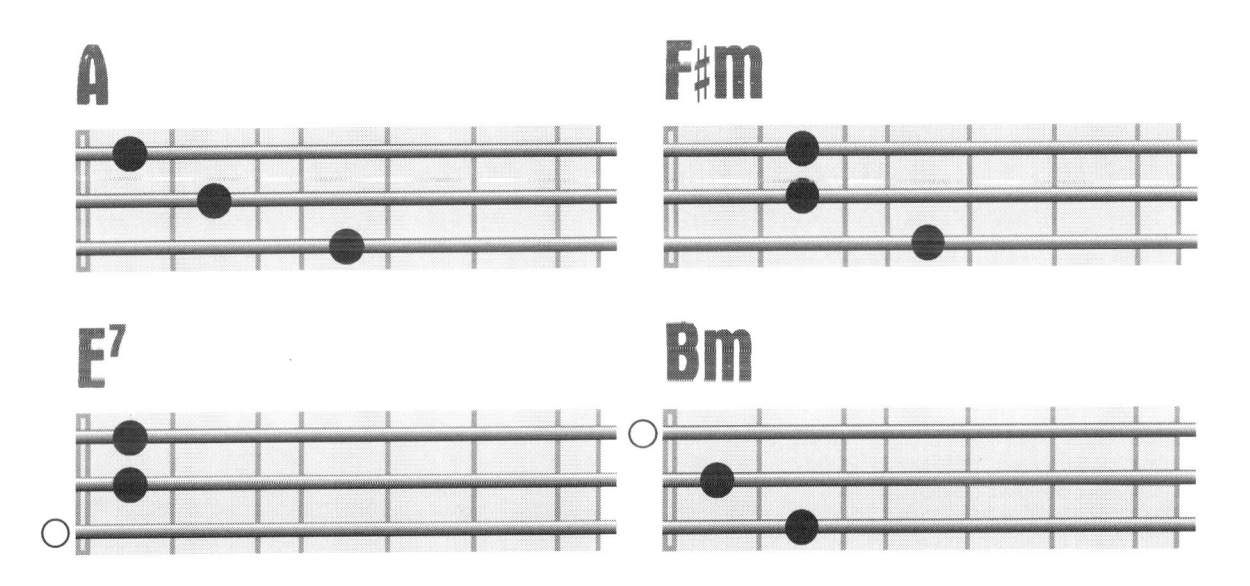

Aura Lee

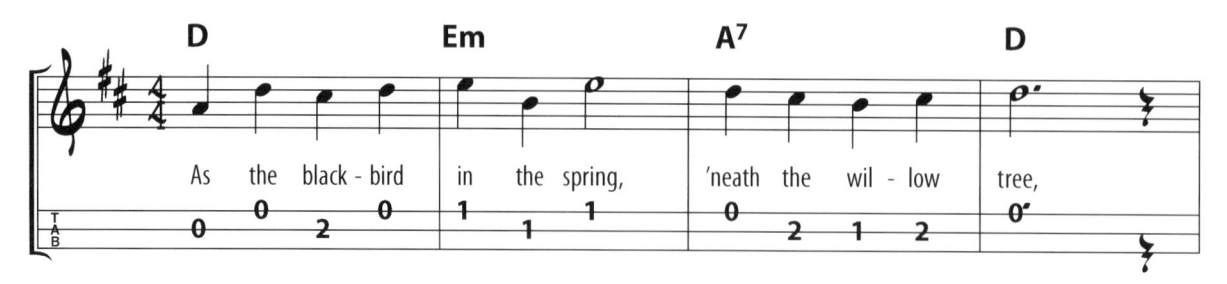

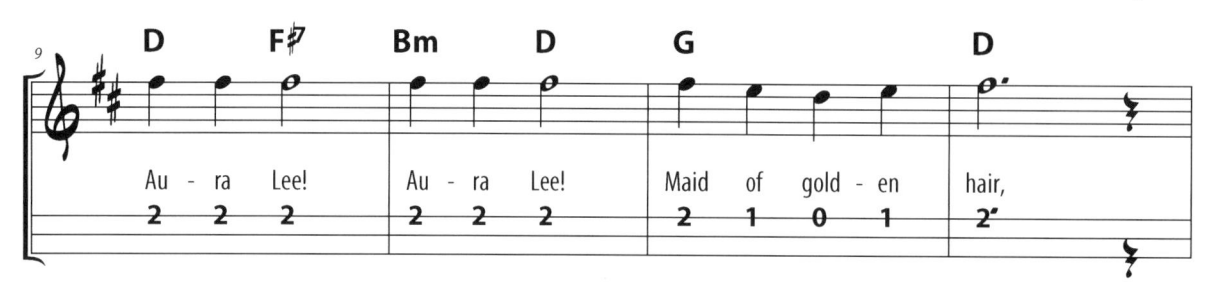

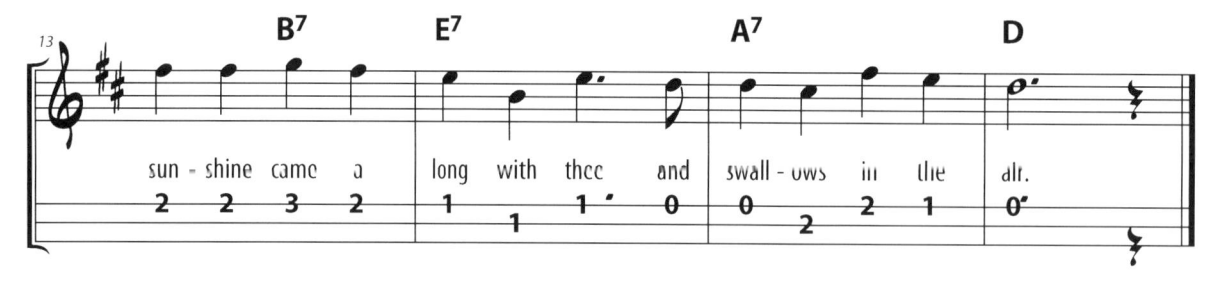

2. In thy blush the rose was born,
   music, when you spake,
   through thine azure eye the morn,
   sparkling seemed to break.
   Aura Lee, Aura Lee,
   birds of crimson wing,
   never song have sung to me,
   as in that sweet spring.
   Aura Lee! Aura Lee! ...

3. Aura Lee, the bird may flee,
   the willow's golden hair,
   swing through winter fitfully,
   on the stormy air.
   Yet if thy blue eyes I see,
   gloom will soon depart;
   for to me, sweet Aura Lee
   is sunshine through the heart.
   Aura Lee! Aura Lee! ...

4. When the mistletoe was green,
   midst the winter's snows,
   sunshine in thy face was seen,
   kissing lips of rose.
   Aura Lee, Aura Lee,
   Take my golden ring;
   Love and light return with thee,
   and swallows with the spring.
   Aura Lee! Aura Lee! ...

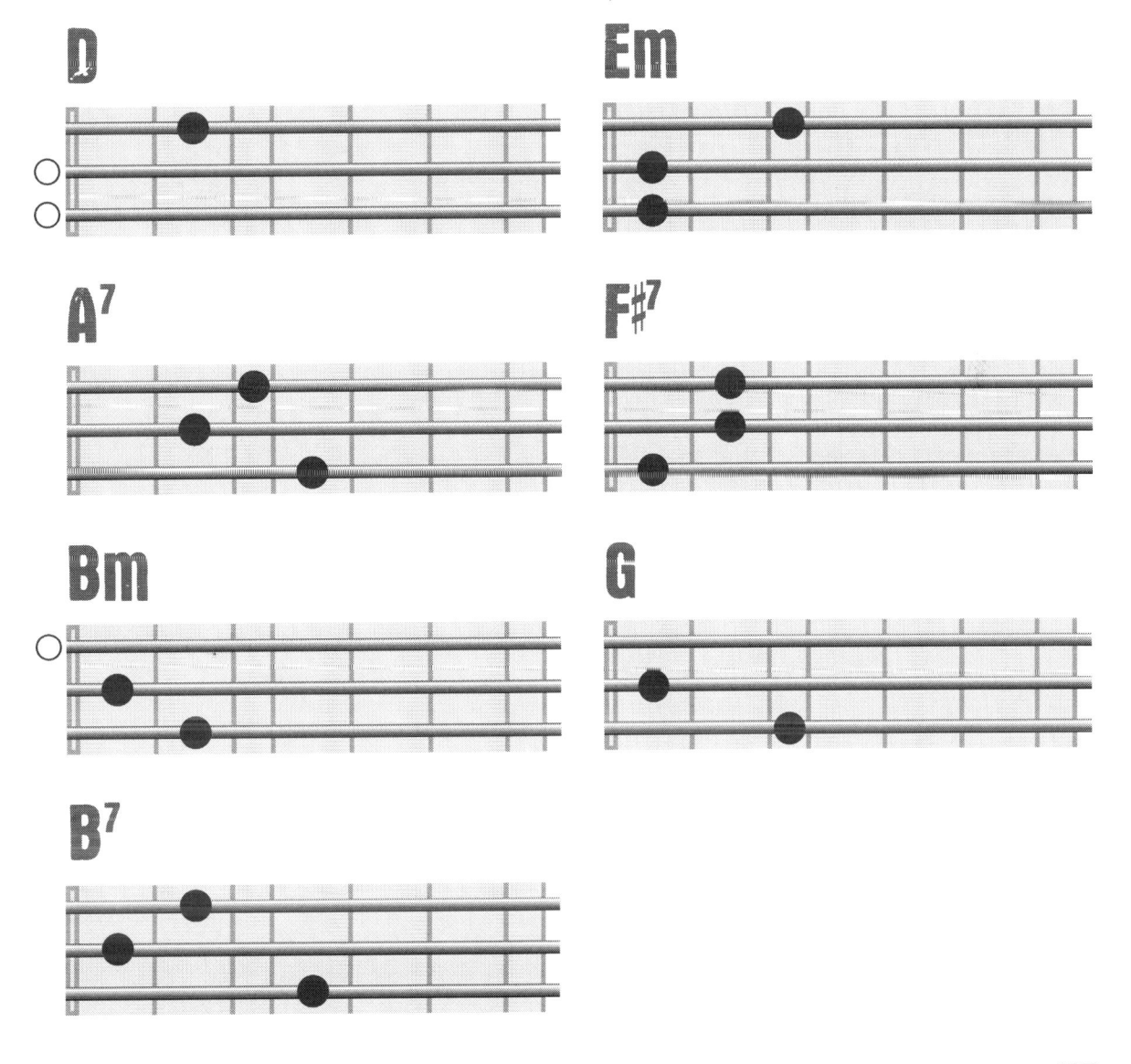

Oh! Susanna

I came from Alabama with my banjo on my knee, I'm goin' to Lou'siana, my Susanna for to see. Oh! Susanna, oh don't you cry for me, for I come from Alabama with my banjo on my knee.

2. I had a dream the other night
   when ev'rything was still;
   I thought I saw Susanna
   a-comin' down the hill;
   the buckwheat cake was in her mouth,
   the tear was in her eye;
   says I, I'm comin' from the south,
   Susanna, don't you cry.
   Oh! Susanna,
   oh, don't you cry for me ...

3. I soon will be in New Orleans,
   and then I'll look around,
   and when I find Susanna
   I'll fall upon the ground.
   And if I do not find her,
   then I will surely die,
   and when I'm dead and buried,
   Susanna, don't you cry.
   Oh! Susanna,
   oh, don't you cry for me ...

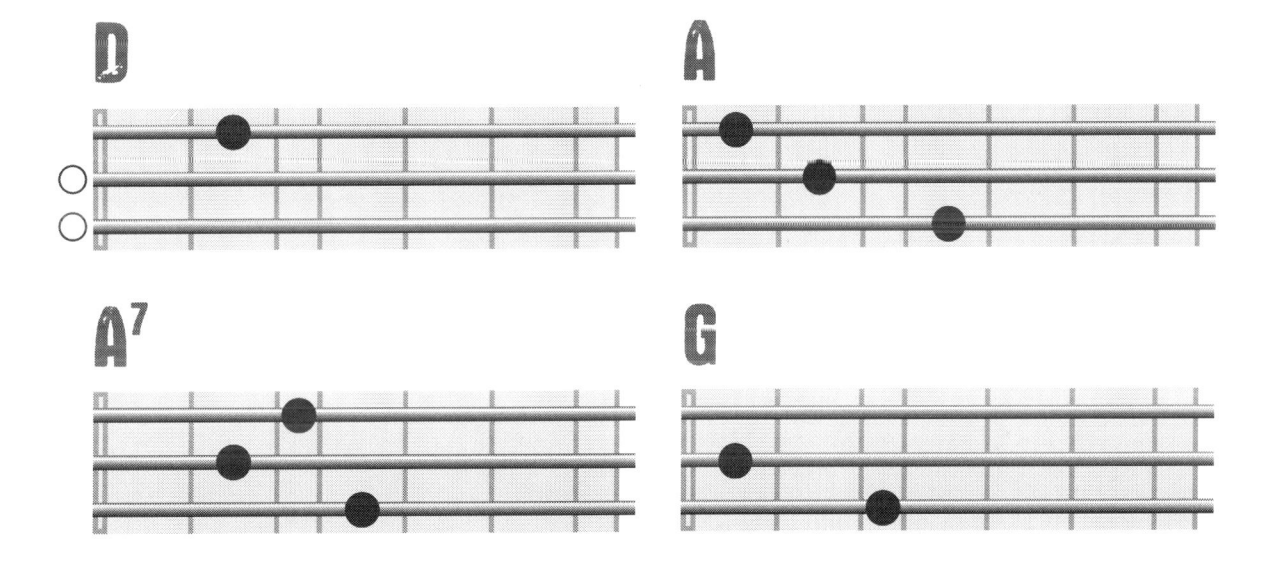

D

A

A⁷

G

Buffalo gals

1. As I went walking down the street, down the street, down the street, a pretty girl I chanced to meet under the silvery moon.

Chorus
Buffalo gals, will you come out tonight, come out tonight, come out tonight,
Buffalo gals, will you come out tonight, and dance by the light of the moon.

2. I asked her would she have some talk,
   have some talk, have some talk.
   Her feet covered the whole sidewalk
   as she stood close by me.

3. I asked her would she have a dance,
   have a dance, have a dance.
   I thought I might get a chance
   to shake a foot with her.

4. I'd like to make that gal my wife,
   gal my wife, gal my wife.
   I'd be happy all my life.
   If I had her by me.

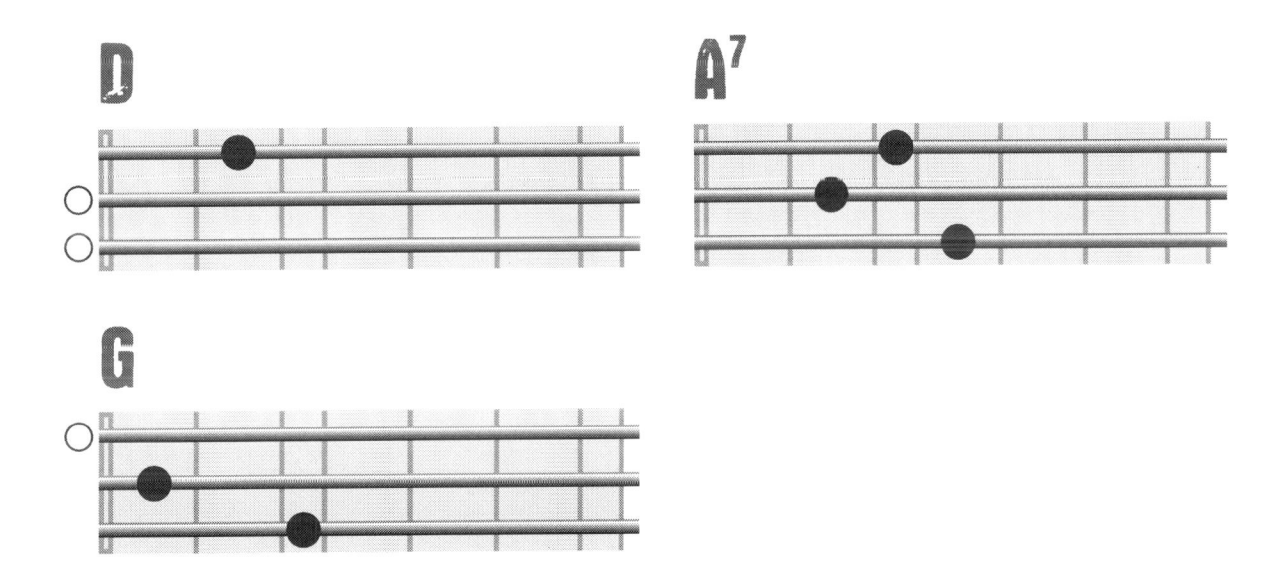

House of the rising sun

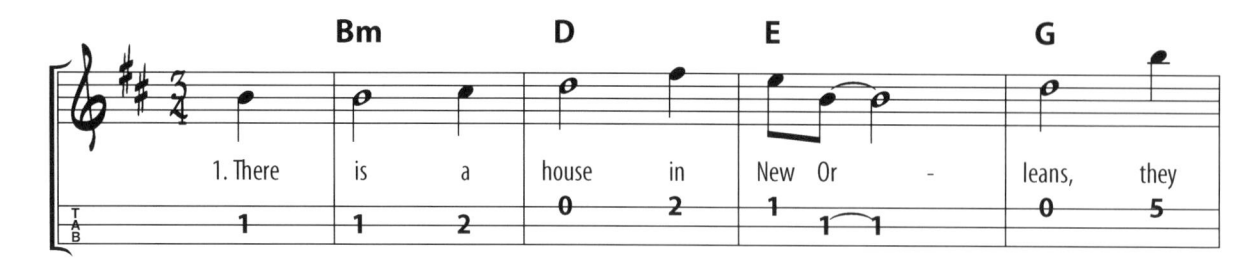

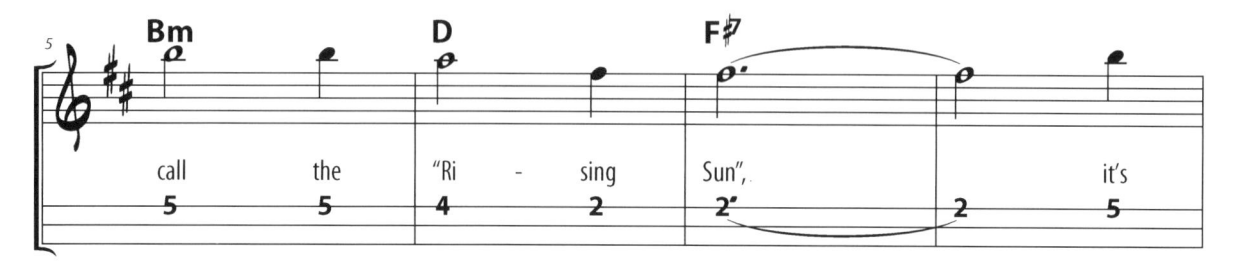

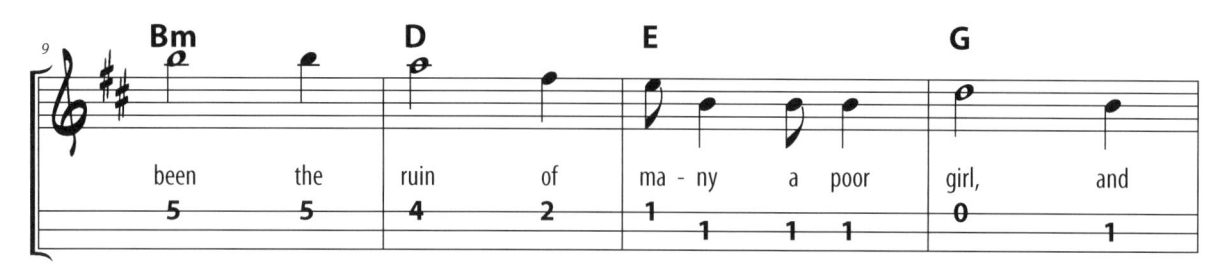

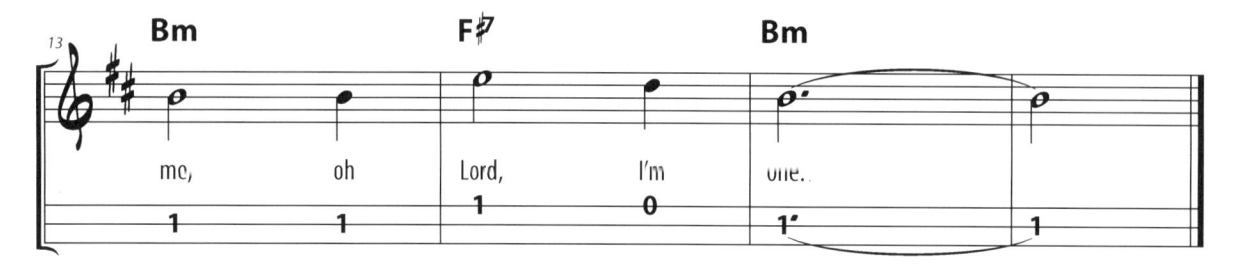

1. There is a house in New Orleans, they call the "Rising Sun", it's been the ruin of many a poor girl, and me, oh Lord, I'm one.

2. If I had listened what Mamma said,
   I'd been at home today.
   Being so young and foolish, poor boy,
   let a rambler lead me astray.

3. Go tell my baby sister,
   never do like I have done,
   to shun that house in New Orleans,
   they call the Rising Sun.

4. My mother she's a tailor;
   She sold those new blue jeans.
   My sweetheart, he's a drunkard, Lord,
   drinks down in New Orleans.

5. The only thing a drunkard needs,
   is a suitcase and a trunk.
   The only time he's satisfied,
   is when he's on a drunk.

6. Fills his glasses to the brim,
   passes them around.
   Only pleasure he gets out of life,
   is hoboin' from town to town.

7. One foot is on the platform,
   and the other one on the train.
   I'm going back to New Orleans,
   to wear that ball and chain.

8. Going back to New Orleans,
   my race is almost run.
   Going back to spend the rest of my life,
   beneath that Rising Sun.

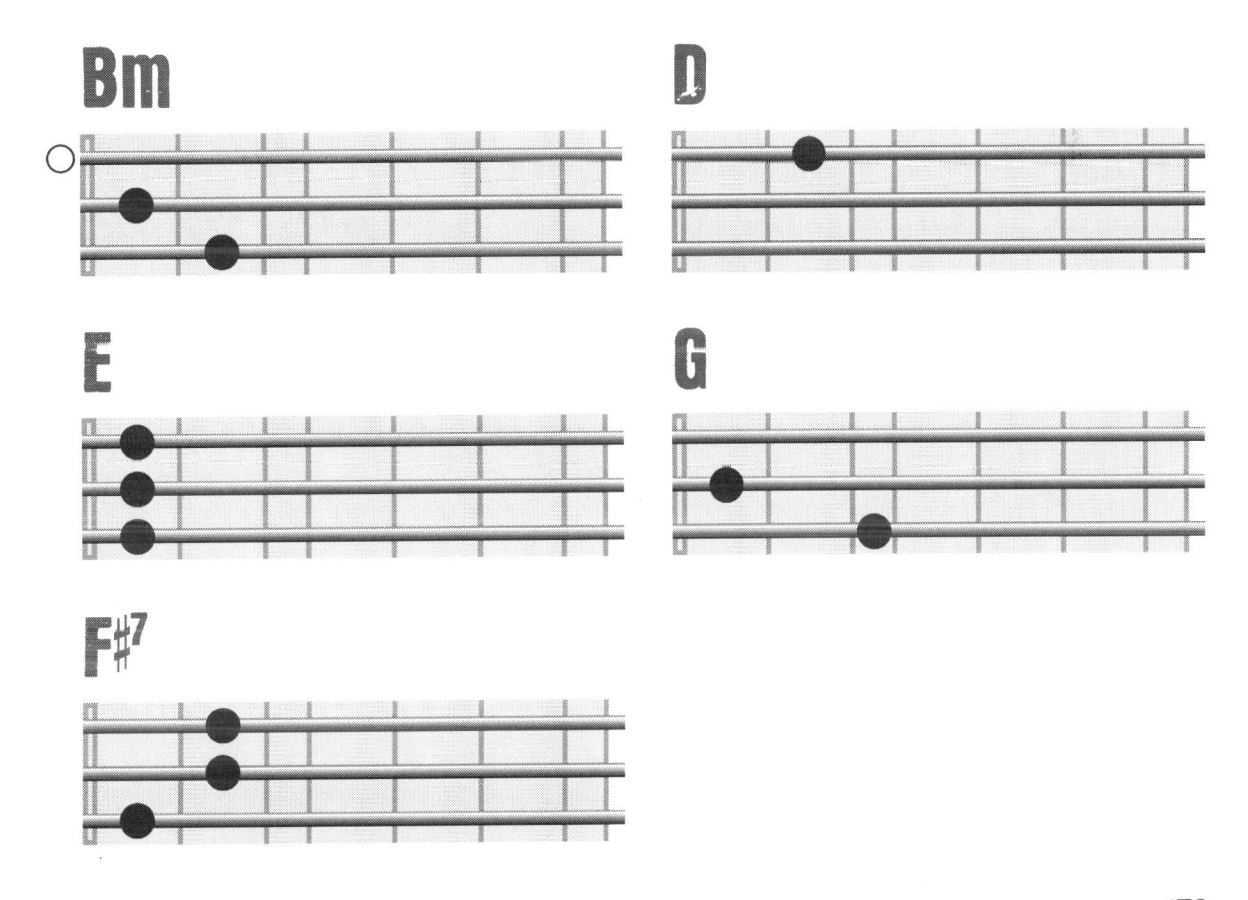

Bm

D

E

G

F#7

Home on the range

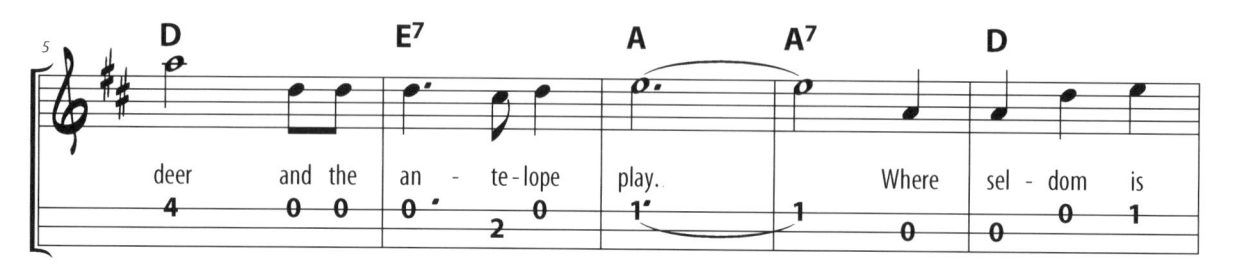

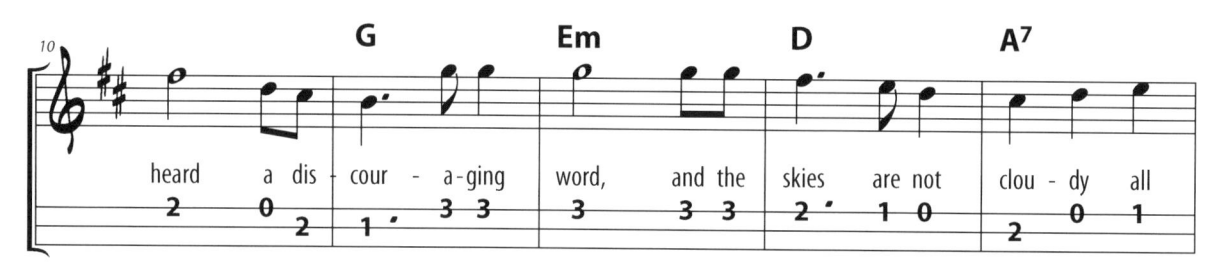

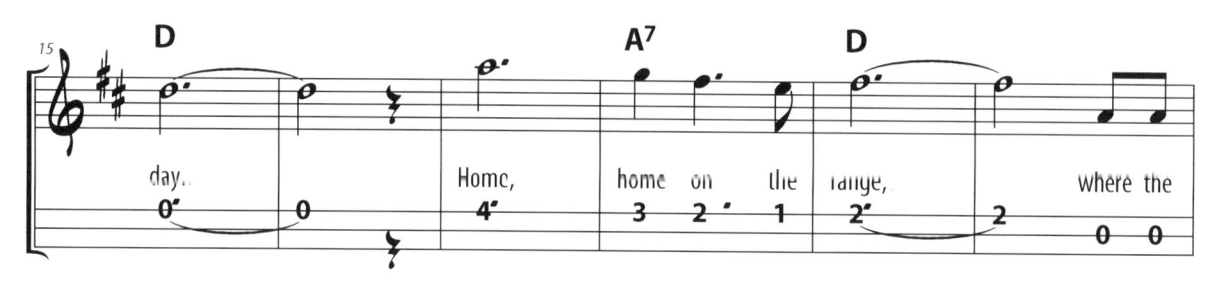

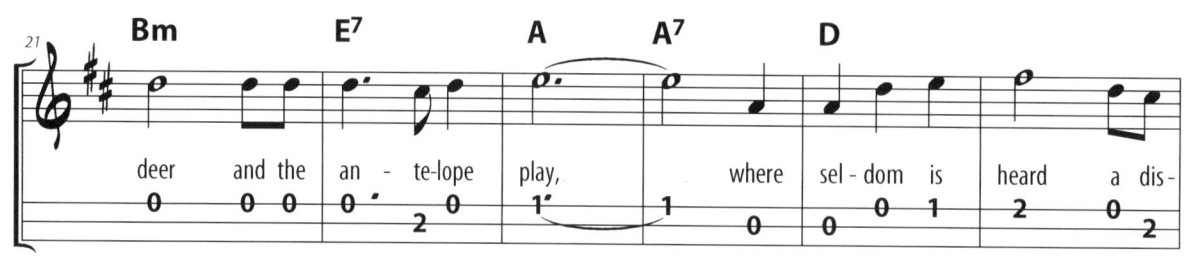

2. How often at night, when the heavens are bright
   with the light from the glittering stars,
   have I stood there amazed and I asked as I gazed,
   if their glory exceeds that of ours.
   Home, home ...

3. Where the air is so pure and the zephyrs so free
   and the breezes so balmy and light,
   that I would not exchange my home on the range
   for all the cities so bright.
   Home, home ...

D

G

E⁷

A

A⁷

Em

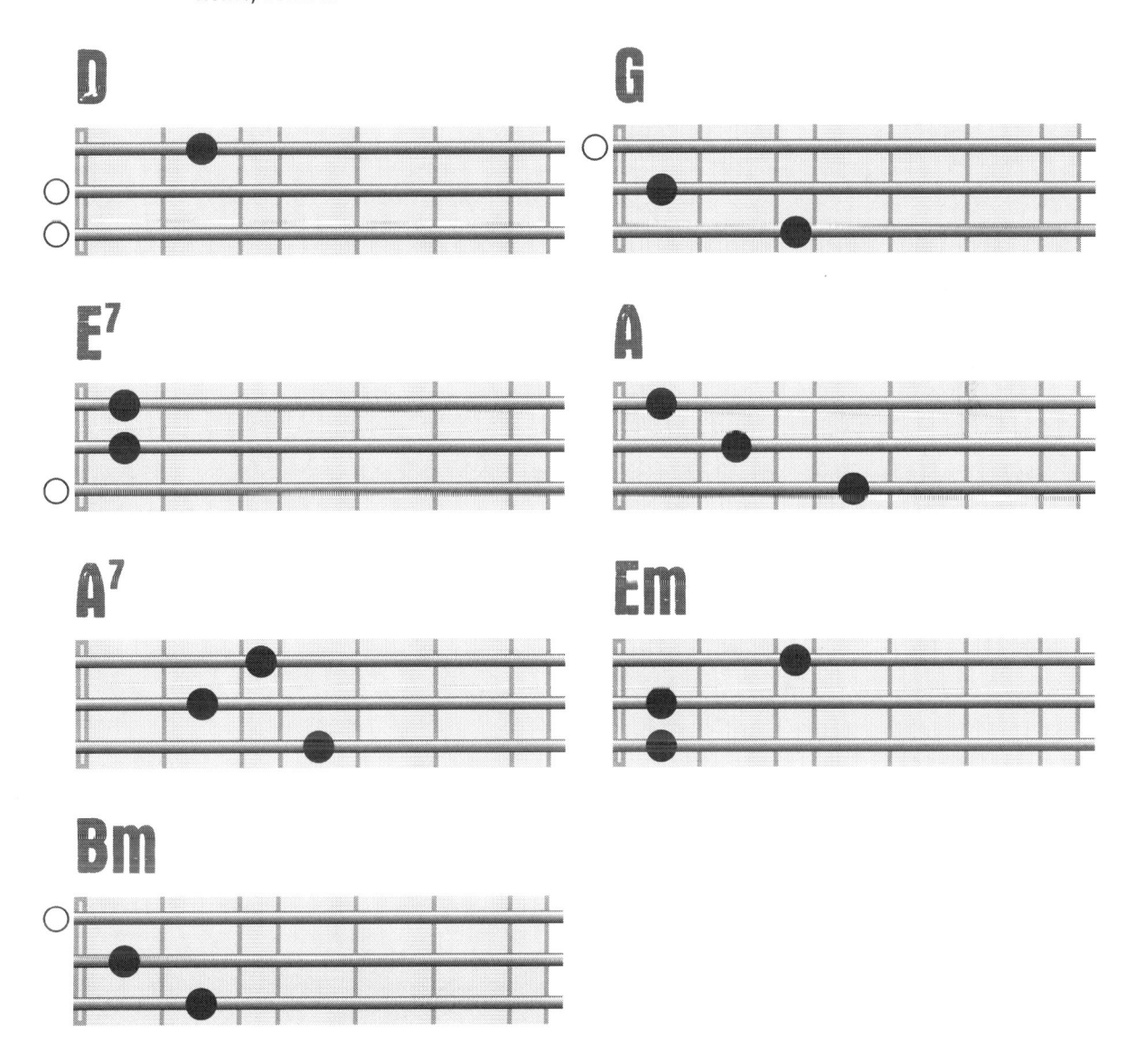

Bm

On top of Old Smokey

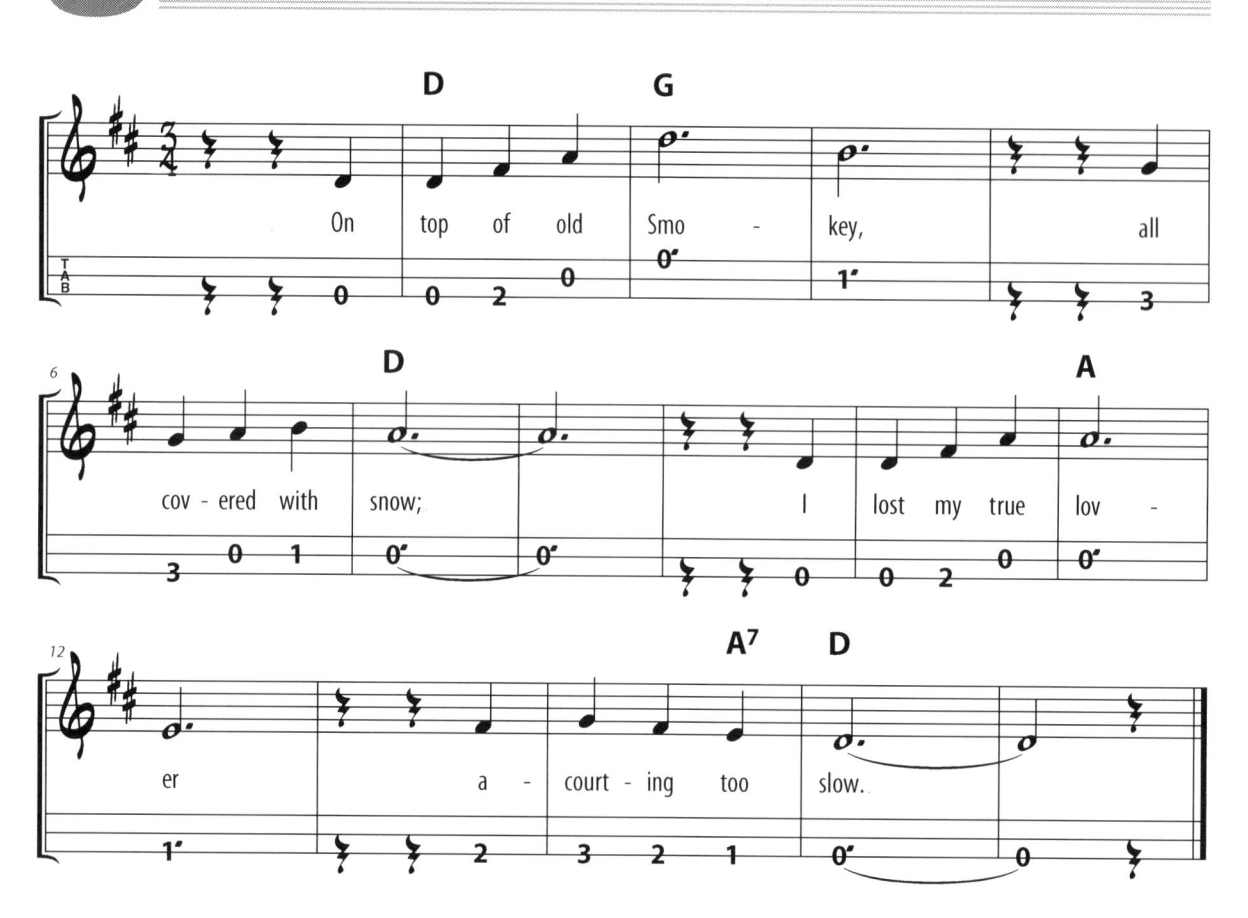

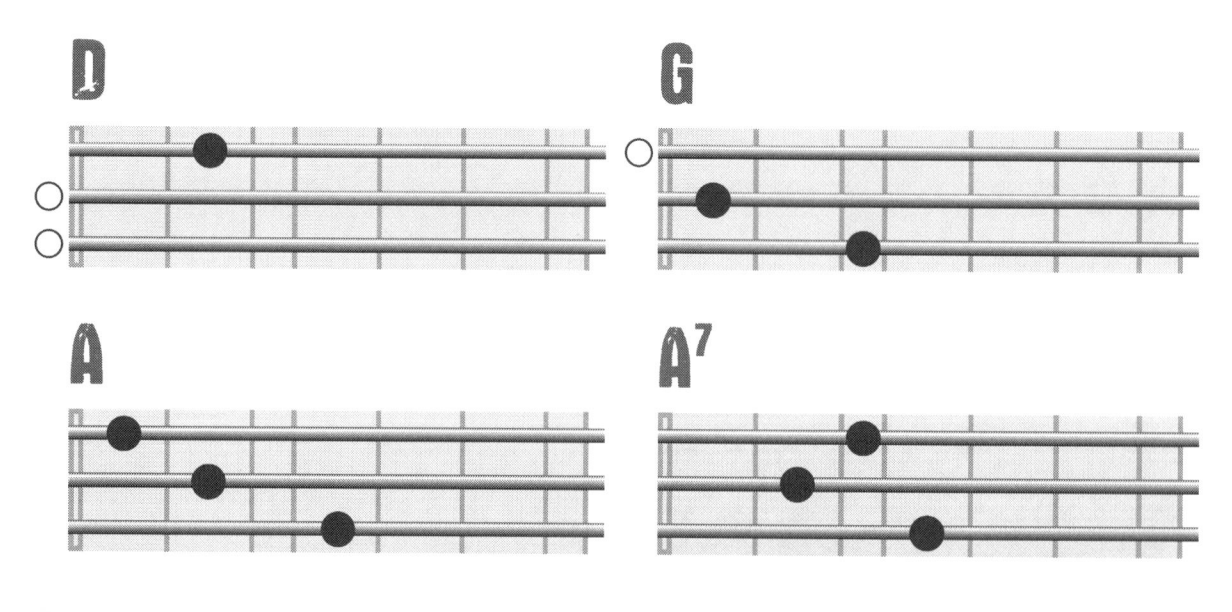

Tom Dooley

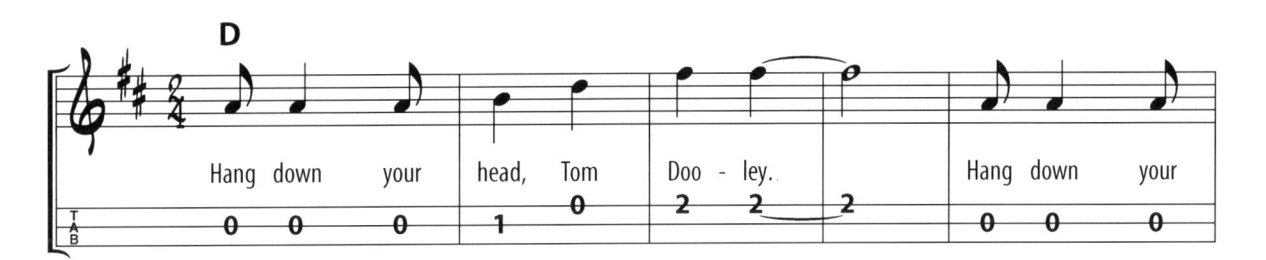

2. This time tomorrow,
   reckon where I'll be?
   If it hadn't been for Grayson,
   I'd a-been in Tennessee.

3. This time tomorrow,
   reckon where I'll be?
   Down in some lonesome valley,
   hangin' from a white oak tree.

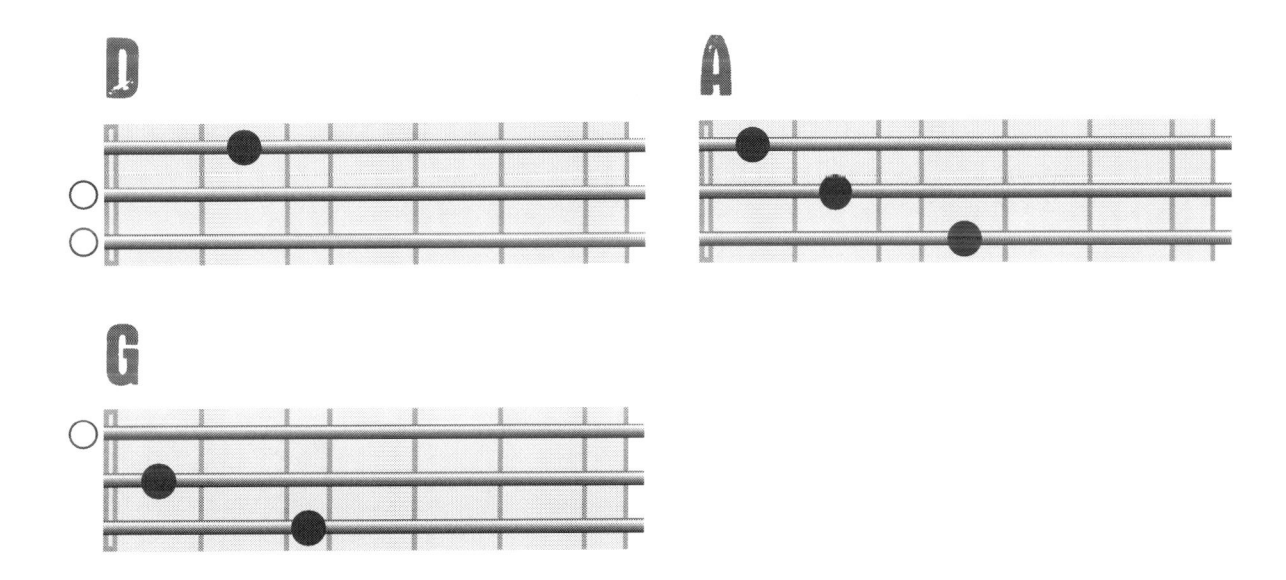

177

Tuning your Merlin

In this book I use standard D tuning.

In this tuning the strings of your Merlin are tuned to:

- D (melody string, double string) - both strings are tuned to D.
- A (middle string)
- D (bass string)

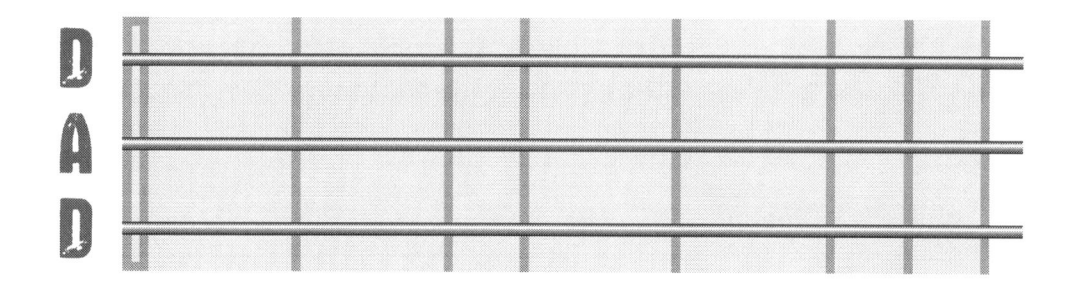

Tuning your Merlin is easiest using an electronic tuner.
Nevertheless, it's a good idea to practice tuning by ear, too.
So here's how to properly tune your Merlin by ear:

1. First, using a reference tone from a guitar or piano, tune the bass string to the note D.

2. Then press the bass string down at the 4th fret and tune the middle A string to this note.

3. Now press the middle A string down at the 3rd fret and tune the melody string(s) to this note (D).

Check your tuning:
Play all strings. This should result in a nice and full sounding D major chord – the easiest chord on the Merlin (strictly said this is a D major chord with the third missing).
If this chord does sound „dirty" or not like a chord at all, check points 1–3 again.

merlin tablature

I've notated the songs' melodies in standard notation and tablature. If you don't want to read music, simply use the tablature. Here's how it's read:

- Horizontal lines represent the strings, vertical lines the frets of your Merlin.
- Numbers indicate the frets.
- Open strings are indicated by an "0".

So the passage below (the first bar of „Aura Lee") reads:

- first play the A string (open string),
- followed by the D string (open string),
- then the A string, 2nd fret
- and the D string (open string).

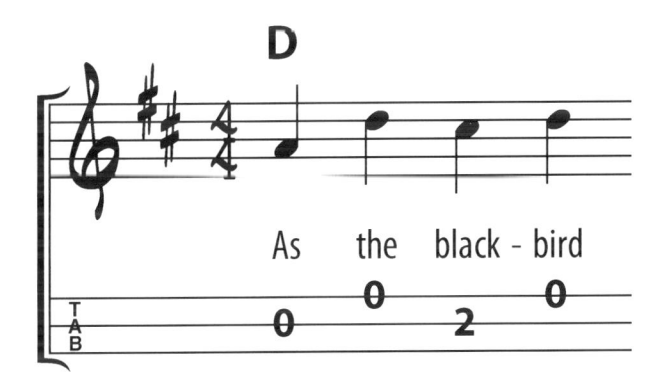

The notes on the Merlin fretboard:

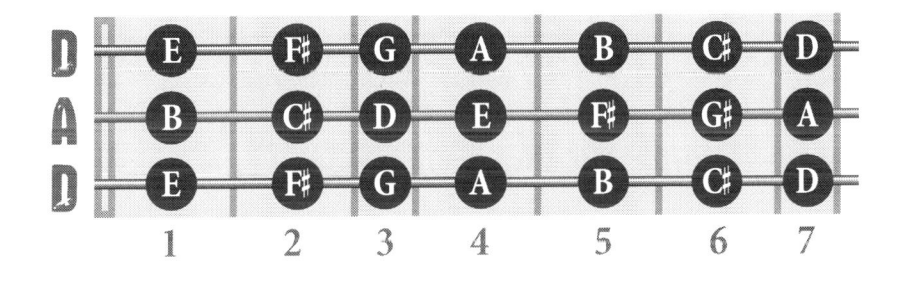

Basic chords

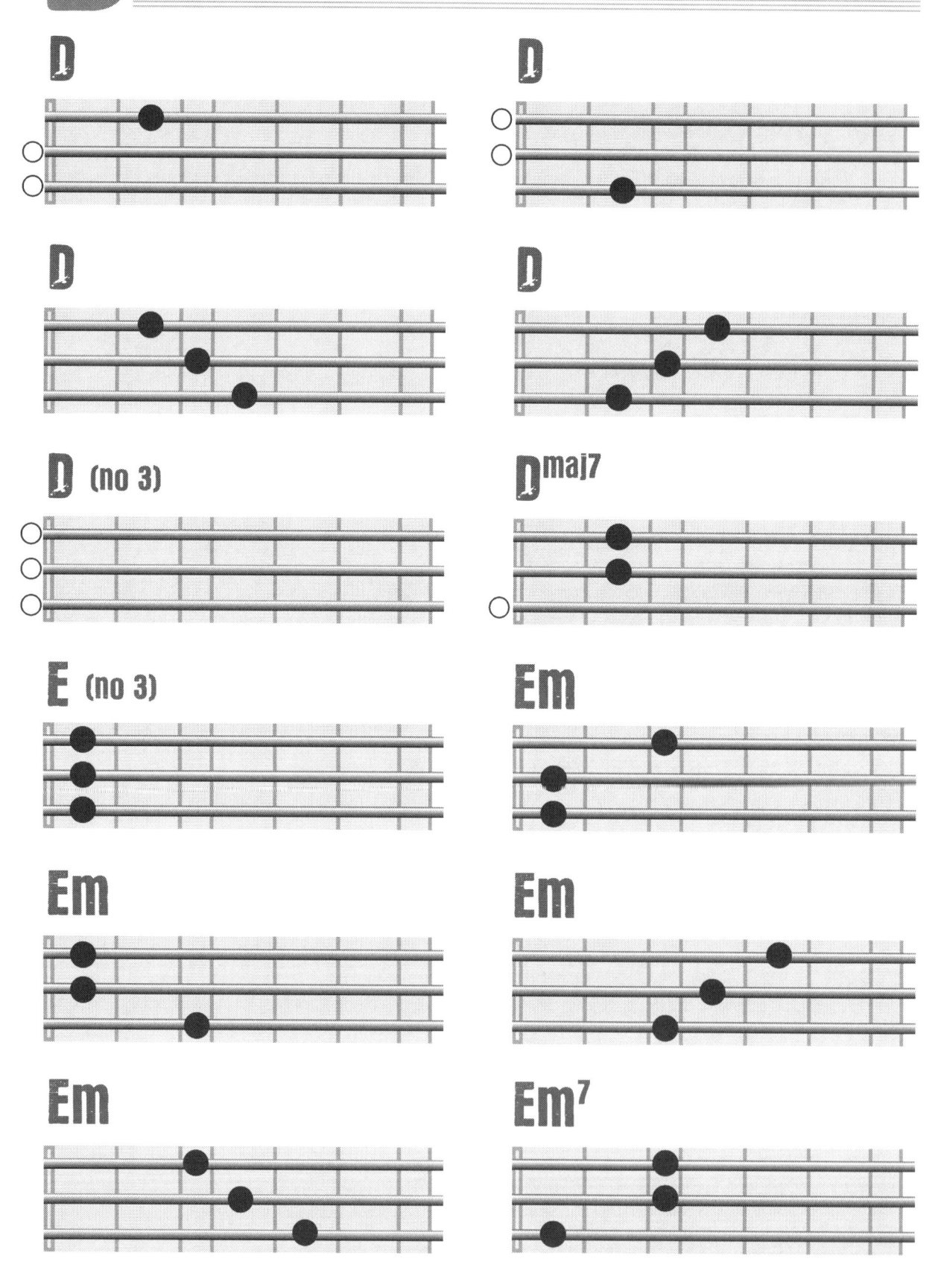

D

D

D

D

D (no 3)

Dmaj7

E (no 3)

Em

Em

Em

Em

Em7

E⁷

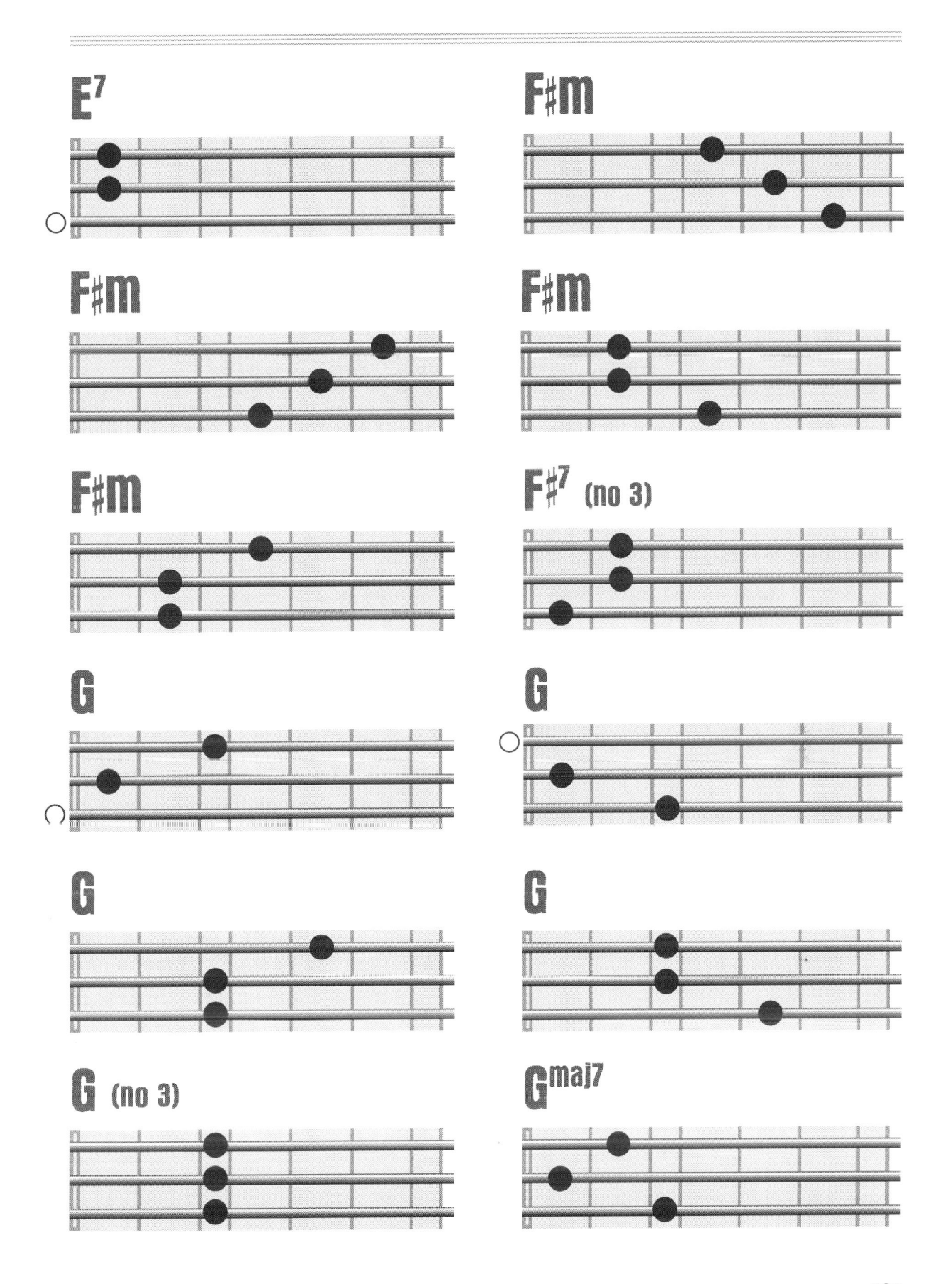

F♯m

F♯m

F♯m

F♯m

F♯⁷ (no 3)

G

G

G

G

G (no 3)

Gmaj7

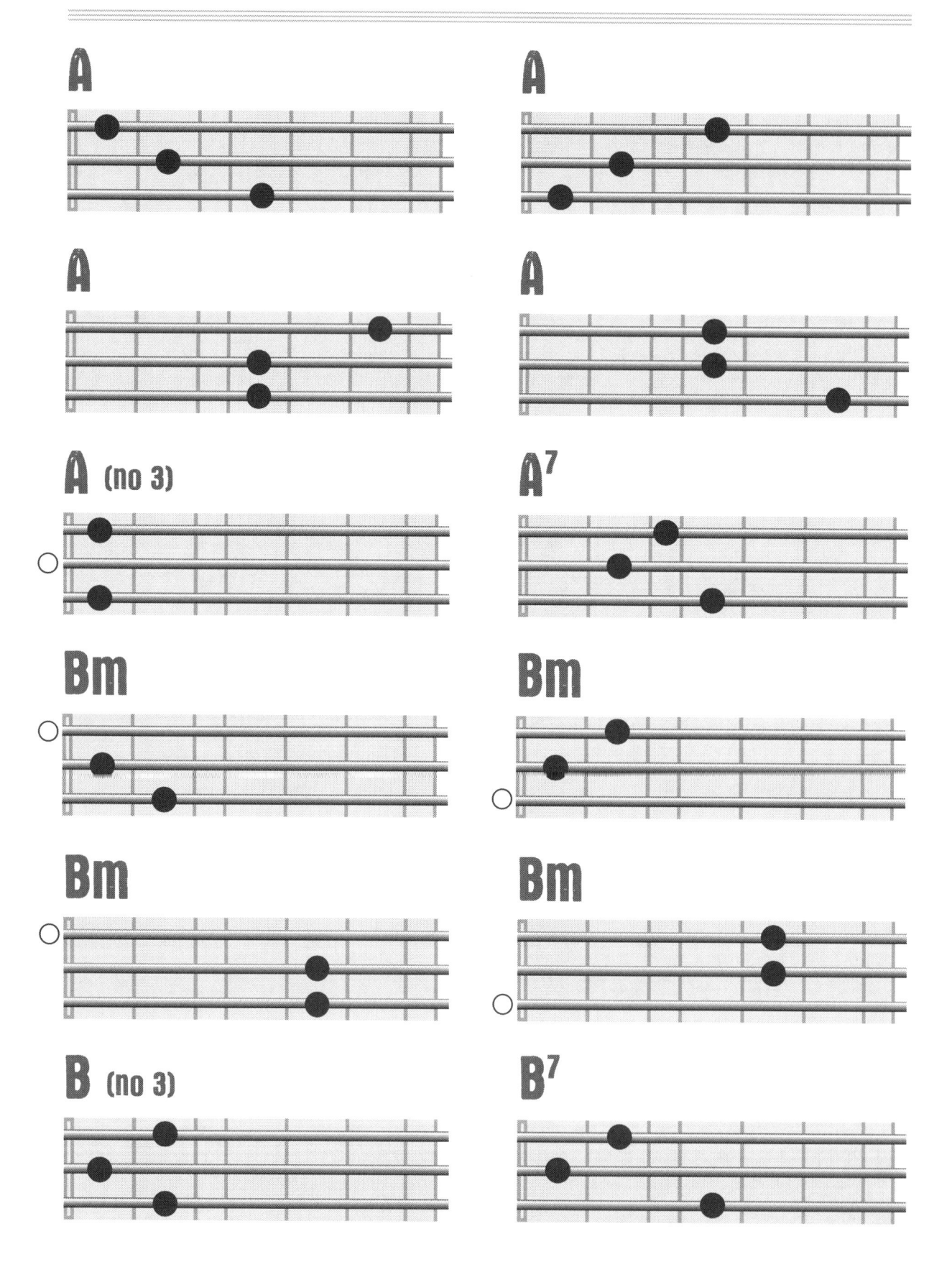

A

A

A

A

A (no 3)

A[7]

Bm

Bm

Bm

Bm

B (no 3)

B[7]

Strumming patterns

The following is a selection of basic strumming patterns which you can use for song accompaniment. These are just for starters – you'll soon use other, more elaborate patterns or invent your own. Feel free to use a pick or your finger(s) for strumming - basically whatever feels best.

Here's how they're read:

- The horizontal lines represent the strings of your Merlin.
  Downstroke (strumming in the direction of the floor): arrow upward
  Upstroke: arrow downward.
- The length of the arrows indicates which strings to strum.
- Each of these pattern shows a whole measure.

For song accompaniment you can choose (and also combine) whatever pattern feels best to you, but keep in mind to match the pattern's time to the time of the song, e.g. for a song in 4/4 time only use strumming patterns in 4/4 time.
Songs in 2/2 time can be played using strumming patterns in 4/4 time.

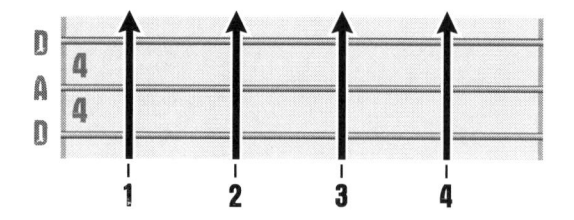

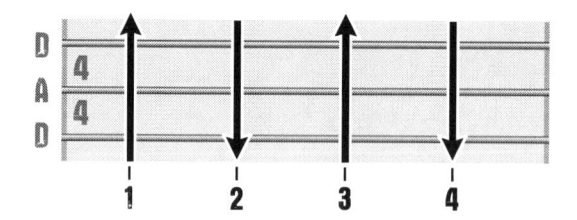

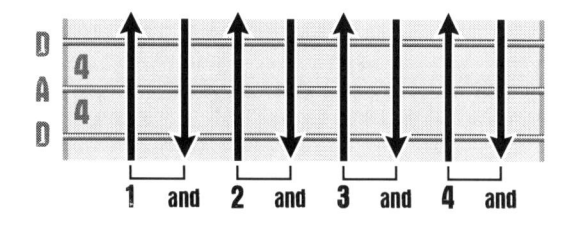

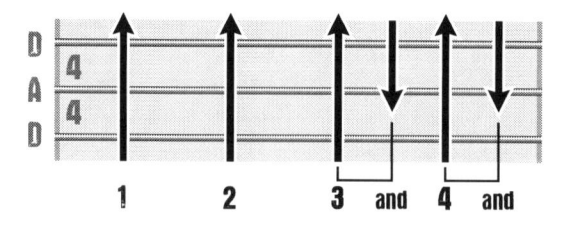

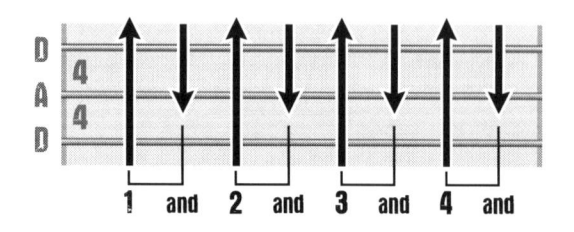

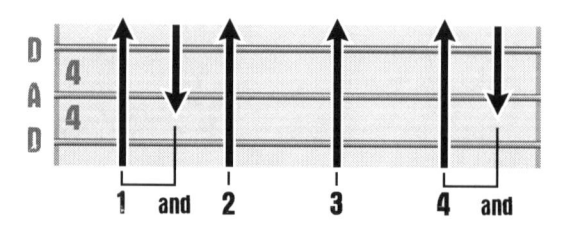

184

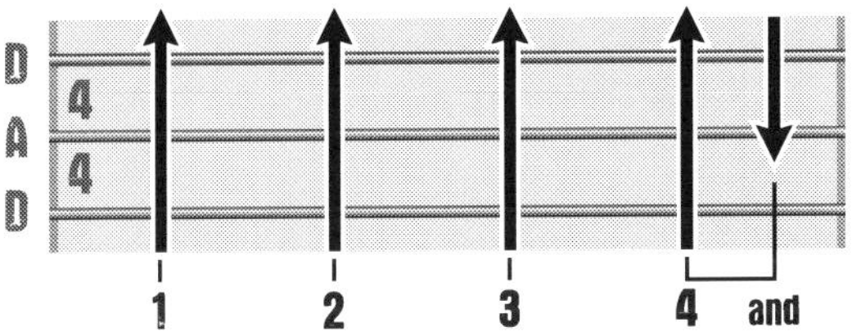
D
A
D
4
4
1 2 3 4 and

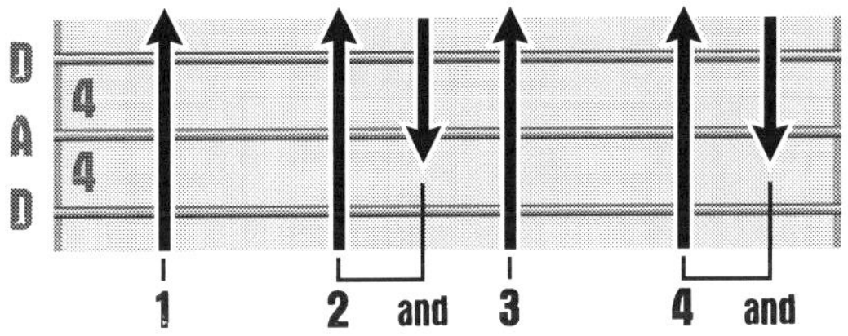
D
A
D
4
4
1 2 and 3 4 and

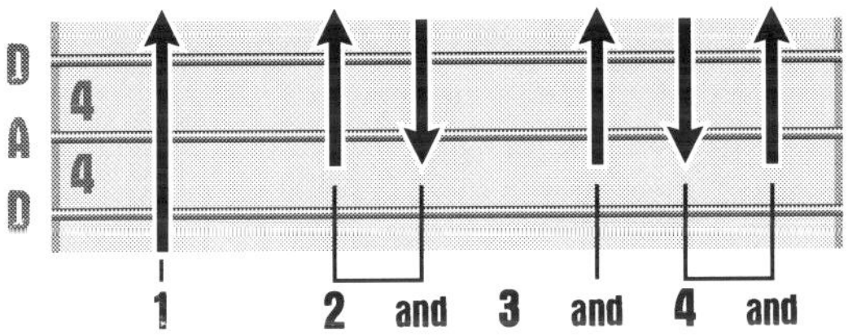
D
A
D
4
4
1 2 and 3 and 4 and

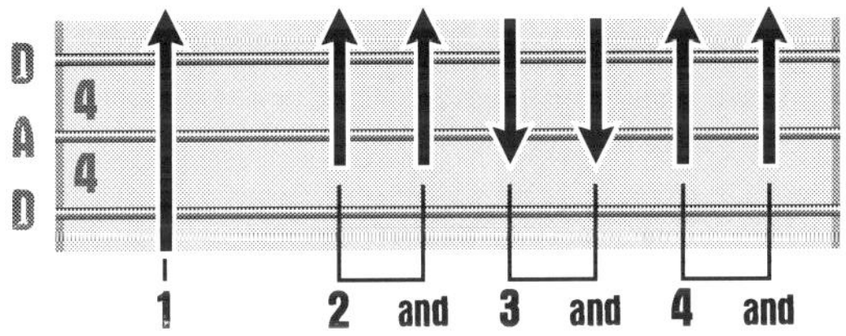
D
A
D
4
4
1 2 and 3 and 4 and

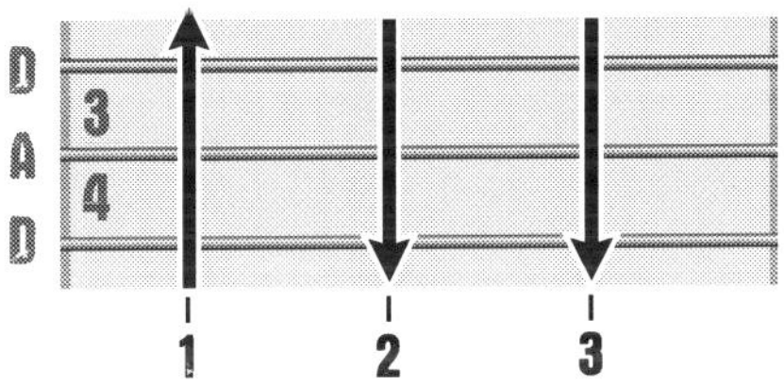
D
A
D
3
4
1 2 3

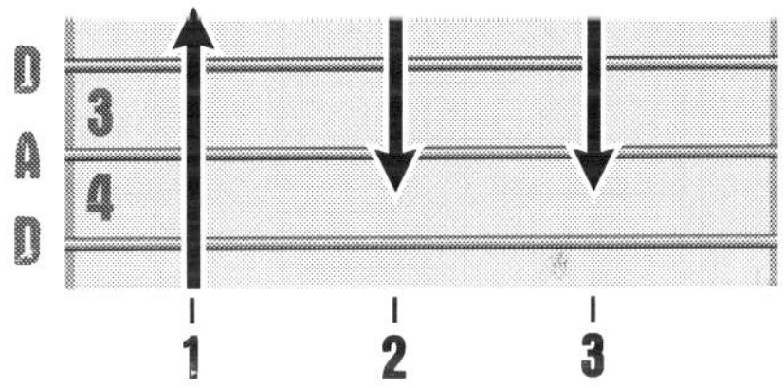
D
A
D
3
4
1 2 3

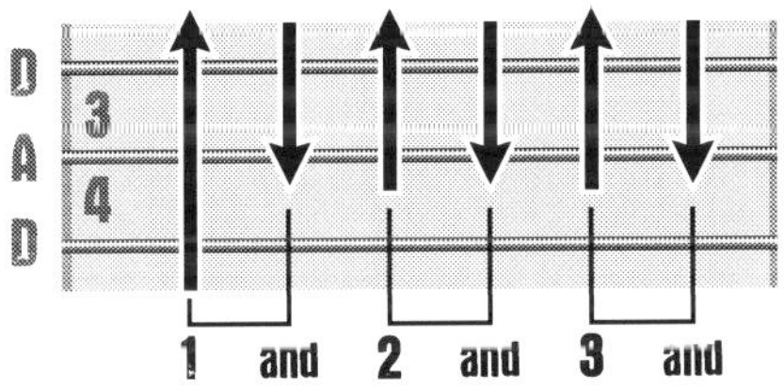
D
A
D
3
4
1 and 2 and 3 and

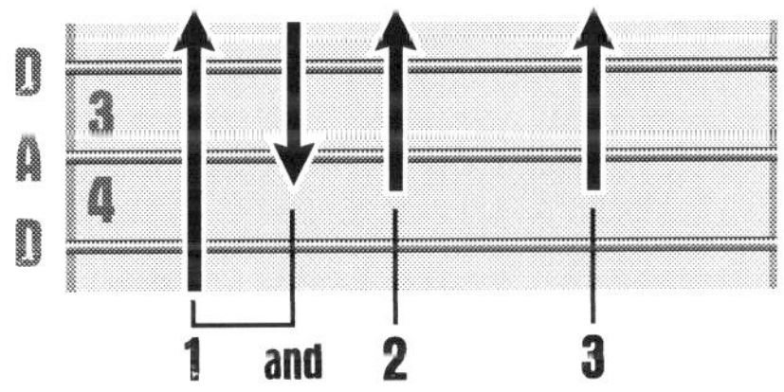
D
A
D
3
4
1 and 2 3

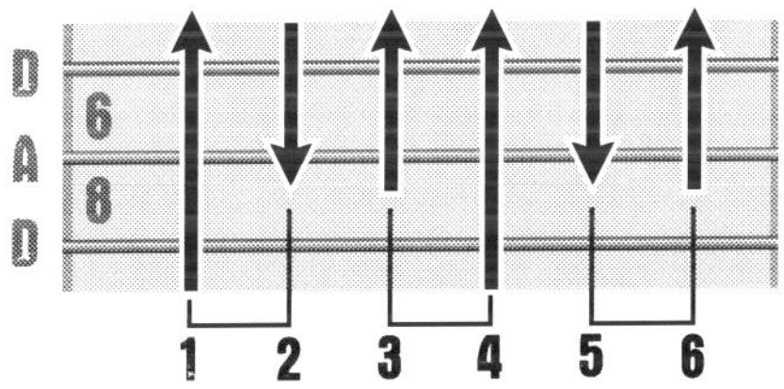
D
A
D
6
8
1 2 3 4 5 6

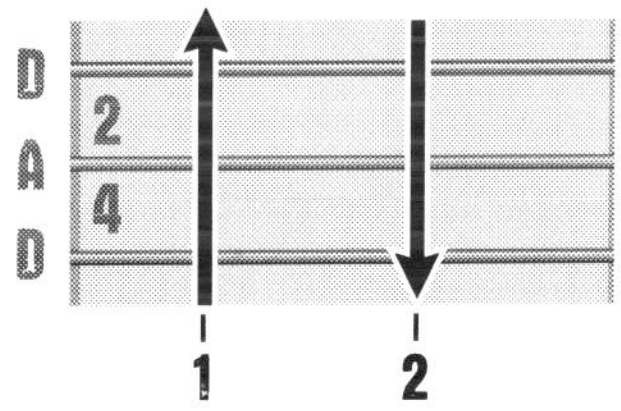
D
A
D
2
4
1 2

Picking patterns

Many songs sound particularly good when played using a picking pattern. The basic ideas is this: instead of picking all the notes of a chord simultaneously with your finger(s) or a pick, you play them successively, one after the other. Picking patterns are commonly used for longer musical sections (or even whole songs) and adapted to the chord changes if necessary.

As in tablature, horizontal lines represent the strings of your Merlin. The time signature is notated at the beginning of the pattern as a fraction (e.g. 4/4 for songs in 4/4 time).
The letters T, I and M indicate the fingers of the picking hand.
There are a few things to keep in mind when using picking patterns:
Obviously, the pattern's time signature has to match that of the song. In some cases, the pattern may have to be adapted to a certain chord or a chord change, but most of the time you can use the following simple rule:

- pick the D (melody) string with middle finger
- pick the A string with your index finger
- pick the D string (bass string) with your thumb

One of the best ways to practise picking patterns is to play them on open strings until the movement of your fingers becomes second nature – practicing this way ensures you'll be able to concentrate on more important things when it's time to play the song. When the picking pattern has been "automized" to a certain degree it's time to add chords and chord changes. Take your time because nothing sounds worse than a "stuttering" picking pattern interfering with a smooth chord change.
On the next page you'll find some basic picking patterns. These are of course just a small selection from the multitude of possible patterns, meant to whet your appetite – you'll soon find varying patterns and inventing new ones can be lots of fun!

For a start, you may want to try:
- Combining different picking patterns
  (e. g. one for the verse and one for the chorus).
- Combining picking patterns with strumming patterns.
- Mixing picking patterns with melody lines and damping techniques.

187

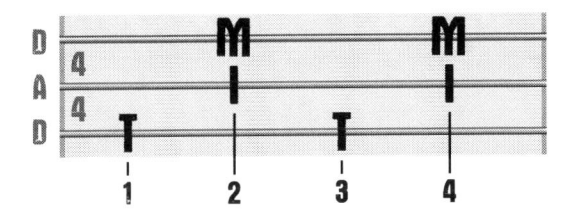

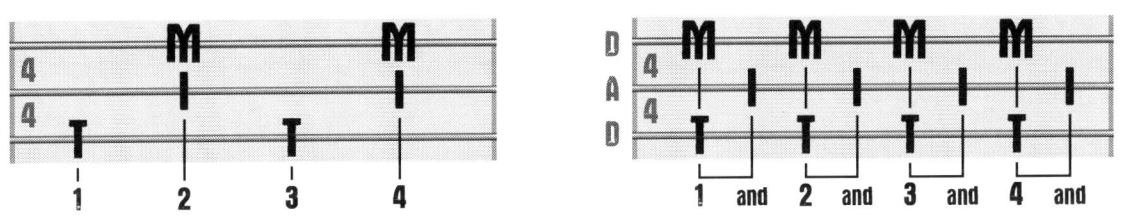

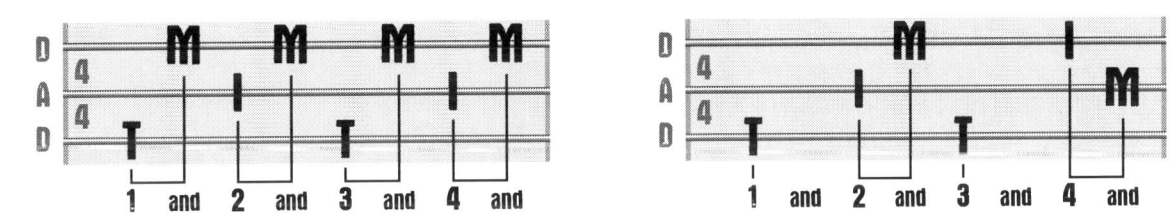

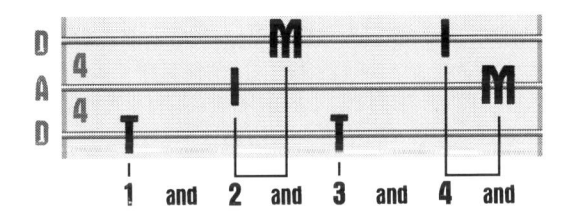

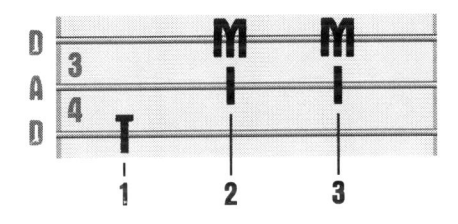

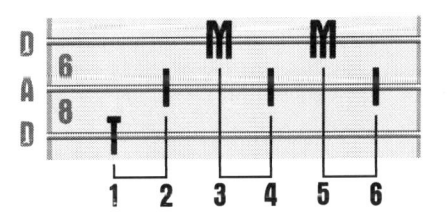

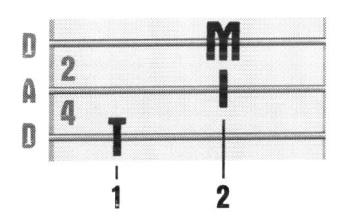

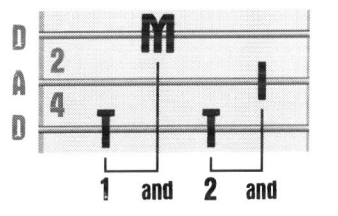

Made in United States
Orlando, FL
28 September 2024